D1207949

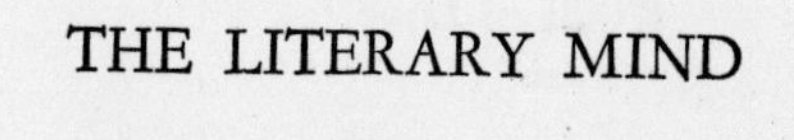

THE LITERARY MIND

Lamont

THE LITERARY MIND

Its Place in an Age of Science

By

MAX EASTMAN

1931
CHARLES SCRIBNER'S SONS
New York · London

A

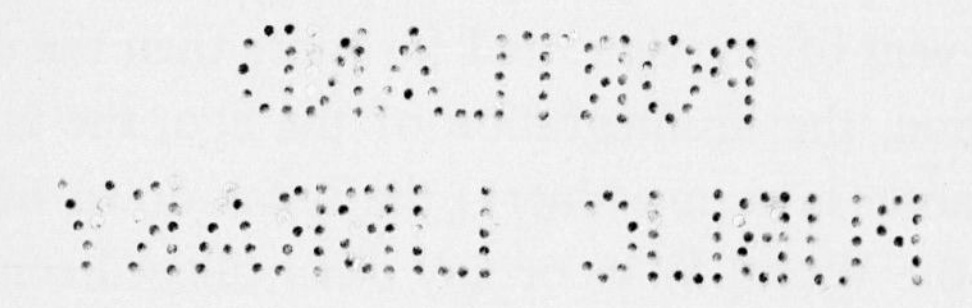

PREFACE

This is a volume of essays on contemporary literature, and any one of them can be read separately if the reader so chooses. But it is also a book about the relations between literature and science, and the essay-chapters are threaded upon a definite argument.

In Part I, I suggest what science is and how it is steadily advancing into fields heretofore occupied by literary eloquence. This I judge to be the great intellectual event of our time, and far more than the decline of religion, the disintegration of the ego, the analysis of romantic love, machinery, the break-down of capitalism, the World War, or any other alleged source of the "modern temper," responsible for the qualities of our literature.

In Part II, I show that the neo-classic criticism and the New Humanism are both, in their essence, only a grandiose effort of the literary mind to resist this advance of science.

In Part III, I show that the tendencies in poetic literature called "modernism" are a retreat before this same invasion. Abandoning all pretence to understand or interpret life, the poets are taking refuge in pure poetry and unintelligibility; the critics are conspiring with them. In explaining these poets, I discover that this contemporary invasion by science of the field of literature is in reality but the last stage in a division of labor between the two which has been in progress since the sixteenth century.

Believing that science alone can adjudicate the resulting conflict and decide what functions remain for the literary mind, I have attempted in Part IV to take the first step toward such a decision by defining poetry scientifically. I have tried to give my definition a biological as well as a psychological foundation. (My criticism of I. A. Richards' psychology of poetry, although placed in a note, belongs to this part.)

In Part V, I have discussed in the light of my definition the future of poetic literature, drama, fiction, criticism, and the peculiar problem of the teacher of literature.

When I boast that my book is so constructed that it can be read either hoppingly or at a steady walk according to the taste of the reader, I am making a virtue of economic necessity. The book grew up in circumstances which bent it to this form. It has all the faults of a natural growth—among them a certain recurrence of theme which I hope the reader, forewarned of the necessity, may find some way to make a virtue of. The theme of my definition of poetry, for instance, is anticipated in a different key—historical rather than psychological—in the essay called *The Tendency Toward Pure Poetry.*

I owe my thanks to *Harper's* and *Scribner's* magazines for printing some of the essay-chapters in slightly altered or abbreviated form. I perhaps owe my apologies to the New Humanists for so vigorously jumping on them after they are dead. My excuse is that if they are dead, it is not because anybody killed them. They rose from the dead once, and we have no assurance that they will not rise again. Besides, I am not really jumping on the New Humanists, but attempting to explain them.

M. E.

August, 1931.

CONTENTS

PART I

PART II

PART III

PART IV

PART V

PART I

THE MARCH OF SCIENCE

I

THE MARCH OF SCIENCE

THE word science, to the popular mind, suggests a limited kind of professional activity. It means working with test-tubes and telescopes, plotting curves, calculating equations. But these activities are not different in kind from what happens when any person makes an earnest effort to judge well and speak general truth about anything. Our judgments about atoms and stars are more exact and mathematical than other judgments, but perhaps only because our acquaintance with these objects is so shallow. If the stars came near, if one atom could be caught and delved into, the astronomers and physicists might find themselves almost as humble and distracted as the student of human nature. They smile at the inaccuracy of his knowledge; he might ridicule the timidity of their ambition—to study only things so far away or minute that a few accurate statements is all you can make about them. His effort, at any rate, is not deeply different from theirs. And if his findings are to be reliable, they require the same discipline—the discipline of suspended judgment, elimination of the personal factor, patience in the attempt to be consistent, a serene passion for verification. In short, they require to be scientific. Science is merely the persistent and skilled use of the mind and the stores of human knowledge about any problem.

Scientists are of course afflicted with a kind of professional vanity, and they occasionally get into a state of rapture over their ability to explain something mechanically, or mathematically, or with the concept of cause. You will see them at such times step out of their laboratories with a very unscientific light in their eyes, blow a horn on the street corner, assemble a few gullible people, and try to make a great impression on them by telling them that all explanation is mechanical, or all reality number, or that causation is such a rigid and exclusive principle as to make human choice a delusion. This never works very well, and need not be taken more seriously than philosophy or any of the other frailties of human nature.

From the standpoint of scientific method, philosophy —except as a criticism of the sciences, a part of their collective labor—consists of jumping to conclusions. This becomes evident when you consider the career of man as a whole, the millions of years of his infancy, the tiny span of time that a few accidentally brainy individuals—not bred, I mean, for the purpose—have been trying to understand the world. In a large view they understand little or nothing. They have, of course, a perfect right to jump to conclusions, but it is only the right that all men have to hazard a belief in their own guesses. As scientists they have achieved their results and established their authority by an opposite procedure. And everybody ought to realize that when scientists abandon their own line and take up jumping to conclusions as an avocation, they divest themselves so far forth of that authority. The assertion, for instance, that all explanation is mechanical—that the world is, in fact, a machine—was not a part of the science of mechanics, nor was it any part of science, nor was it consistent with the method of science as a whole. That method demands that before dogmatizing about what explanation is, one should study the process of explanation as closely at least as one has studied the objects explained. But this is at present impossible, for explanation involves motions in the brain which are not accessible to observation. If we had the means to see or even directly infer what happens in the brain when a person explains something, nobody would dream of dogmatizing about the nature of explanation—or about the nature of the world, either—until the returns were in. To dogmatize now, when the returns are inaccessible, is of little help to the progress of knowledge. I suspect that to future ages the recent vogue of mechanomorphism will seem rather a hysterical flight from anthropomorphic tendencies. There is no sign that we are going to receive any soft comfort from real knowledge such as various superstitions have supplied us. But nevertheless it is the sceptical poise, and not the rushing to immolate ourselves upon uncomfortable beliefs, which distinguishes science from immature attempts at knowledge.

The most progressive scientific men in these days realize that their methodological assumptions are not ultimate descriptions of the universe. They know where ends their technical preoccupation with problems which they might solve, and where begins that weakness—whether soft-headed and benevolent or hard-headed and boastful—for getting up in meeting and making large statements. Professor Eddington, appending to his brilliant exposition of the new physics a rather sentimental venture in religious philosophy, may serve to indicate this line of division on the soft side. And Professor Watson, manufacturing out of the ideas of Pavlov and his own brilliant experiments a patent mechanical philosophy-of-life called "Behaviorism," may warn us against the same danger on the hard side. Professor Watson when he retired from science went into the advertising business, and very appropriately too, for Behaviorism was little but a philosophic selling-device for a valuable scientific method. It is necessary to my argument that the reader have clearly in mind this line of division between scientific method and the use of scientific ideas as a spring-board from which to jump to some grandiose conclusion. When I talk about science and use the word scientific, I am doing so in full consciousness of the fact that the few hundred years in which a few Western minds have been occupied in the systematic search for verified knowledge are a fraction of the first second of a minute in a single day's work of the mind of man as a whole.

One other thing must be understood or my argument will go astray, and that is that knowledge originally grew out of purposive activities and is still much bound up with them. Knowing is not a state-of-being in which "the mind" becomes a copy or reflection of "things." Knowing is an act of comprehending the elements of experience in their relations to each other and to our human interests and modes of behavior. One need not be a pragmatist philosopher in order to recognize this. One need only study the process of knowing as one studies any other biological function. For my part I think the initiation of this mode of study, and the fertile pursuit of it, is the great contribution of John Dewey to the sum of wisdom, and that his tendency toward a philosophy of pragmatism is, like others of its kind, a tendency to jump to conclusions where no conclusion has been reached, and where the conclusion when it is reached will probably be less neat and single than the one jumped to. To say that all knowledge, even that which issues from reflection, is experimental, that the idea which succeeds in reorganizing the environment, removing trouble and perplexity, is the true one, seems to me in a sense legitimate. But to make this statement an ultimate definition of truth, entailing a conflict with those who wish to examine the relations between the idea and the environment which enable it to perform that function, seems to me illegitimate. It reveals that same desire to get somewhere and sit down—that search for the one or the absolute—which is so admirably denounced by the pragmatists in all other philosophies.

At any rate it is not necessary to my thesis that the relation of knowledge to action should be made to overshadow its relation to the material acted upon. It is necessary only to recognize that knowing is itself active, and that science consists not in the "contemplation of things as they are," as Francis Bacon described it, but in the conceiving of things as they are importantly related together. I could base my argument upon the statement of Clarence I. Lewis, who calls himself a conceptual pragmatist, that "the interest of knowledge is for action, and action proceeds by way of relation." Or I could base it upon the statement of Morris R. Cohen, who hates pragmatism, that "the nature of things which rational science tries to formulate consists of laws or invariant relations of order of possible phenomena." Only I should ask leave to remind Professor Cohen that if science is interested only in invariant relations of order—dull and monotonous things, it would seem, in their own character—and finds no permanent satisfaction in variant relations and disorder, that is no part of its rationality. It would be quite reasonable, if one were driven by an organically disinterested curiosity, to spend a life-time working out the decimal points in the number π, the disorderly ratio of the diameter of a circle to its circumference, or in ascertaining the annual changes in the ratio of the number of potatoes grown in Chemung county to the number of people bitten by fish in the South Sea Islands. If invariant relations of order have so absorbing a fascination for our brains, even when we have no end in view but knowledge, it must be because our brains are in a deep sense instruments for finding them out. And our brains are such instruments because these invariant relations of order are what have been, and will always be, of practical and necessary relevance to action. It is in this sense, and not that of a pragmatist philosopher, that I think even of theoretical science as belonging, by contrast at least with poetry, to the practical functioning of our natures.

I am of course offering a remark where a treatise might seem inadequate. It is because my argument is not about the nature of science, and yet it is necessary to indicate what I mean by science or the argument will be misunderstood.

I must also disclaim any wish to exalt scientific method itself, or the word science, into a new benevolent godhead to which are attributed all the mystic potencies of the supernatural powers it has displaced. Each distinct step forward in experimental knowledge has been followed by a burst of childlike hope that now all problems are to be solved in fact as in the fairy tales. Copernicus was followed by Giordano Bruno, sowing through Europe his flaming evangel of the Universal Art of Knowledge; Galileo, by Thomas Hobbes with his cooler but no less compendious dream; Newton, by Voltaire and the visionaries of Reason; Adam Smith, by the utopian socialists; Darwin, by Herbert Spencer, the credulous agnostic, crying "Progress is not an accident but a necessity—it is certain that man must become perfect." In our own day Freud, the discoverer, was followed by a myth-making Freud, and by a whole flock of doctors who did not quite know for a time whether they were practising magic or medicine. These divinely comforting or miracle-working agencies made out of the name of science are the last gods to be conquered. But the only power which can conquer them is science. It is still only a question of the better use of the mind. To denounce science as "the false Messiah," basing the denunciation upon scientific knowledge, is utter sophistry, unless you mean merely to warn people against quack prophets, and remind them that true science cannot offer itself as a Messiah. True science is only one half knowing; the other half is never pretending to know.

The intrusion of this disciplined and sceptical attitude of inquiry, into the world-old business of chatting about human nature, has been one of the principal events of our time. It is unhappily named psychology, the science of the soul—although its first step was to dismember the soul—and it is unhappily associated with all the most profitable forms of hocus-pocus. It is more tightly associated, however, with biology and the physiology of the brain and nervous system. Deriving a convincing force from these sciences, it advances steadily, a formidable although imperfect machine of purgation, from one sphere of our loose chatter to another. It arrives at last in the fields occupied by literary essayists and the professors and critics of literature, penetrating here slowly indeed because of the mountains of great eloquence that have been built up, and because the building of this eloquence is a well-paid profession. But it penetrates inevitably. There can be no ultimate resistance, unless you would rather be foolish than wise.

When Matthew Arnold wrote his discourse on "Literature and Science," the question was merely whether the "natural sciences" should replace "humane letters" as the predominant factor in education. And his conclusion that "letters will not in the end lose their leading place" was based upon the necessity to relate the findings of those "natural sciences" to the problems of human conduct. "This the men of science will not do for us," he cried. But those times are gone. The men of science now quite rigidly insist upon doing exactly this. Indeed, it is no longer a question of the relation between *natural* sciences and *humane* letters. It is a question whether scientific method shall replace the method of "letters" in the study of man himself. And since scientific method is merely the method of acquiring reliable knowledge in any field, the answer is obvious. "Letters," in so far as they deal with general truth and yet hold aloof from science, will lose their leading place not only in education but in the entire scheme of social values. It would be truer to say that they *are* losing their leading place, and losing it rapidly. In 1880 Professor Huxley complained that "No reply to a troublesome argument tells so well as calling its author a 'mere scientific specialist.'" To-day Hilaire Belloc complains that "A thing having been said to be established 'scientifically' there is no questioning of it."

This change in the relative estimation of the scientist and the man of letters is the most important change in social opinion that has occurred in the fifty years intervening between Huxley and Belloc. It is one of the most important changes that has ever occurred anywhere. You might sum it up by saying that science, having displaced magic and religion and abstract philosophy as a source of help and guidance, is now successfully attacking "literature." This explains, in my opinion, the whole contemporary agitation among critics and literary professors; it explains the present tendencies in fiction; it explains the "modernist" poets. And it raises questions about the nature of poetry, and the future of the literary mind, which demand a thoughtful answer.

PART II

LITERATURE ON THE DEFENSIVE

I

THE SWAN-SONG OF HUMANE LETTERS

At the present moment two groups of essayists and critics seem to be opposing each other in the literary arena. There is a young and cocky group who pride themselves on being "intellectual," and believe that they are leading us out of the romantic swamp into a new era which they call classical. Allen Tate, Ezra Pound, T. S. Eliot, Ivor Winters, Edith Sitwell, Robert Graves, Laura Riding—readers of modern essays will recognize the group, or rather tendency, to which I refer. Then there is an older or more solemn group who regard themselves as the champions of moral discipline, and consider that they are rescuing us from "naturalism" and guiding us back or upward into the life of the spirit. These two groups—the neo-classics, as I will have to call them, and the humanists—exchange arguments from time to time, and also from time to time hit each other over the head with the flat of a sword or some other antique weapon. Robert Shafer recently gave Allen Tate a resounding thwack in the pages of *The Bookman* and received as loud a one in return. But the battle although loud is not very interesting, because the hostility is not deep. The two groups are quarrelling with each other only incidentally, and so to speak sideways. And what they are quarrelling about is the *plan of campaign* against their common enemy, science. The real war which they are both waging with all their hearts—the one under the banner of "intellect," the other under the banner of "morals"—is a war in defense of the ancestral preserves of humane letters against the encroachments of verified knowledge. They are fighting for the right of literary men to talk loosely and yet be taken seriously in a scientific age.

In order to prove this, I have gathered one or two of the choicest blooms of their literaryness. I want to show by concrete example that scientific knowledge and a sense of its method would only make these critics do what they are doing better than they are doing it.

I begin with Miss Sitwell, a brilliantly colorful poet, fitfully brilliant in prose, the daughter of an aristocratic British family, a typical "neo-classic," with the most earnest conviction that she is intellectual. In a little volume on *Poetry and Criticism* Miss Sitwell undertakes to explain how the modernist poets are "bringing a new and heightened consciousness to life." She begins by flying from the contemporary knowledge of her subject to "those halcyon days"—she dates them with intuitive accuracy—just before Francis Bacon called attention to the possibilities of verified knowledge. Invoking upon her effort the purer spirit of those days, she proceeds as follows:

"The senses of many people are practically unused. . . . The result of this is that there is no connection between their senses and their brain, and it irritates them excessively when these are brought into relation with each other. The modernist poet's brain is becoming a central sense, interpreting and controlling the other five senses; for he has learned the truth uttered by Blake, that 'Man has no body distinct from his soul. . . .' His senses have become broadened and cosmopolitanized; they are no longer little islands, speaking only their own narrow language, living their sleepy life alone. When the speech of one sense is insufficient to convey his entire meaning, he uses the language of another. . . . Modernist poets are not difficult to follow if the fact of different sense-values is remembered."

In this untidy huddle of ideas, which might be the preparation for a rummage sale of the half-antique furniture of the literary mind, it is hard to know where to pry in with a little modern information. Suppose that, instead of knowing all about Thomas Lodge's *Defense of Poetry* in 1579, and Sir Philip Sidney's in 1583, and about Ben Jonson's *Discoveries* and Sir William Davenant's theories in his Preface to *Gondibert*—suppose that Miss Sitwell knew a little something about the senses and the brain! It sounds ludicrous, but when you consider that these are the subjects about which she is writing, it is not perhaps an altogether preposterous suggestion. If Miss Sitwell knew, for instance, that the senses are not five but nearer twenty, if she knew that the retina is in a peculiar sense a part of the brain, if she knew how integral is the entire experience and action of the nervous system, how this soul-brain that she has concocted out of a mixture of mediæval theology and modern newspaper jargon falsifies the facts and the ascertained relations among the organs of consciousness, is it not possible that she might have said something more pointed and more relevant than she has, to the problem of "bringing a new and heightened consciousness to life"? It seems to me that without destroying any of Miss Sitwell's charm, which I indeed should posit as indestructible, we might safely offer this amendment to her intellectualness.

What she is really trying to say here is that the modernist poet heightens consciousness by comparing the impressions of one sense with those of another. And the whole passage is a mere clumsy and blunt approach to a subject that has been studied with subtle attention for fifty years. Francis Galton first observed a close association, and at times a confusion, between the impressions of one sense and those of another, and named it *synæsthesia.* It does not matter about the name, but it does matter that both he and others who followed him established the fact that while such an identity or likeness between one kind of sensation and another may be experienced faintly or occasionally by almost anybody, its vivid and frequent occurrence is a rare eccentricity—not pathological, but capable of becoming in extreme cases an affliction.

It becomes clear as you continue to read Miss Sitwell's essay that she is not so much concerned with modernist poetry as with an extreme trait of her own poetry. And the fact that this trait rests upon an eccentricity of her mind, so that many of these metaphors which heighten consciousness in her will as surely becloud and depress it in others—this fact, whatever conclusion you may draw from it, is of crucial relevance to her essay. In my view of the world it is precisely for the sake of Miss Sitwell and her essay that those plodding and meticulous investigators have been laboring away upon this seemingly trivial subject for these fifty years, and have reached at least one statement of fact about it which may be relied on as general truth. There is no "classicism" in Miss Sitwell's ignorance of this truth, no intellectuality, or nobility, or dignity, or beauty, or bravery—no value of any kind. Her very delightfully arrogant essay would merely be better, if she knew what she is talking about.

Not knowing what you are talking about is no mere accidental default, however, in most of these neo-classic writers. It is the substance of their faith. The extremists among them are not only ignorant of the scientific investigations of their subject-matter but militantly opposed to them. The word "intellect" upon their lips is a veritable battle-emblem—a challenge to mere knowledge, or intelligence, or any other crude enterprise of the kind, to compete with the exalted abstract talk which they produce after reading the history of literature. Miss Laura Riding, a young woman who in a brief span of years leapt from the dull level of the American backwoods to the very heights of British intellectuality, has written a book called *Contemporaries and Snobs,* in which she attacks science and belabors it as though it were a no less despicable thing than ignorance itself or stupidity.

A "fetish of the concrete intelligence," she calls it, "a mere by-way of the suggestive intelligence, or intellect, a digression. . . ." Miss Riding's book is a torrent of uncontrolled cerebration in which few have had the patience to discover any coherent message beyond the quite obvious one that the writer is young, literary, and indignant. If you study the book with a certain diagnostic sympathy, however, seeking rather for the causes than the meanings of what is said, you will find it a most significant document. The source of Miss Riding's indignation is the demand of this age that statements made by literary people shall have a definite reference and be valid. That is what she means by denouncing "the contemporary mind, or the concrete intelligence, or whatever we please to call it," and setting off against it a far nobler thing called "intellect" or the "suggestive" or "poetic" intelligence. What Miss Riding denounces as the concrete intelligence is the scientist's habit of *meaning something definite by what he says.* What she extols as intellect, or the suggestive, or poetic intelligence, is *literary loose talk.* With that much interpretation, her essay becomes a veritable tiny signal-post in the cultural history of man, being at once the most frantic defense, and the most extreme example of literary loose talk ever yet penned or published—so extreme and so frantic as to suggest irresistibly that the end is near.

Let us add, then, to our anthology this purest and highest bloom from the neo-classic tree, the tree of intellect:

"The concrete intelligence suffers from the illusion of knowledge since it does not recognize a degree in knowledge at which all its laws and implements cease to operate and at which another order of intelligence enters. It is at this degree that the poetic intelligence begins, an illuminating ignorance in which everything is more than certain, that is, absolute because purely problematical."

T. S. Eliot belongs in his foundations to this same school of "illuminating ignorance." Indeed, I am not sure but he and Ezra Pound were the prime movers in this vain last effort to be at once intellectual and ignorant of science. Eliot at least did more than any other, with his serious historical scholarship and flair for the upper circles, to give an appearance of modern knowledge to what was really a rather frivolous contempt for the efforts to achieve it. His attitude to these efforts, particularly where they plunged into the fields occupied by polite letters, may be seen in the following passage on what he called "the present day":

"This day began . . . with Tylor and a few German anthropologists; since then we have acquired sociology and social psychology, we have watched the clinics of Ribot and Janet, we have read books from Vienna . . .; social emancipation crawled abroad; . . . and we have a curious Freudian-social-mystical-rationalistic-higher-critical interpretation of the Classics. . . ."

Conscious, perhaps, of a slightly hoity-toity flavor in this irony, he interrupts it with the benign remark:

"I do not deny the very great value of all work by scientists *in their own departments. . . .*"

The italics are mine, and their purpose is to stress the identity of Eliot's attitude with that of Miss Riding. *Thus far shalt thou go* is what they both say to the spirit of verified knowledge as it begins to encroach upon fields sacred to the free, the pure, the literary eloquences. Stay in your own departments—here "another order of intelligence enters."

It is with this "other order of intelligence" that Eliot has defined his position as a critic and offered leadership to the modern tendency.

"I believe," he says, "that the modern tendency is toward something which, for want of a better name, we may call classicism . . . a higher and clearer conception of Reason, and a more severe and serene control of the emotions by Reason."

Had he not been dragging a generation behind the energetic brains of his time, T. S. Eliot would know that Reason with a capital R was long ago carried out and reverently dropped on the scrap-pile. "A higher conception of Reason" is as relevant to the present problems of psychology as a lower conception of the high-wheeled bicycle is to the problems of locomotion. And as for the emotions—Eliot tells us here that they are to be controlled by Reason. Elsewhere he has announced that they are to be "disciplined" by religion. In still another place they are to be "transmuted" by poetry—in still another, "worked up into poetry," and in still another, "depicted in poetry." On one page poetry is "an escape from emotion"; on the next page the thing to appreciate in poetry is not only "the sincere expression of emotion," but "the expression of significant emotion." Speaking of the "pernicious effect of emotion," Eliot tells us that the emotions provoked by a work of art "are, when valid, perhaps not to be called emotions at all." A few pages later he tells us that, "In the *Agamemnon,* the artistic emotion approximates to the emotion of an actual spectator: in *Othello* to the emotion of the protagonist himself." In one essay Eliot affirms that "the business of the poet is . . . to express feelings which are not in actual emotion at all"—whatever that may mean. In another he praises one poet above another because he gives his subject "a connection with that inexhaustible and terrible nebula of emotion which surrounds all our exact and practical passions and mingles with them"—whatever that also may mean. The citations are sufficient to indicate that, even in literary terms, Eliot has thought nothing through and has no position in the very matter in which so many of the literary lost sheep of the moment are looking to him for guidance. But even should he undertake to arrive somewhere and stay there upon this problem of emotion which so troubles him, he could not accomplish it with any cogency for modern minds in the unenlightened terms so far chosen. Whatever emotion may be, it is not an interior lake of nebulous and semi-explosive fluid to be "escaped from" or "worked up" by poets, swum in and out of by "feelings," and "mingled" with passions. It might be pertinent—if also a trifle impertinent—to suggest that had Eliot watched a little longer "the clinics of Ribot and Janet" and read the "books from Vienna," he might have found some solution of that particular emotional problem which is so obviously reflected by these sad fits and starts in the theory of poetry.

I have culled my next blossom of literaryness from our American champion of the modern tendency, Gorham B. Munson. Mr. Munson occupies a mid-position between those elegantly hell-raising critics I have described as neo-classical and the more decorous and moral ones who call themselves humanist. He has a deep admiration for Paul Elmer More and Irving Babbitt, but he is also a great advocate of "intellect" and the younger generation. In passing on his intellectual way through

Wesleyan University, Mr. Munson must evidently have heard of the science of psychology, for in the passage I am about to quote he speaks of the imagination as a "psychological faculty." The word psychological has no meaning here, but serves to remind us of the existence of reliable knowledge and the possibility of making definite statements in the field in which Mr. Munson is about to release a piece of pure literature.

"As a psychological faculty," he tells us, "the imagination appears to be superior to reason, feeling and action: a higher development. Its processes occur in a flash and the word for them is simultaneity. The range of its simultaneous *perceptions* is not less than the whole of the given field. That is to say, the imagination in a flash *takes in* the whole of a given object—its origin, its history, its constituents and relations, its uses and its future: it *covers* at once all the actualities and possibilities included in what was . . . *seen!*"

Mr. Munson will excuse the italics and the exclamation, but that word *seen,* arriving after I had loyally struggled with *perceive, take in,* and *cover,* as describing the concrete operation of this truly remarkable faculty, was too much for the distending powers of my intellect. After reading this definition of imagination, I can think of only one experiment which might cast any doubt on its "superiority" to reason, feeling, action, or indeed any other faculty, function, or phenomenon yet observed in this humble world of fact—and that would be to allow as irresponsible, undisciplined, immature, inconsequential, and, in short, humanistical-neo-classic an intellect as Mr. Munson's to define these other faculties and functions.

If we wish to learn something about a "zoological" animal, we go to a zoologist; about a "gynecological" woman, to a gynecologist. This is becoming an established practice, and is at times so important that I do not see how it can be stopped. How long shall we continue to go for information about "psychological faculties" to literary critics who apparently never glanced in a text-book in psychology—who still skate gaily over such rudimentary distinctions as that between seeing, perceiving, and imagining, to say nothing of "taking in" and "covering"? Is it not obvious that this state of affairs can be prolonged only through a general stoppage of all growth?

It is perhaps unfair to base an argument upon Mr. Munson, for he is a kind of specially privileged infant-of-letters. He shows us the "superior order of intelligence" so blithely on the rampage as to relieve us of the labor of the *reductio ad absurdum*. But take Professor Babbitt himself. He is praised by his admirers as a "psychologist," and I have culled from his vigorous and splendidly erudite books three typical examples of his "psychology":

"The part that conceives, that reaches out and seizes likenesses and analogies, may be defined as imagination; the part that discriminates and tests the unity thus apprehended from the point of view of its truth may be defined as analytical reason; the part that perceives is, in the case of the humanist, primarily concerned with the something in man that is set above the phenomenal order. . . ."

"We may . . . distinguish two main orders of intuitions corresponding closely to the two main types of enthusiasm . . . : on the one hand the sensuous or æsthetic, and on the other the spiritual. . . ."

"Three planes may be distinguished—the religious, the humanistic, the naturalistic—though there are, of course, numerous intermediary stages . . . by which man may mount or descend from one level to another of his being."

Is this psychology? Is it not rather to be described as capricious and undisciplined homiletical talk, standing in the same relation to psychology that alchemy and astrology did to the physical sciences—destined as surely to lose its suave tone of authority and disappear? Professor Babbitt himself is quite aware that his home-made apparatus of "parts," "levels," and "orders of intuition" will not survive the advance of disciplined inquiry into his field.

"The humanist is not hostile to science as such," he assures us, but he is hostile to "a science that has *overstepped its due bounds.*"

Again the italics are mine, and their purpose is to show that Professor Babbitt is at one with Miss Riding and Mr. Eliot. The litterateur, the professional critic, the professor of literature—they are all defending, at some last ditch or rampart, the territorial preserves of their trade against the advance of technical and specialized understanding.

Professor L. T. More, himself a physicist—an ally in the opposing camp—is bold enough to attempt to define the exact position of this last ditch or rampart. He says in his essay contributed to the volume *Humanism and America:*

"In a general way, we may say that the scientist should follow in his investigations the phenomena of the objective world only until their special forms of energy are absorbed by our nervous system. It is in the province of the humanist to study the phenomena of the subjective world after these stimuli have been translated into thought and emotion."

This was an indiscretion which the literary defenders of humanism would never commit. Indeed it was a fatal indiscretion, for I fear it must be conceded that by blundering in with this scientific formulation of a literary attitude, Professor More has given the whole game away. The strength of the humanists lay in the fact that while they were defending literary loose talk, the weapon with which they were defending it was also literary loose talk. That made their position well-nigh impregnable. They were protected by the mere automatic operation of their instincts, much in the manner of a small cuttle-fish called the squid, to whom I once dedicated these brief lines of appreciation:

> "There is a fish-like thing, the Squid,
> Who chews a philosophic quid,
> And at the merest wish or wink
> Spits up a cloud of purple ink,
> Which hides himself and all he did.
> He is a literary kid."

Professor Babbitt, who is a master of the inky manœuvre, writes an article called *Humanism: An Essay at Definition.* He begins by denouncing our whole epoch—the epoch, let us remember, of exact science—for its "loose and irresponsible use of general terms." He states that the first step of the humanists must be to define what they mean. Then he writes fourteen pages full of the loose and irresponsible use of general terms without concretely defining a thing, and closes by reminding us that "the first step . . . must be, as I remarked at the outset, right definition." That is successful eloquence, you see! That is literature. But now this naïve physicist, Professor More, glancing up rather casually from his graphs and equations, and seeing an esteemed colleague struggling and squirming in these foul clouds of his own ejaculation, steps forward magnanimously—professors *are* human, as a matter of fact—and offers to lend a hand in the rather technical and, to speak plainly, *scientific* business of definition.

He might as well have shot the esteemed colleague and set a tombstone on his grave: "Here lies the last enemy of knowledge." For when you have once designated the exact spot at which an activity called "science" loses its validity, and must surrender to another activity called "humanism," any amateur in matter-of-fact thinking can train his batteries on that exact spot, and you will find it untenable no matter where it is.

The scientist, says Professor More, may study the phenomena of the objective world only "until their special forms of energy are absorbed by our nervous system." But if you hold to that formulation, it will be necessary for the surgeon to consult a humanist before puncturing the spinal column or injecting his serums into a diseased nerve. Professor More of course would not hold to it; he would retire upon his second position, which is that "processes of consciousness" mark the limit which scientific interpretation may not pass. And here we might merely remind him of the family doctor, whose benign function consists, assuredly 90 per cent of it, in offering a scientific interpretation of our "processes of consciousness"—namely, in telling us that we are not as sick as we think we are. Would you compel the poor man to call in a literary critic before daring to assure us that our stomach-ache is not a cancer?

Professor More has demonstrated the folly of attempting to locate scientifically—that is, really to locate—the "due bounds" which science must not overstep, the "department" in which it must abide, the "degree" at which it must surrender to a "higher order of intelligence." There is no such bound, department, or degree.

Science cannot make your choices for you; that is true. But it is true of all science and of every choice. Physics cannot tell you whether to put lightning-rods on your house, it can only give you reliable general information about lightning. But you do not on that account call physics a pseudo-science, and turn to the literary critics for some "higher" kind of information on this subject. Psychology and sociology cannot tell you whether to commit divorce, murder, marriage, or adultery, but if you are going to choose, these sciences can offer you some clearly defined and fairly reliable information, in place of the vague, uncertain, and contradictory deliverances of humane letters, upon which to base your choice. I believe the majority of laymen who are marching in the humanist procession imagine that they are defending their right to make important choices. What they are defending is their right to make important choices on the basis of amateur, accidentally inherited, unchecked, and unverified information, while taking care, when making unimportant choices, to assemble the best information available.

This accords so ill with any conception of moral responsibility or human dignity, that after you have once realized it, you will find it impossible to believe that responsibility or dignity is what the humanists are genuinely concerned about. They take these words into their mouths, but in the depth of their hearts these solemn critics are no more especially interested in morals than the gayer ones are in intellect. What they are both especially interested in, like so many of the human beings around them, is their own profession. They are brandishing every weapon of idea they can lay hold on —brandishing God himself if they can still hang to Him—in a vain effort to defend the prestige of humane letters against the inexorable advance of a more disciplined study of man.

II

THE RESURRECTION OF THE SCHOLAR-GENTLEMAN

THE literary high-brows of the moment, both young and old, seem to me to speak with a strangely hollow voice. They seem abstracted. They discuss vital questions, but they never seem to care vitally about just the question they are discussing. Take religion, for example. The young men argue about God as though they were choosing a talking-point for a sales campaign, or a nice location for a battery of eloquence. It is not a question whether God exists, but whether it is a good idea to believe in Him. "Religion is highly desirable if it is really available to the individual," Ivor Winters tells us. And Allen Tate issues an earnest paper proposing a kind of generalized family soup of religion, containing all religions in its mysterious deeps, but each so dilute and dissolved in the surrounding extract of polite letters that nobody will be disturbed by their differences. He frankly calls his religion by the name of "technique," a technique for "validating values," not a value in itself, as it would be if its postulates were true. T. S. Eliot, we remember, not long ago notified his readers, adopting the brief but unhurried style of the engraved announcement of a social event, that he is "classicist in literature, royalist in politics and anglo-catholic in religion." And the volume in which he flung us this majestic morsel left us with a feeling that he might more accurately describe himself as classicist in literature, royalist in literature, and anglo-catholic in literature. "The spirit killeth," he has assured us, "the letter giveth life."

And it is the same way with the older men. The "Humanists" as a group have not even made up their minds whether they believe in God or not. Their religion seems to consist of the opinion that those who do believe in God do not believe in Him *enough* to prevent their co-operating in all practical matters with those who don't. "Though I see no evidence," says Irving Babbitt, "that humanism is necessarily ineffective apart from dogmatic and revealed religion, there is, it seems to me, evidence that it gains immensely in effectiveness when it has a background of religious insight." Is not that a rather cool way to discuss the question whether this world is God-ruled and guided to a divine goal? And Paul Elmer More, the other humanist father, poses the question in the same fashion. "Can humanism, of itself, unaided, provide the purpose and values it needs for its fulfilment and without which it cannot pass from the purely critical to the productive state? Must it not for its driving force depend on religion?"

One may well doubt whether the humanists will ever pass from the critical to the productive state without supernatural assistance, for in the natural order the productive state usually comes first. But one may also doubt whether a God believed in for this express purpose—the need being acknowledged "reluctantly," as Mr. More confesses, "almost wishing my answer were mistaken"—will supply the missing electricity. God, at least, was never approached by the most willy-nilly pragmatist with a less flattering indifference to the problem of His real existence.

Another problem which these men seem to approach with their minds on something else is that of political democracy. Irving Babbitt has written a fervent and strong book on the need of this country for real leaders. He goes so far as to say that one should "in the interests of democracy itself seek to substitute the doctrine of the right man for the doctrine of the rights of man." One waits eagerly for his unfolding of the new plan by which the "right man" shall be picked out and moved into his place. He has no plan. He is blandly indifferent to the propriety of his suggesting a plan. Having pointed out that a multitude of men are being "mechanized in order that the captain of industry may . . . live in a state of psychic unrestraint," having warned us that "a leading class that has become Epicurean and self-indulgent is lost," and having assured us that thanks to the inadequacy of our leaders, "both progressive and conservative," we are "moving through an orgy of humanitarian legalism towards a decadent imperialism," and that moreover "the whole elaborate structure that has been reared by the industrial revolution is in danger of collapse," he leaves the job right there, and wanders off vociferating about Confucius and the "inner life"—the "superiority" in fact "of inner over outer action." It seems to me that anybody who cared about the state-of-affairs Professor Babbitt depicts so eloquently, would want to analyze the process by which those miserable leaders got into their positions, and think up some scheme for getting some better ones in.

Of course if he meant by the "inner life" some miracle-working divine event or preoccupation, we might understand his turning this way for a solution of the desperate situation he has depicted on the outside. But the "inner life" turns out to be nothing more miracle-working, and for that matter nothing more "inner," than decorum or the art of behaving like a gentleman —"moderating and harmonizing" one's desires "with a view to living to the best advantage in this world." It is obvious that this programme cannot solve the problem of democracy and leadership. It does not even approach the problem. And moreover it seems nothing less than absentminded to identify decorum with the "inner life." It seems as though the man started to say something and then forgot what it was he was saying.

Another question on which these professors talk as though they were thinking about something else is that about controlling nature. They denounce Zola and Theodore Dreiser and other realistic novelists for having apparently abandoned the purpose to control nature. They tell us that these novelists regard nature, and particularly human nature, as wholly bad and nothing to do about it. Then, while we are wondering whether this is quite true or not, they suddenly bundle them all up into the same abstraction with Rousseau, who thought that human nature was wholly good and everything could be done about it! They call this abstraction "naturalism." And while we are still gazing at this with a slow-witted amazement, like a cow at a new gate, they make another quick motion, and we find in the same package—Francis Bacon, whose one thought was by means of experimental knowledge to get control of nature!

It is a brilliant feat, and I do not see how anybody

could fail to admire it. The idea that human nature is wholly bad, you see, is the same as the idea that human nature is wholly good, except that it is at the opposite extreme. Obviously they belong together and both mean a renunciation of control. And then it is well known that the effort of experimental science to control nature was so successful in the sphere of mechanics, that some rather wild men jumped to the conclusion that the mind itself is nothing but a machine, and the control is an illusion. Therefore Bacon and the whole experimental-scientific movement, Rousseau and the whole revolutionary movement, Zola and the whole realistic movement, are one and the same thing—"naturalism." Deny it if you can!

For my part I should not dream of denying it. You can classify things any way you want to, and your classification will depend in the long run upon your interests. I only assert that a person interested in controlling nature in any concrete part or aspect, human, animal, vegetable or mineral, could not possibly make or accept this classification. For such a person the distinctions it ignores are the vital ones. And so here too the literary *illuminati* seem to be caring about something else besides what they are discussing.

What is it they are caring about?

I have stated in the previous essay my opinion that their opposition to the employment of scientific methods in the study of man is dictated by a protective interest in their own profession of literature. I think I can prove that all these other positions defended by them in so hollow a tone are defended for this same underlying reason. What they are caring about vitally and concretely, while inattentively discussing so large and various an assortment of abstractions, is the defense of "humane letters" against the encroachments of disciplined and verified knowledge.

In order to do this, I must first suggest how far-sweeping and momentous an enterprise it is to defend literary as against scientific knowledge. It does not mean merely that men-of-letters are trying to keep up the price of their product in a competitive market—trying to outsell statistics and laboratory reports with exploits in traditional eloquence. That would be as one-sided as to imagine that they are merely defending a deep habit of enjoyment, which is also a part of the truth. In order to understand the wide reach and dignity of the forces engaged—and particularly the important position occupied by college professors—it is necessary to realize that the literary profession, and that profession of being occupied with the history of literature which goes by the name of the "Higher Learning," has always enjoyed a social and academic prestige superior to that of experimental science. It is this superior prestige, and the whole social, economic and political system, and system of ideas, in which it inheres, that the embattled men-of-letters are fighting to preserve. They are defending the last relics of that nobler status which was accorded in the feudal society to the study of "polite literature," to an impeccable acquaintance with "the classics," to a mastery of "the humanities," as opposed to the rather low social rating of the vulgar pursuit of useful knowledge.

It was Thorstein Veblen who first observed the class

distinction involved in the conflict between science and the humanities. He showed that the "superiority" of futile knowledge is in the last analysis identical with that pecuniary superiority which makes possible a life of leisure. The sciences are given a lower status in a caste society exactly because they are useful, because they are serviceable to the community. Having this general value, they have no value as a symbol of the special power of their possessor to consume his time in non-gainful employment. A word will recall the unique flavor of Veblen's book[1] to those who have read it—and I offer my condolences to those who have not.

"Neither does good repute attach to knowledge of facts that are vulgarly useful. Hence it should appear probable that the interest of the invidious comparison with respect to pecuniary or other honorific merit should occupy the attention of the leisure class, to the neglect of the cognitive interest."

Although Professor Babbitt does not realize that the higherness of the kind of culture he advocates consists *essentially* in this pecuniary elevation, he does realize, and quite frankly state, that it is a culture for gentlemen only. He loves to quote the saying of Burke that "All the good things which are connected with manners and with civilization, have, in this European world of ours, depended for ages upon two principles; . . . I mean the spirit of a gentleman and the spirit of religion." And he never fails to make it clear that the spirit of a gentleman is here the critical thing—religion being of the essence only in so far as it may be, so to speak, *de rigeur* with the gentlemanly class.

[1]*The Theory of the Leisure Class* (1899).

"The ideal of the finely poised gentleman . . . was often allied with Christianity ('devout humanism') but it was also found among the free-thinkers ('libertines') who were hostile to every form of belief in the supernatural." "Why should not the humanist . . . refuse to take sides too decisively in the great debate between the naturalists and the supernaturalists?"

Professor Babbitt also realizes that his "ideal of the finely poised gentleman" can be attained only by those who possess plenty of free time. Indeed he is admirably frank in depicting humanism as a leisure-class philosophy of life.

"Economic and other conditions," he tells us, "are more favorable in this country than elsewhere for the achievement of a truly liberal conception of education with the idea of leisure enshrined at its very centre." He says elsewhere, to be sure, that it is "the quality of a man's work that should determine his place in the hierarchy that every society requires," but only after making it clear that the highest quality of work—that of the "natural aristocrat, as Burke terms him"—is neither manual nor mental, but is an invisible kind of "ethical working" exemplified in the ideal ruler of Confucius who "sat gravely on his throne and that is all."

To put it very simply, the humanists are defending the noble status of their profession, or attempting to regain it, against two "principles" which unite even more firmly than religion with a gentleman: the spirit of a plain man and the spirit of science. Experimental knowledge is plebeian, not only because being useful it carries a flavor of work rather than of sport. It is plebeian also because it develops in close association with productive work, and looks mainly to successful working for the test of its validity. It is plebeian because it continually suggests the possibility of changing things, and the patrician, being well placed in the *status quo,* is disinclined toward any too wonderful generalization of this idea.

Once it is understood that a question of social status is thus involved in the defense of humane letters against science, all those strangely abstract preoccupations of the literati will be seen, I think, to find a concrete motive here. Their cool and yet cordial attitude toward God is quite understandable when you realize that the Higher Learning which they are defending was until recent date an almost exclusive possession of the priestly caste. Its *higherness* derived, in fact, originally from this intimate association with the personal attendants of the *Most High.* But the Most High, whatever may hold as to the problem of His existence, has suffered an undeniable decline in our industrial era as a source of prestige. And therefore the modern defender of the higher status of the humanities, while retaining a grateful memory of that happier relation in the good times gone, is unable to count on any effective assistance from the King of Kings. Professor Babbitt is shrewd enough—and Paul Elmer More, we may say, is not quite shrewd enough—to cast loose from the Most High God and stake his game altogether on the "Higher Immediacy" of the moral will.

When I say "shrewd," I do not mean to attribute to these men-of-letters a wilful deceptiveness either of themselves or others. Of what passes in their minds I cannot judge. I merely attribute to them a vital and concrete motive which I think can explain their strangely detached preoccupation with a set of abstractions not actively conceived and not evidently belonging together. After all, the outstanding fact about that New Humanist programme of salvation is that it was drawn up and issued by literary critics and professors. There is a very general difficulty in finding out just what the programme is. Professor Babbitt himself confesses that in a whole "series of volumes" he has been unable to "make entirely clear" what he means by humanism, and it would be rash on the basis of this experience to cling to the faint hope that another volume might dispel the clouds. If these experts in literature are not able to make clear just what their plan is for saving the world, I do not see how they can take offense if we suggest in our perplexity that perhaps it is not the world, but the prestige of literature, that they are trying to save. Mr. More has himself expressed the opinion that "literature may not too presumptuously be cherished as the final end of existence."

This motive also explains their incredible reluctance to do anything, or even admit that anything should be done, about the "external" problems of our industrial civilization. It explains why Professor Babbitt breaks our hearts with his desolating picture of democracy and its leaders—the whole outfit hell-bent for destruction, if I may so paraphrase his dignified language—and then proposes to save the day by persuading these same leaders to renounce their preoccupation with "humanitarianism," resist the temptation of the ideal of "service," and learn to "limit their desires in so far as this limitation can be shown to make for their own happiness." He does not, of course, really propose to solve the problem in this juvenile manner. He merely turns away from the problem. And he turns away from it, not because it is a trivial problem, but for the opposite reason—because it has become so vast and critical a problem that only science can solve it. There is no longer any parade-ground here for the man-of-letters. Nobody will pay any attention to him; the situation is too serious. Nobody would consult a literary critic if a member of his family went crazy—not even a New Humanist. He would consult an expert in the "pseudo-science of psychology." And nobody is going to consult humane letters about the mortal problems of our industrial civilization; he is going to consult sociology and economics. The defenders of humane letters have no choice therefore but to draw us away from these problems to the problems of the "inner life." The situation in the "inner life," bad as it is, is not critical, and the data moreover appear to be less firmly in the hands of science. Here are both occupation and complacency for the professor of literature.

Not only does this explain why these professors turn with exaggerated dogmatism to the "inner life," but it explains the peculiarly uninspiring stretch of mud flats which this "inner life" turns out to be. It explains why they find it necessary to rear up all that complicated and imposing apparatus of Dualism of Consciousness and Insight of Faith and Supra-Rational Intuition and Conscience and Ethical Will and *Frein Vital* and the Three Levels of Being, and deafen our ears with the old ethico-deifical hullabaloo, only to advocate at last the ordinary routine business of learning to behave yourself. I think everybody who has passed through the ceremonies of initiation and been led up to the inmost altar of the New Humanism has had an involuntary giggle escape him when he found out what it was all about.

Malcolm Cowley, in a desperate attempt to understand this inner vacuity of the New Gospel, jumped to the conclusion that what these men of letters really believe in, and what they mean by all that suspiciously abstract talk about "refraining," is chastity. It would seem a plausible hypothesis, but upon investigation it turns out that they don't even mean that. Professor Babbitt, although modestly draping himself for the purpose in Latin, has issued a most lenient decretal upon this point: "The humanist would moderate rather than deny entirely the most imperious form of the *libido sentiendi*. . . ." I am afraid that even the Freudian wisdom cannot explain the extraordinary fuss which these literary men are making about the obvious fact that it is necessary to hold-in a little in order to have as good a time in leisure as possible.

The fuss consists essentially of taking the attitude of the Christian toward a moral code regarded as the revealed word of God, and attempting to attach it to the code of Aristotle, which was merely a thoughtful formulation of ordinary bourgeois good-sense. Professor Babbitt calls this uniting the Christian and the Classical traditions, and it is uniting them in a way, but in a very tricky way. The essence of the Greek view of morals, and the underlying assumption of Aristotle's Ethics, was that virtue is intelligent conduct. "Knowledge is virtue," as Plato's Socrates says. The brave man is the man who knows when to fight and when to run away; the right act is the act based upon the best information. That is the fundamental "classical tradition" in morals, and Aristotle's rather conservative and gentlemanly ethic merely remarked that this right, or intelligent, act will usually be a moderate one. Professor Babbitt seizes this ethic of Aristotle because he wants to be a gentleman. But he abandons Aristotle's underlying assumption that the good act is the act which results from true knowledge, because he also wants to be a literary scholar and oppose the encroachments of science. It is to keep science out of the discussion of moral problems that he clings to those Christian ideas of "conscience" and "inner vision" and "higher will," which combine so ludicrously, and indeed combine not at all, with Aristotle's quiet effort to describe intelligent conduct. And since he does not really believe in Christianity or any other revealed religion, he finds himself in the ridiculous position of asserting that this higher ethical will is one of the "immediate data of consciousness," and yet also asserting that it lies beyond the purview of psychology, which is merely the name for any serious study of the immediate data of consciousness. He finds himself dismissing as a "corruption of ethics" Freud's attempt to improve the technique of self-control through the knowledge of self—dismissing it in the name of Socrates and Aristotle and the Greek tradition. "Deny this ethical will and the inner life disappears," he cries in a most un-Aristotelian flurry. Deny this ethical will—understand it, rather, as a will to act intelligently and with full relevance to the facts—and nothing whatever disappears but the superiority of literary loose talk to scientific knowledge.

A like motive explains the wilful blindness with which the humanists toss about that manufactured abstraction called "naturalism." They despise Francis Bacon because his zeal for controlling nature holds a chief place in the advancement of science to which as scholar-gentlemen they are professionally opposed. They despise Rousseau because with his wild idea that nature needs no control he furnished a slogan to that revolution which overthrew the system of caste in which the superiority of the scholar-gentleman was secure. That is why they roll these two contrary characters and attitudes up into one abstraction called "naturalism," and tell you that this abstraction is the concrete essence of evil. If it is true that Professor Babbitt cannot go to sleep until he has looked under the bed to see if Rousseau is there, this is not because he foolishly imagines that anybody is still taken in by Rousseau's nonsensical idea that "all men are good in a state of nature." It is because he wisely knows that Rousseau with all his romantic nonsense was the herald of a democratic revolution. And that revolution is what exalted—or will yet exalt—the knowledge which is useful to the community, the real and reliable knowledge heralded by Francis Bacon, above the polite preoccupations of the Higher Learning.

That is how Rousseau and Bacon come to be rolled up together, and I suspect that Zola and Dreiser find their way into the same company for a similar reason. The opposition of our literary professors to extreme and bitter realism is not due to the suggestion of fatality or hopelessness of action which it conveys to weak and enervated minds. It is due to the suggestion it conveys to strong minds that action is necessary. They want to preserve in literature that complacent composure which properly accords with the gentlemanly status they demand for it. It is not that they oppose reality, or think that art should confine itself to the ideal, but merely that there is a certain limit beyond which seeing the plain facts becomes uncomfortable, and indeed impossible, to a reasonably sympathetic gentleman suitably engrossed in "living to the best advantage in this world." For that reason they oppose a "fatalistic" attitude which they attribute to these describers of sordid facts, and at the same time oppose "humanitarianism" which can only be defined as the attitude of those who refuse to be fatalistic about these same facts. And they oppose the ideal of service, except it be "service to God," by which they mean the pompous monument of temporal pride and spiritual humility which the feudal caste system erected upon the burial place of the ideal of human service. And they oppose "progress" as an idea, because progress as a fact has departed inexorably from that feudal system. And they preach "tradition" as an abstract good, incredibly pretending that there is only one tradition or at the most two, because the prevailing traditions in literature and the humanities are aristocratic. In short, they wish to be gentlemen-and-scholars with the full status and prerogative, complacency, composure, authority and reward which of right appertained to that order in the times gone.

If this is true of the New Humanists, it is even more

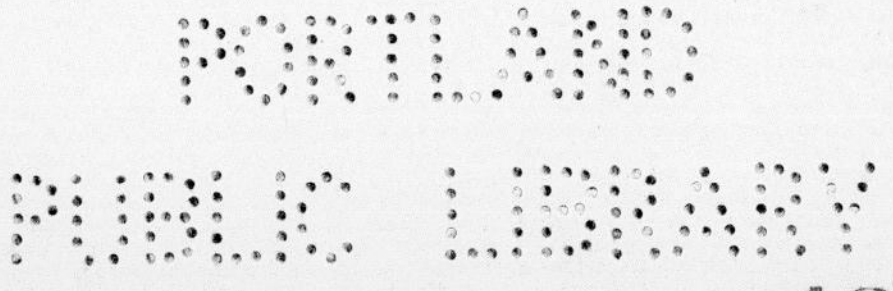

obviously true of those younger critics whom I call "neo-classical." The humanists are resisting science in the name of a Higher Morality and demanding that we should "subordinate intellect to the ethical will." These other critics are resisting science in the name of Intellect itself, or "Reason," or a "Superior Order of Intelligence." But they are resisting it with the same motive—because it threatens the prestige of their profession. And so they not only talk with the same queer abstractedness about God, but dismiss with a bland gesture of superiority all the pressing perplexities of our industrial civilization, naïvely imagining that in thus pushing out of their purview questions upon whose solution depends the future of our race they are outgrowing a childish obsession of the writers of a previous decade with economics. They are merely retreating to a safer position in the struggle to defend against verified knowledge the narrowing domain of the "literary intelligence."

And since they are waging the same struggle as the humanists, they show of course the same homesickness for feudalism, the same antagonism to the masses of mankind and to those interested in their destiny. It was no accident that in expressing his polite scorn for the early efforts of psychology and sociology, T. S. Eliot should have tossed in among them the movement for social emancipation. "Social emancipation crawled abroad" was the phrase in which he expressed his feeling. And it is no accident that in advocating a revival of "intellect" and a "control of the emotions by Reason," he should deliver the essential force of his attack against Bernard Shaw and H. G. Wells and Bertrand Russell, three men essentially distinguished by intellect, but who have devoted their intellects, not to literary scholarship, but to mastering some essentials of the advancing sciences and trying to make literature say something of contemporary force and meaning. "They all exhibit intelligence at the mercy of emotion," Eliot tells us.

I have suggested elsewhere that this critic would speak more wisely about emotion if he knew what is known—and also the limitations of what is known—about this subject. But I do not think it requires technical knowledge—only a little shrewd sense—to see that he is here merely opposing one emotion to another. His phrase "social emancipation crawled abroad" is saturated with sentimental emotion. His whole reaction of distaste for experimental science and what he calls "social emancipation" is but the complacent squeamishness of one dominated by the sentiment of caste. And this state of feeling is not even perceived, to say nothing of being illumined or led into its results and relations, as are the contrary emotions of Shaw and Wells and Bertrand Russell, by an activity of intellect. The instinct is enough, since it is the instinct of a gentleman. "Tradition" will supply the place of reason, and the police—at least so it is hoped—will make intelligence unnecessary.

There is indeed a shallowness in the passion, as there is pettiness in the ambition, of those who can aim no higher than toward an incomplete identification with a leisure class. Futility in the object is for them the sanction of pure feeling, and in those enterprises whose crown and glamour is futility, try as you will, the deep organic passions will not enter. Dryden cared clearly about the nice graces of a panegyric and its place in the history and among the forms of poetry, but confusedly about the question whether it was addressed to Cromwell or King Charles. He revelled in a somewhat Rabelaisian wit, but was quite ready to repent and pray public forgiveness for his best jokes at the dictate of a changing fashion. Pope, in order to polish the meter of his philosophy and promote its favor in the market, changed the statement that human life is "a mighty maze of walks without a plan," to read "a mighty maze—but not without a plan." A passion that so picks the path of its loyalty is a passion none too vast in force. If that is what it means to be "intellectual," we shall have to concede that some of the neo-classicists have risen so high. As I turned the pages of *The Sacred Wood* after copying Eliot's cavalier reference to the problems of science and to the social problem, my eye fell upon this opening sentence of another essay:

"It is a question of some nicety to decide how much must be read of any particular poet."

A nice question indeed—not one which would have stirred a riot in the Mermaid Tavern, but one into which a perfect gentleman, a gentleman and a scholar, an anglo-catholic and a royalist, need not to be too fastidious to enter with full abandon.

It is this drift of his ambition, this tendency of his nature toward small elevations, and not any urgency of intellect or classic restraint of great passion, that has determined Eliot's position as a critic of letters. His bizarre predilection for Dryden, the incredible pretense, I should say—for Eliot has underlying his trivialities a fine and solid taste—that Dryden is a poet comparable in any great point of his art with Milton, belongs in my opinion to the same ambition. Eliot himself suggests that Dryden's subject-matter is what has averted so many critics from him. His subject-matter—or rather, perhaps, his attitude in life—is what brings Eliot with homage to his feet.

To me it seems obvious beyond dispute that it is not the forms of poetry, but the feeling-tone of the Restoration, toward which this critic and his literary friends have gravitated with so gallant a step. How else can one perceive the fact, for instance, that he and Edith Sitwell, while advocating a return to that period of temperate clarity in verse, should be composing, he as cloudy, and she as decadently ornamental, a poetry as our language knows? Edith Sitwell is a kind of color-lavishing Aubrey Beardsley of poetry; I do not know how she could go farther away from Pope. And T. S. Eliot, if he should survive as a poet, would survive to disprove the opinion of John Dryden himself that "The first end of a writer" is "to be understood." It is possible to comprehend this contradiction only when you remember that the period toward which these poets are yearning back was not merely a period of clarity and spare color in poetry. It was also the last period when gentlemen and ladies felt undisturbed by "social emancipation," and literary scholars safe in their superiority to science. In the age of democratic and proletarian revolution, a wilful extreme of artifice in beauty, a decorating of all adornments, is the natural protest of a lady. And in the age of science, an obscurity impenetrable by acid, lens or scalpel, is the sole refuge of the literary gentleman and scholar.

Thus in their more diverting way the neo-classic critics are waging the same struggle as the New Humanists. The difference between them, indeed, is almost as significant as their deep accord. The neo-classic group are lighter in their step, more elegant, more graceful in impertinence, and more assured. You might convey the flavor of the difference by saying that they are more interested in "polite" than "humane" letters, more busy being literary gentlemen than scholars. Disguising their reaction against the vulgar pursuit of useful knowledge as a revival of Intellect, and deceiving themselves even more perfectly perhaps than others with the disguise, they do at times achieve the ease and witty irresponsibility of those cultivated gentlemen of the Restoration. Many of them, too, have had either the foresight to be born in England, or a sufficiently driving sense of republican inferiority to make them move over there where the Puritans were actually kicked out and the king restored. The humanists have had to fight their battle where the Puritans landed, and where the kingly and feudal system never got a hold. They have the task not only to revive a gentlemanly tradition, but to create one and make it take root in alien soil. It is the strain of this effort that makes them so much more serious than their British confrères. It is to meet this necessity that they dress up their defense of humane letters not as an intellectual but as a moral revival. Only from a somewhat international point of observation does it become evident that the "Higher Immediacy" of their ethical will, and the "Superior Order" of the neo-classic intellect, occupy the same real altitude—an altitude measurable in terms of the "predilections of the leisure class" and the "canons of pecuniary merit."

In his chapter on "The Higher Learning," Veblen makes this seemingly prophetic remark:

"Habituation to war entails a body of predatory habits of thought, whereby clannishness in some measure replaces the sense of solidarity, and a sense of invidious distinction supplants the impulse to equitable, every-day serviceability. As an outcome of the cumulative action of these factors, the generation which follows a season of war is apt to witness a rehabilitation of the element of status, both in its social life and in its scheme of devout observances and other symbolic and ceremonial forms."

The war to which this passage alludes was the American Civil War, and Veblen was explaining the sudden adoption by our Middle-Western universities of the academic cap and gown. He would explain in like words, I imagine, the revival in this generation of a sudden devotion to "those fields of speculation and investigation which are reputable and futile, rather than to the quest for scientific knowledge." And I think we may safely predict that the present efforts toward a literary rehabilitation of the régime of status will have as little permanent success in stemming the tide of vulgar but real knowledge as did the academic cap and gown in our Middle-Western universities.

The time will come, of course, when we shall have to stop explaining everything that happens as a result of the World War, and we might begin by regarding this literary apparition, not merely as an echo of that predatory period, but as the premonition of a dictatorial régime to come. It seems probable to me that if Irving Babbitt should begin to think a little less with isms and dead men's names, and more with his own living brain, he would soon pass from bewailing the loss of the "inner check" to advocating an outer one in the Italian form. He has already ascribed to Julius Cæsar "the merit of seeing that . . . as the result of the breakdown of religious restraint (for which Stoical 'service' was not an adequate substitute), the Romans were rapidly becoming unfit for republican institutions." And he has given us a fair warning in the remark that "Circumstances may arise when we may esteem ourselves fortunate if we get the American equivalent of a Mussolini." In those circumstances, I suppose that a majority of the critics and professors I have been discussing would flock with Professor Babbitt to the fascist banner. But I think they would be disappointed of their dearest—at least of their most romantically "classical"—hopes. A modern dictatorship is not a return to feudalism. The Black Shirts are not imbued either with "the spirit of religion" or "the spirit of a gentleman." Nor can they lay the foundations of a régime in which those lost attitudes might renew themselves and flourish. The foundation for that was a predatory and agrarian life with a primitive technique of industry. The feudal lord was a glorified warrior and land-owner. The fascist dictator is a glorified financier and factory boss. He may flirt a little for his own purposes with an existing Pope or king, but there is no hope in him —not even on the fringes of his glory—for the revival of the intellectual grandee, the noble scholar of the humanities, the high-priest of "literary truth." He is impelled by the technique, and compelled by the vital problems, of machine industry, to be scientific. He is compelled, too, by the fact that science is in the hands of his enemies, of those who would overthrow him and go deeper with the experiment in democracy. If he stops us on that course, he will stop us with the scientist and not the literary scholar seated beside his throne.

In my opinion the knell of this whole cultural incident—this little wild-goose chase into history of the demoted men-of-letters—is sounded in the recent confession of T. S. Eliot that he is dissatisfied with the meaning of his own "statements in criticism," dissatisfied also with "the terminology of the Humanists," and disposed to ask himself, "whether there is still any justification for literary criticism at all, or whether we should not merely allow the subject to be absorbed gently into exacter sciences." He has travelled far from his pre-Darwinian gods, from Campion, Boileau, Dryden, from the benign pronunciamento of *The Sacred Wood:* "I do not deny the very great value of all work by scientists in their own departments." He has grown more proud and humble, fame having perhaps assuaged the provincial self-distrust which made him hasten to those sophomoric heights. I do not mean to express a hope that T. S. Eliot will soil his fingers by joining in the work of these "exacter sciences," or that he will grow up to the stature of any rigorous aspiration in his social feeling. I think he will shrink more deeply into the protecting elegances of the church. But he has at least pronounced the words which may ring the curtain down upon this whole gentlemanly anti-scientific interlude.

PART III

LITERATURE IN RETREAT

I

THE CULT OF UNINTELLIGIBILITY

Two tendencies are confused in the literary movement called modernist which ought to be distinguished. They are clearly distinguished for me, because I like one of them and the other I regard as an affliction. But many people see only one tendency here and are puzzled to define it. The tendency that I like is toward the cultivation of pure poetry. The tendency that I do not like I call the Cult of Unintelligibility.

If you pick up a book by Hart Crane, E. E. Cummings, James Joyce, Gertrude Stein, Edith Sitwell, or any of the "modernists," and read a page innocently, I think the first feeling you will have is that the author isn't telling you anything. It may seem that he isn't telling you anything because he doesn't know anything. Or it may seem that he knows something all right, but he won't tell. In any case he is uncommunicative. He is unfriendly. He seems to be playing by himself, and offering you somewhat incidentally the opportunity to look on.

All poetry, according to I. A. Richards, is an act of communication. It is that, whether the poet thinks so or not, because words are in their very nature communications. All literature, indeed, Mr. Richards would define as a verbal communication of values. I defer to him because he is a psychologist who teaches literature —the sole living example of this long-awaited species.

I accept his assertion that all literature is *in some degree* a communicative act, and I say that modernist literature is characterized by an increasing stinginess in the performance of this act.

A dominant tendency of the advancing schools of poetry for the last twenty years has been to decrease the range, the volume, and the definiteness of communication. To my mind that statement, which has a verifiable meaning, might take the place of about one-half the misty literarious talk of the poets and the poet-critics of the modernist movement. They are not "abandoning romanticism," "returning to the eighteenth-century tradition," "inaugurating a neo-classical era" —it is the height of romanticism to imagine that they are. They are not "overcoming the distinction between subject-matter and form," "revolting against the tyranny of the general reader," being "primitive," being "intellectual," being "æsthetic," instituting an "artificial barbarism," or clinging to the "hard matter-of-fact skeleton of poetic logic." There is no such skeleton and no such logic. What they are doing is withdrawing into themselves. They are communicating to fewer people, they are communicating less, and what they communicate is less definitely determined. And this is true of the whole movement, all the way from free verse to free association.

Free verse decreases the definiteness of communication by introducing into the transcription of poetry a gross mark of punctuation which has no significance commonly agreed upon. Suppose that instead of this arbitrary line-division I made up a new character, a semicolon composed of two commas with the tails going opposite ways. And suppose I announced that as a poet I was going to use that comma-colon wherever and whenever I wanted to, like the joker in the pack, without any agreement as to its value, either rhythmical or grammatical. It would be obvious, would it not, that the freedom I had acquired was not a freedom to communicate more to my readers, but a freedom from the terms of communication—a freedom to play by myself? This is the principal thing accomplished by the line-division in free verse, except in a few poems where it is employed, as Blake and Whitman usually employed it, to divide the actual phases of a chant.[1]

From free verse it was a short step to free punctuation. I mean the habit of turning loose a handful of punctuation marks like a flock of bacteria to browse all over the page, and even eat their way into the insides of apparently healthy words. Let us see an example of this from the poetry of E. E. Cummings. We have to *see* his poetry because it is composed so largely of punctuation that it cannot be heard. In fact we shall soon have to exhibit Cummings in a projection-room; for undoubtedly the next step in modernism will be to show these punctuation marks in the actual process of entering a word, and show how the nucleus of the word, its meaning, divides, and the new and more delicate meanings are formed by a process which the biologist would describe as endogastric proliferation. For the present

[1]After further reflection I would revise this statement. The principal thing, or at least the best thing, accomplished by the typographical arrangement called free verse, is to notify the reader, and keep him notified, that he is reading poetry and is to give his attention to the rhythm. In this way it does sometimes, if the author desires and the reader consents, promote a subtlety of rhythmic communion. Its commonest effect, however, is to loosen the bonds between them.

we must content ourselves with examining the poem first in its normal condition, and then seeing how it looks when infected or impregnated with punctuation marks.

"Among these red pieces of day—against which, and quite silently, hills made of blue and green paper, scorch-bending themselves, upcurve into anguish, climbing spiral, and disappear—satanic and blasé, a black goat lookingly wanders. There is nothing left of the world, but into this nothing 'il treno per Roma signori?' jerkily rushes."

That is the poem. It hasn't any title; it just jumps at you like a robber out of the brush and says "Listen or run!" However, somebody has been indiscreet enough to make revelations about this poem, and I happen to be in a position to explain that it has to do with a ride on an Italian railroad train. It is evening, and the sun is just setting over the mountains—the day, that is, is breaking to pieces and the pieces are red. And the poet also is going to pieces in a manner of speaking. At least he is feeling a little heart-sick or car-sick, and I imagine him leaning against the window in that rather frantic quietness which seizes one on such occasions, and as the train swings into the hills, the hills rise and seem to bend around and climb up spirally the way scorching paper bends, and this process gives the poet a feeling of anguish which it is hardly necessary to locate in the vicinity of the solar plexus. And then suddenly the hills disappear, a black goat slides by in the twilight, and then nothing, a blank—it is dark—or the poet is dead, or something—but the conductor calls out, "The train for Rome, gentlemen?"

It is quite a poem, you see, after all—quite an experience. But it is a very expensive one, because you have to hire a couple of detectives and have the poet shadowed for a month or two until you catch him in a temporary fit of common sense and get him to admit what it is he is talking about.

Now let us see how this already sufficiently obscure poem looks after an attack of punctuation:

Among
  these
          red pieces of
day (against which and
quite silently hills
made of blueandgreen paper

scorchbend ingthem
-selves-U
pcurv E,into:
          anguish(clim
b)ing
s-p-i-r-a-
l
and,disappear)
          Satanic and blasé

a black goat lookingly wanders

There is nothing left of the world but
into this noth
ing il treno[1] per
Roma si-gnori?
jerk.
ilyr, ushes

You can see from this that punctuation is a serious affliction. And yet it is quite possible that if you put this poetry under a microscope you would find that the

[1] I venture to correct Mr. Cummings's spelling of this word, hoping that "trene" was an orthographic mistake and not a part of his lyrical inspiration.

commas and parentheses themselves have been attacked by still more minute grammatical organisms, and that the whole thing is simply honeycombed with punctuation.

To show the length to which a sane man will go when he sets out to be literary, let me quote the comment of Paul Rosenfeld on Cummings's use of punctuation marks:

"The typographical display exists upon his pages never in the intention of picture-writing, and always for the purpose of marking the acceleration and hesitation of the rapid, capricious, and melodic line."

What would a man who was trying to be scientific say about this same question? Or rather what would he do about it—for science has a way of answering questions by doing something. He would take two of the most enthusiastic admirers of this poetry—Paul Rosenfeld might be one, and E. E. Cummings another—lead them into separate sound-proof chambers and permit them to read this poem in the august presence of a sphygmograph, a machine designed to record in a white line on a black roller the actual pulsations of the "rapid, capricious, and melodic line" as it is "marked" by these signs of punctuation. Is there any reason to believe that, punctuation being what it is and human nature being what it is, the two readers would produce curves showing the same "accelerations and hesitations" at the points where these punctuation marks appear? Of course they would not. It is only necessary to mention the experiment. The critic, therefore, is not talking sense. He is talking what I call literarious nonsense.

Science is nothing but a persistent and organized effort to talk sense. And science would tell us that these punctuation marks on the rampage do not promote accuracy of communication, but destroy it. They may have a very subtle, fine, and real value within the poet's mind. It is a mere conspiracy of folly to pretend that they have an identic value in the mind of any reader.

From free punctuation it is an easy step to free grammar—or rather, freedom from grammar. I use this inexact expression to characterize the kind of freedom attained, in its ultimate purity, by Gertrude Stein. Let us examine a passage of Gertrudian prose:

"I was looking at you, the sweet boy that does not want sweet soap. Neatness of feet do not win feet, but feet win the neatness of men. Run does not run west but west runs east. I like west strawberries best."

One can hardly deny a beauty of ingenuity to these lines. They have a fluency upon the tongue, a logical intricacy that is intriguing. But any deeper value they may have, value for the mind or the passions of a reader, will be composed of elements not objectively implied but accidentally suggested by them. No doubt any one who dwells with idle energy upon their plausible music will find impulses from his own life rising to employ them as symbol or pattern for a moment of realization. But the impulses that rise to these lines from the reader's life will never by any chance be the same as those that dictated them in the life of the author. Communication is here reduced to a minimum. The values are private—as private as the emotional life of the insane. In fact the passage quoted was not from Gertrude Stein, but from the ravings of a maniac cited by Kraepelin in his *Clinical Psychiatry.* Here is a passage from Gertrude Stein:

"Any space is not quiet it is so likely to be shiny. Darkness very dark darkness is sectional. There is a way to see in onion and surely very surely rhubarb and a tomato, surely very surely there is that seeding."

It is essentially the same thing, you see, except that Gertrude Stein perpetrates it voluntarily, and—to judge by the external appearance—not quite so well. It is private literature. It is intra-cerebral art.

Edith Sitwell says, in her *Poetry and Criticism,* that Gertrude Stein is "bringing back life to our language by what appears, at first, to be an anarchic process. First she breaks down the predestined groups of words, their sleepy family habits; then she rebrightens them, examines their texture, and builds them into new and vital shapes." If this engaging statement means anything except what every good and vivid writer does, it means that Miss Stein is emptying words of the social element. Words are vessels of communion; she is treating them as empty vessels, polishing them and setting them in a row.

James Joyce not only polishes the words that he sets in a row, but moulds them and fires them in his own oven. From free grammar he has taken the farther step to free etymology. All boisterous writers have made up words, but they have made them in such a way or placed them in such a context that their meaning or value was conveyed to the reader. Joyce, in his recent writing, makes up words to suit the whim-chances of a process going on only in his own brain.

"For if the lingo gasped between kicksheets were to

be preached from the mouths of wickerchurchwardens and metaphysicians in the row and advokaatoes, allvoyous, demi-voyelles, languoaths, lesbiels, dentelles, gutterhowls and furtz, where would their practice be or where the human race itself were the Pythagorean sesquipedalia of the pan-epistemion, grunted and gromwelled, ichabod, habakuk, opanoff, uggamyg, hapaxle, gomenon, ppppfff, over country stiles, behind slated dwellinghouses, down blind lanes, or, when all fruit fails, under some sacking left on a coarse cart?"

This literary form also finds its involuntary parallel in the madhouse. There too the inevitable step is taken from free grammar to free etymology. That automatic "flight of ideas," the result of some pathological drying upward of the deeper associational roots of words, naturally passes over into a mere flight of syllables. Indeed any one can imitate both these symptoms by compelling himself to talk faster than he can think or feel. But he cannot imitate them with the rare and various genius of James Joyce. Joyce is equipped for creative etymology as few men ever were. He has a curious and wide learning in languages and their ways; he has a prodigiously fine ear. You feel that he lives in a world of spoken sounds, through which he goes hearing as acutely as a dog goes smelling, that all the riches of his mind are but an ingenious complication of the neural paths from ear to tongue. The goal toward which he seems to be travelling with all this equipment of genius is the creation of a language of his own—a language which might be superior poetically, as Esperanto is practically, to any of the known tongues. It might be immortal—as immortal as the steel shelves of the libraries in which it would rest. But how little it would communicate, and to how few. When it is not a humorous emotion—as praise God it often is—that we enjoy with Joyce in his extreme etymological adventures, what is there that we experience in common with him? A kind of elementary tongue dance, a feeling of the willingness to perform it. To me reading Joyce's *Work in Progress* is a good deal like chewing gum—it has some flavor at the start but you soon taste only the motion of your jaws. Of course a more permanent flavor can be got, if you want to sit down with dictionaries and work over it as you would over a Chinese puzzle, or a foreign language, or a few dozen foreign languages. But even if you should do that, nobody else would, and therefore the total amount of communication would remain as before infinitesimal. Until we establish an international bureau for the decoding of our contemporary masterpieces, I think it will be safe to assert that Joyce's most original contribution to English literature has been to lock up one of its most brilliant geniuses inside of his own vest.

For better or worse, it results from the indefiniteness of the matter communicated in these extreme kinds of freedom that only one genius can distinguish himself in each kind. Gertrude Stein discovered the flight of ideas as a literary form some twenty years ago, and she has been hammering away at it, lonely and immortal, ever since. No one else can distinguish himself in this form, because there are no definite distinctions in it. A similar thing is true of Joyce in so far as he speaks a private language, and of Cummings as the discoverer of intraverbal punctuation. They cannot be rivalled; they can only be imitated. Their glory is secure.

Younger modernists ought not be discouraged by this fact, however, for there are other freedoms still to be won. There is alphabetical freedom, for instance. Why should the letters within a word be permitted to congregate forever in the same dull, old, conventional and sleepy groups? Why not a little spontaneity of arrangement here, and the occasional eruption of an Arabic or Chinese or Russian letter that happens to linger in the memory and chime with the whims of the poet? The Russians have a great, fat, double-squatting letter that looks like a toad sitting on his grandmother making pious motions with his arms. One poet might enrich the alphabet with borrowings like this. Another might abandon the alphabet altogether and make a new one more congenial to his inner life.

Moreover, with all respect to the typographical genius of E. E. Cummings, he is a mere infant in the free art of punctuation. Why content oneself with meagrely redistributing a handful of tame signs, dried up, stale, dead and familiar to all Western European civilization for upwards of three thousand years? Can you wake a man up with an exclamation point that was known to his father and his grandfather and his great-grandfathers before him? Can you stop the modern breath with a colon that was a bore to Cleopatra? Let us have a little real creative activity in these fields. A little cross-breeding between plus signs and semicolons would be a good beginning. By crossing the minus sign with the colon we got the sign of division; a cross between a plus sign and a semicolon might give us something even more remarkable. That has never been tried. And why not introduce a few foreign strains here, too?

Spanish question marks behave in very queer ways, standing on their heads in front of a question as well as jumping up and making faces behind it. All these things would help to jazz up the rapid, capricious, and melodic line. Each of them would give one more uncommunicative poet a place of distinction.

And then there is free type-setting still to be adequately exploited in English, although known long ago to the futurist poets of Italy. And there is free photo-engraving still to be imported from Russia. I have a volume given me by the Russian poet Maiakovsky, in which a large part of the total effect is produced by a series of scrapbook designs made out of reproduced photographs and magazine half-tones. The cover design is a picture of the poet's wife, a charming girl in real life, apparently entering the first stages of an epileptic fit. On another page she appears, more tranquilly, as an insert in a menagerie. Another page shows Maiakovsky himself being shampooed by a dinosaur while engaging in a long-distance telephone conversation through an automobile horn with his cook, who seems to be standing on the poop-deck of an astronomical observatory getting ready to do the family wash. If Paul Rosenfeld thinks that E. E. Cummings's typography is not picture writing, it may be so, although the question is subtle. But here is a far more powerful poet than E. E. Cummings—the most gifted Slavic poet of his generation—and several volumes of his rhapsodical mixtures of poetry with picture writing of the most childlike type have been published by the State Printing House and sold in Soviet Russia by the tens of thousands.

Maiakovsky's crazy-quilt photo-designs are actual illustrations of the themes of his poems. Both the themes and the illustrations are infected with unintelligibility, and I find the designs distasteful because they are inexpressive and old-fashioned. Even in progressive kindergartens the scrapbook has been replaced by picture writing of a more active and original kind. Nevertheless, in so far as these typographical experiments *are* picture writing, and overtly so, they are not so much a part of the cult of unintelligibility as an effort to escape from it. The marks in the book, having lost their clear character as signs suggesting imaginary experience to the reader, begin to be cultivated as an offering of actual experience to him. This development appears in E. E. Cummings—even if not in his punctuation—in his fondness for printing poems in queer, funny, fancy, or grotesque ways upon the page. Every once in a while he turns a poem upside down. And that too is a good idea, if there is no danger of anything falling out of it. But I do not suppose he writes them upside down. I doubt whether he conceives them upside down. This way of printing them is something else besides poetry; it is a pictorial art, an art of making designs out of printer's ink and paper. And that is of course what you have left when all the social communication is withdrawn from words.

Following this road, the modernist poets might become exquisite painters of letters as the poets of ancient China were. They might give their creative attention to the mixing of inks, the selecting or inventing of textures and tints of paper, and the binding of books. They might even anoint their verses, as once the

Persian poets did, with an appropriate odor—not always as in those days, you may be sure, a pleasant one. And in this manner they could revive, if they had money enough, on a small cultural island in the midst of our machine civilization, some of the charms of a past age of the world. But in so far as they are really modern, and not wealthier than is usual with poets, I do not see how they can go very far in this direction, except to abandon poetry altogether and became either painters, on the one hand, or on the other, printers and manufacturers of ink and paper. And that is, perhaps, the logical outcome of the tendency I am describing—a tendency to ignore the terms of the act of verbal communication.

I have described only the cruder manifestations of this tendency. It appears, however, in poetry that is quite sociable in the matter of verse-form and grammar and punctuation and etymology. A freedom to make unlimited use of all the foreign languages that happen to be known to the author is one of its manifestations. A freedom to make unexplicit allusions to some book or manuscript he happens to have been reading—accessible perhaps only in the Bibliothèque Nationale or the British Museum—is another. Mr. Graves and Miss Riding in their *Survey of Modernist Poetry* speak with great enthusiasm of this kind of freedom.

In a single volume of Ezra Pound's *Lustra,* they tell us, "occur literary references to Greek, Latin, Spanish, Italian, Provençale, and Chinese literature—some of these incorrectly given. Mr. Eliot, who is a more serious scholar, has references in *The Waste Land* to Greek, Latin, Spanish, Italian, French, German, and

Sanskrit. The English classics quoted or referred to are not now the stock-classics to which Victorian and post-Victorian poets paid tribute, not Chaucer, Spenser, Shakespeare, Milton, Burns, but others known only to the cognoscenti—Peele, Kyd, Lyly, the less familiar Shakespeare, Webster, Marvell, Dryden, Swift, Darley, Beddoes; making the succession of English poetry wear a more varied look. The same enlargement is made with the Greek, Latin, Italian, and French poets."

The authors call this a method of "civilizing and enlarging poetry." Its actual effect is to narrow the circle of communication to a small group of specialists in a particular type of learning—by no means the most important type—and to communicate even to the members of this circle only a part of the content of the poem. Most of the "cognoscenti," as I know them, will be so tickled by the poet's assuming they know everything he is alluding to, that they will get along better than others without the more specific pleasure of finding out what he is alluding to. Even those who do find out will have enjoyed a cerebral exercise rather than the emotional and intellectual experience of the poem.

I use the word *cerebral,* because it is the firm conviction of the modernist poets and their admirers that they are extremely intellectual, and it is my firm conviction that they are not. They have a great deal going on inside their heads in proportion to what goes on in their organs of vital emotion, but so has a bridge player or a tired business man devoting his idle moments to cross-word puzzles. In my opinion, the admirers of modernist poetry as a distinctively intellectual phenomenon may be divided into two classes. First, those who think they understand what is unintelligible because they do not know what it is to understand. They are the same people who listen in a theatre to a foreign actor speaking an unknown tongue, and come home and tell us his acting was so wonderful that they understood the whole play. Second, those who do know what it is to understand, but find so little in real life to exercise their understandings upon that they develop a devout passion for conundrums, riddles, rebuses, acrostics, logogriphs, and games of solitaire and twenty questions. My own playful tastes lie very strongly in the opposite direction. Life itself as I try to live it is puzzle enough, and there is no dearth of riddles even when the talk is clear. Therefore, when the modernist critics object to Mr. Cummings's poems that they are too lucid—"they do not present the eternal difficulties that make poems immortal"—I can only bow and retire. I do not live in that world. When they object to the established punctuation of Shakespeare because it "restricts his meaning to special interpretations of special words," and say that "if we must choose any one meaning, then we owe it to Shakespeare to choose . . . one embracing as many meanings as possible, that is, the most difficult meaning," I feel that they have never touched the mind of Shakespeare. And when they describe one of the great sonnets, punctuated in a manner that they consider, on very flimsy evidence, to be Shakespeare's own, as "a furiously dynamic cross-word puzzle which can be read in many directions at once," I feel that I am confronted with beings of a different species. It seems to be a species in which the cerebral cortex is severed from the midbrain and the rest of the vital system, and seeks the experience of life in speeding up all by itself like a racing motor.

T. S. Eliot has discovered another kind of freedom that deserves comment. It is to be found in a series of explanatory notes which he appends at the end of his poems. A similar device was adopted by Dante in his *Vita Nuova*. But Mr. Eliot's notes differ from Dante's, and from all other explanatory notes, in being entirely free from explanation.

Another friendly custom of the older poets has been abandoned by the modernists—the custom of giving the poem a title which tells us what it is about. The modernist titles tell us what the poem is not about, and they usually tell us that in a foreign language. Here, for example, is a poem by Edith Sitwell. Edith Sitwell is, in my opinion, the most gifted of the modernist poets—the one who is most unaffectedly expressing a genuine and inevitable poetic character—but she is also one of the most wilfully unfriendly to me, her admiring reader. She has entitled this poem "Aubade," and if you do not happen to know what "Aubade" means, that is your good luck. You will have less difficulty in finding out what her poem is about.

"Jane, Jane,
Tall as a crane,
The morning light creaks down again.

Comb your cockscomb-ragged hair,
Jane, Jane, come down the stair.

Each dull, blunt wooden stalactite
Of rain creaks, hardened by the light,

Sounding like an overtone
From some lonely world unknown.

But the creaking, empty light
Will never harden into sight,

Will never penetrate your brain
With overtones like the blunt rain.

The light would show, if it could harden,
Eternities of kitchen garden,

Cockscomb flowers that none will pluck,
And wooden flowers that 'gin to cluck.

In the kitchen you must light
Flames as staring red and white

As carrots or as turnips—shining
Where the cold dawn light lies whining.

Cockscomb hair on the cold wind
Hangs limp, turns the milk's weak mind.

Jane, Jane,
Tall as a crane,
The morning light creaks down again."

This is not, to be sure, one of the most unintelligible of modernist poems. I have chosen it because it is one which the author has been gracious enough to explain to the non-cognoscenti. She has used it indeed to prove that modernist poetry in general is quite easy for intelligent people to understand. Her way of doing this is to pretend that the poem is not her own, and then offer her own understanding of it as proof that it can be understood. "Let us, as an example of the new scale of sense values," she says, "use an 'Aubade' by a modern poet —a poem which many people pretended was incapable of an explanation. Whereas it is, in reality, extremely simple and quite explainable. . . ." Then she takes up her own poem and explains it line by line as follows:

"*'The morning light creaks down again.'* The author said 'creaks,' because in a very early dawn, after rain, the light has a curious uncertain quality, as though it does not run quite smoothly. Also, it falls in hard cubes, squares, and triangles, which, again, give one the impression of a creaking sound, because of the association with wood. *'Each dull, blunt wooden stalactite of rain creaks, hardened by the light.'* In the early dawn, long raindrops are transformed by the light, until they have the light's own quality of hardness; also they have the dull and blunt and tasteless quality of wood; as they move in the wind, they seem to creak. *'Sounding like an overtone from some lonely world unknown.'* Though it seems to us as though we heard them sensorily, yet the sound is unheard in reality; it has the quality of an overtone from some unknown and mysterious world. . . ."

So far we are still somewhat in the dark—are we not? We have found out that the author is rather hypnotized by the idea that sights can be compared to sounds, sounds to things touched, and so forth. We knew this long ago, have observed it in poetry as far back as the *Rig-Veda*—"the fire cries with light"—and read about it also in the text-books of psychology. But we have never seen it piled on quite so thick before. We have never seen a poem in which these comparisons were coldly and deliberately and, therefore, unconvincingly, perpetrated throughout twelve or fourteen stanzas by a poet seeking to exemplify what she imagines to be a new psychological discovery. So far, then, her explanation has made us aware of her capabilities in bad taste, but we are still unaware of the subject of her poem. But now she suddenly, and quite recklessly it seems to me, condescends to tell us what she is talking about:

"The poem is about a country servant, a girl on a farm, plain and neglected and unhappy, and with a sad bucolic stupidity, coming down in the dawn to light the fire."

Is not that a wonderful relief? And how beautifully it is expressed! We must say one thing for the modernist poets—they all write excellent prose. When they do want to tell us something, they tell it with lucid and luminous precision.

As poets they do not want to tell us. They do not want to sacrifice, in order to tell us, any least value that their poems may have for them untold. The act of communication is irksome to them. It is irksome at times to us all. It is inadequate. How much can we communicate, indeed, by this elementary device of tongue-wagging or by making these tiny ink-wiggles on a sheet of paper? Little enough. Every one who has composed poems knows how often he has to sacrifice a value that is both clear and dear to him, in order to communicate his poem to others. Abandon that motive, the limitation it imposes, and you will find yourself writing modernist poetry. I know this because I have tried it. During the very days while I was writing this essay an experience came into my life out of which I felt that it would be peculiarly appropriate to make a private poem. The poem reflects, I suppose, a certain preoccupation with the mannerisms of the modernist poets I had been reading, but still it is in no sense or flavor of the word a parody. It is a poem just between us two, I and myself.

ON LEARNING THAT NINA HAS FALLEN

Skin-whitishly
this cataract
pain (or importance)
bell-glasses your
heretofore
Clothedly so naked
bell breast.
Glows through the rose
rings loud
rings rose.

LOLLING TONGUED BELLS TOLL BEST

Lash-push of also-anger
A with worm gnawing
with with.
Crimson-skinned eye-rims peeping
preeeping
Bared iris of (also and) Priapus
Hands all awake doing
all organs like hand organs doing, singing
linger-hunger
lingerandhunger
Pained Puritan crank up the old Ford right after dinner

DUB

dub dub
drub-a-dub
drub-a-dub
druble druble
drouble drouble
droubble droubble droubble droubble droub. . .
Afterward
frigidairily

remembering

SIGN ON THE DOTTED LINE

(ex ante facto)

Cocu!

So far from offering this poem as a proof by parody that the "modernist" style of writing is a hoax, I offer it in proof of the opposite thesis—that modernist poetry is the most sincere and natural thing in the world to write, that any poetry will be modernist which ignores the reader or looks upon him as a mere excuse for speech. The modernist tendency may be defined then—in this first and least lovely aspect—as a tendency toward privacy, combined with a naïve sincerity in employing as material the instruments of social communion.

II

THE TENDENCY TOWARD PURE POETRY

In the previous essay I described "modernism" as a tendency of poets to keep the values of their poems to themselves—or offer them to the reader incidentally to be enjoyed as a kind of colored puzzle. If all literature may be described as a verbal communication of values, the modernists may be described as absorbed in the values to the neglect of the act of communicating them. They are unsociable poets, unfriendly, and in extreme cases their language approaches that of the insane or idiotic. Indeed, the word *idiot* means in its origin nothing more slanderous of the character of much of their writing than "private."

But that describes only one-half of its character, the unlovely half. The modernists are distinguished not only by their absorption in values, but also by the kind of values in which they are absorbed. It seems to me that what they are cultivating in their privacy—and what they communicate at such times as they do consent to a social relation with their readers—is the values of pure poetry, isolated, so far as that is possible, from values which belong properly to practical, or scientific, or prose language.

By pure poetry I do not mean a "mystic essence" supposed to reside in certain lines which happen to be beautiful or moving, or to suggest perfection, for reasons not easily analyzed.

"La fille de Minos et de Pasiphaë"

is one of the lines chosen by French critics to illustrate this mystic essence. (You will destroy it neatly if you neglect to sound the final *e.*) In English we have *Kubla Khan,* or

"The sedge is withered from the lake,
And no birds sing."

And lately we have been instructed that T. E. Hulme, with the few rather prosy poems he published in a volume with Ezra Pound, entered into the inner shrine of the temple of this mystic essence. To my mind this way of talking about poetry, proper to the age of alchemy, has in this day a rather sophomoric flavor, and I mention it merely to avoid a misunderstanding. By pure poetry I mean to designate a real thing—a way of using words that can be identified, and to some extent at least explained, by the psychologist.

Perhaps the best way to see what poetry is in its own nature is to imagine it originating in the incantations of medicine-men or magicians. Names are supposed by all primitive people to have an occult power over the thing named. They have the power of evoking the being of that thing and compelling its obedience. But in order to do that, they have to be just the right names. And the medicine-man or shaman or poet-magician, who had also some of the gifts of the quack-doctor, would get the idea spread abroad that he knew the right names of things. He could bring rain, for instance, by standing out under the sky and saying the right words. That is a very wonderful and exciting way to use words, and yet totally unrelated to science or everyday practical communication. The ordinary way to use words when the garden goes dry is to say, "Well, don't you think we'd better find the old sprinkling pot?" And the scientific way is only a little more elaborate, "Let's build a dam and dig ditches and irrigate the whole valley." But the sorcerer, the poet, this wonderful and deep-eyed man who is in touch with the heart of reality through language, gets out there in the middle of the valley, and spreads out his hands, and says words which *do not mean a thing.* And then the rain falls. Or else it doesn't. But in any case it ought to. And among almost all primitive peoples, all human tribes who have not yet passed under the affliction of statistics, the opinion is that if the poet has got the right words, the rain does actually fall.

Mr. Briffault tells us that the Greek words *ode* and *epode,* the German *lied,* the English *lay,* and similar words in other languages, have meant in their origin a magic spell or incantation. The Latin *carmina* meant indifferently verses or "charms." *Vates* was a magician or a poet. In several languages the word for magician, like the word poet itself, means "maker." And so we infer that the poet was so named, not for any of the edifying Carlylian reasons that we tried to believe in when we went to school, but because this sing-song man was supposed to be able to bring things into being by naming them. He was a sorcerer; his rhyming language was a magic spell; his function was not to edify soulful people, but to "produce the goods."

That was undoubtedly the principal mother-lode from which poetry arose. But that is not what poetry is. In the mind of that verily gifted magician, naming the raindrops right out of the sky, there was an actual vision of the drops he named. His words did have the power to evoke the being of things—in his imagination. For him, moreover, the line between imagination and sense was not too clearly drawn. He was not entirely a sorcerer, but something also of a child. And he had an *interest* in raindrops, an absurd and altogether important interest in raindrops, which had nothing whatever to do with agriculture or the problem of watering the soil. He had a like interest in the sky. It is not too much to say, in view of what we know about his successors, that he sometimes loved the sky in a mournful way even when it failed to rain. Whether with joy or sorrow, he loved—or was fascinated by—the whole business of "being" in this world. And, like all people who love a thing, he enjoyed calling it pet names. Set free by his profession from any other very steady occupation, he developed a great habit of sitting around thinking up these names for things—the names that would most exactly and vividly evoke their beings into his imagination. That was how he kept awake when he was not working, and that was pure poetry.

The American Indians believed that a good poem could accomplish almost anything. Putting a child to sleep was a mere hint or routine application of its almost omnipotent occult powers. And yet there were pure poets among the Indians also, as is shown very aptly by Natalie Curtis in her *Indians' Book*. She quotes the following song, or tuneful incantation designed to bring rain, from a young Navajo poet:

"Yellow butterflies,
Over the blossoming virgin corn,

> With pollen-painted faces,
> Chase one another in brilliant throng.
>
> Blue butterflies,
> Over the blossoming virgin beans,
> With pollen-painted faces,
> Chase one another in brilliant streams. . . .
>
> Over your fields of growing corn,
> All day shall hang the thunder-cloud;
> Over your fields of growing corn,
> All day shall come the rushing rain."

The magical intention or, at least, the surviving form of such an intention, is here quite obvious. And yet the poet, when he was questioned by Miss Curtis as to the "meaning" of his song, had nothing whatever to say about this form or intention.

"My song," he said, "is about butterflies flying over the cornfields, and over the beans. One butterfly is running after another like the hunt, and there are many."

I set this answer apart from my text, because it is, in effect, another poem—another pure act of realization through language. The poet is asked for the meaning —or as Walt Whitman would say, the "purport"—of his poem, and he only attempts again, and by a fresh manipulation of the magic contained in names, to evoke into consciousness the being of the things he named.

It is to this original and pure form of poetry that the modernists, with all their sophistication and their city things, are tending back. They too are abandoning purports, themes, meanings, preachments, all that so recently and extravagantly admired stuff of edification that led Matthew Arnold actually to the definition of poetry as a "criticism of life." In place of a criticism, these poets are offering us in each poem a moment of life, a rare, perfect or intense moment, and nothing more. They offer us awakening—they even offer to keep us awake for the few moments while we are reading their poem—and that seems to them enough. Poetry is a thing like music or the morning, which stands in no need of meaning anything for those who are sensitive enough to perceive it.

Edith Sitwell, in her *Poetry and Criticism,* says that "the modernist poets are bringing a new and heightened consciousness to life." Hart Crane describes the whole province of the poet's art as "added consciousness and increased perceptions." Neither of these poets clearly conceives what he is saying as a psychology of poetry, or holds with any continuous force to its implications. But at least for a moment they forget the mystic essences, and speak of their art with the same modern intelligence with which we speak of "locomotives and roses." For the length of that moment they confess themselves to be devotees of pure poetry—understanding by that term the original simple thing as it emerged from the practical employments of the magician.

"Paris; this April sunset completely utters
utters serenely silently a cathedral

before whose upward lean magnificent face
the streets turn young with rain,

spiral acres of bloated rose

coiled within cobalt miles of sky
yield to and heed
the mauve
          of twilight (who slenderly descends,
daintily carrying in her eyes the dangerous first stars)
people move love hurry in a gently

arriving gloom and
see! (the new moon
fills abruptly with sudden silver
these torn pockets of lame and begging colour) while
there and here the lithe indolent prostitute
Night, argues

with certain houses."

It is only necessary to select such an example as this—where by accident, or by some momentary act of grace, a modernist poet has actually communicated his whole poem—in order to see what in their privacy these poets are trying to do. They are trying to surrender themselves, more utterly than this has been done before, to the mere uninterpreted qualities of experience. And it seems quite possible—to judge, at least, by this exquisite example from E. E. Cummings—that they are succeeding.

Of course all poets have written pure poems upon occasion. No genuine poet has ever accepted the obligation to support with a criticism of life his every offering of an increased perception of it. Mr. George Moore not long ago compiled an *Anthology of Pure Poetry* which contains verses from all the great periods of English literature. Through a predilection for lyrical song—or perhaps through an influence from the mystic essences—Mr. Moore left out of his volume some of the more rich and slow-moving of pure poems. He left out Keats's "Ode to Autumn," which says absolutely nothing throughout thirty-three lines except just this one very thing—Autumn. But, upon the whole, his anthology accords with our definition, and it proves that there is nothing new in abandoning "ideas," or the problem of adjusting man with his environment, and devoting oneself to the pure art of heightening or diversifying his consciousness.

The new thing about the modernists is the extreme to which they carry this devotion. Pure poetry is not an occasional exploit with them, but a regular duty. In all their poems you feel, not so much a tendency as a determination, to avoid all valid or verifiable judgments or opinions about anything. In their critical essays they boast of this attitude of detachment. They call it "intellectual" or "classical"; but I do not think we need take that very seriously. When T. S. Eliot dismisses Bernard Shaw and Bertrand Russell as "emotional" and offers in the name of "intellect" to replace their arduous thinking about important problems with his wilfully meaningless poetry, his narrowly literary learning, and rather pedantic prose, it is quite obvious that words are being misapplied. Still more obvious, when our American propagandist of modernism, Gorham B. Munson, lays Randolph Bourne away among the "emotional," and brings forward Ernest Hemingway and E. E. Cummings as showing a revival of interest in ideas! In my opinion, if Mr. Eliot and Mr. Munson had the intellect of which they boast, they would not be found, fifty years after the birth of genetic psychology, still taking seriously this old-fashioned dichotomy, intellect versus emotion. Virginia Woolf repudiates her predecessors as resolutely as T. S. Eliot does, but she puts her finger more knowingly upon the line which divides her from them. In order to complete their books, she says, "it seems necessary to do something." The reader must "finish them actively and practically for himself." The kind of book she admires in contrast is "complete in itself; it is self-contained; it leaves one with no desire to do anything." In short, it has no meaning, in the matter-of-fact and practical sense of the word.

The modernists not only abandon meanings more persistently than other poets, but they abandon, whenever they want to, those logical and grammatic forms which are the established vehicles of meaning. They allow their poems to move without the support of these emptied vehicles—without a certain false dignity that they have in the past imparted to the procession of the poet's images. Let us compare, for illustration, a pure poem by E. E. Cummings with one by William Shakespeare. And let us give Shakespeare—for the moment—the precedence. Here is a pure poem which he contributes to Mr. Moore's anthology:

> "When all aloud the wind doth blow
> And coughing drowns the parson's saw
> And birds sit brooding in the snow
> And Marian's nose looks red and raw,
> When roasted crabs hiss in the bowl,
> Then nightly sings the staring owl,
> Tu-whit;
> Tu-who, a merry note,
> While greasy Joan doth keel the pot."

This is, you see, in its grammatical form, not a poem

at all, but a scientific observation. *When* all those first things happen, *exactly then,* simultaneously with them, the owl sings, "Tu-whit; tu-who." Moreover it is, I believe—provided neither the owl nor the roasted crabs are moving with the velocity of light—an accurate observation. And even people who do not know what poetry is would be able to read it through with composure and concede that Shakespeare was sane and of sound mind, and that he might perhaps have discovered something original or important about owls—about the hibernal habits of the *strigidæ,* I should say—if he had carried his observations a little farther. Poetic people know that the scientific observation, as well as the grammatic form which conveys it—the compound declarative sentence—is a mere accidental convenience, a piece of old clothes-line upon which the acts of imaginative realization are strung.

Now the great revolution accomplished by the modernists, in their more extreme and Presbyterian devotion to pure poetry, has consisted of occasionally throwing that piece of old clothes-line away. In Mr. Cummings's realizations of a mouse, for instance, we are not led astray from the poetry by any compound declarative sentence, or by any sentence whatever:

"here's a little mouse) and
what does he think about, i
wonder as over this
floor (quietly with

bright eyes)drifts (nobody
can tell because
Nobody knows, or why
jerks Here &, here,

gr(oo)ving the room's Silence) this like
a littlest
poem a
(with wee ears and see?

tail frisks)
(gonE)
'mouse', . . ."

Here the scientific people will throw up their hands in disgust—the thing doesn't make sense. But poetic people will be satisfied to receive the mouse, and leave the business of making sense *about* mice to the zoologist.

In still another way the modernists carry pure poetry to an extreme. Pure poems in the past have always been single or closely unified moments of realization. If two or more of these moments were joined together, some narrative or argumentative connection was supplied. The modernists unite them arbitrarily, at the dictate of taste or a purely creative impulse. They pile up poems out of imaginative moments as architecture is piled up out of blocks of stone and stone images. Walt Whitman did this same thing, but always contrived to give a hint as to some theme which was, however invisibly, hovering behind and holding it all together. Hart Crane has also been accused of hiding a theme behind the intemperate procession of his images, although "the vision," according to his friend Allen Tate, "often strains and overreaches the theme." But to this his British admirers reply emphatically that "Mr. Crane is preserving his vision from a theme . . . The movements of his poems are the fluctuations of surfaces: they give a sea sense of externality: the moon, the sea, frost, tropical horizons. . . ." It is difficult for a mere reader to decide between these opinions, for it has become a custom in this cult for the poet to tip off a few chosen friends as to what he is really talking about, and allow them to appear before the public as critics with "contact" and with more than usual penetration. I do not know which of these critics has been properly tipped off. But I can at least say as a humble reader that whether Mr. Crane has preserved himself from a theme or not, he has at least preserved me from one, and I regard his poems as wilfully pure of purport. I think it is only by recognizing the right of poetry like any other art to speak life without speaking about it, that one can intelligently approach these poems which abjure even grammar and logic as a bondage, and which evolve upon threads of connection as tenuous as those of a musical symphony. Remember that they are the legitimate children of a magic incantation. They have abandoned their pretense to call forth actual events and objects into the air; but they have not on that account acknowledged the empire of practical sense. They remain proud. They refuse to deck themselves out with meanings. They stand there, offering you nothing—only themselves, and that only if you will surrender to an invisible spell.

It is absurd to describe this arrant and absolute revolt of the motive in the heart of all poets against the central mechanism of practical civilization, meaningful language, as a neo-classic revival, a return to the eighteenth-century tradition, a revolt against the tyranny of the general reader. That is a poor and weak way to defend a crusade that takes its force from the aboriginal fountains of life. The revolt is not against the tyranny of the general reader, but against the tyranny of the practical mind. Instead of describing it as a return to the eighteenth-century tradition, it would be more adequate to say that there have been throughout human civilization three fundamental schools of poetry—three distinct positions of the poet.

First he employed his meaningless but life-enhancing words, under the impression that they performed a magic function. He so justified them to the practical common sense of the race. That was the first school of poetry—the incantation school.

When the belief in word magic declined, he began to offer his words as a kind of colored clothing in which to dress up meanings, and make them more alluring and exciting. Even when he did not actually intend a meaning in the creation of his poem, he would look around until he found one and stick it in somewhere (as Poe confesses he did), because it was now only in this way that he could justify himself to the practical common sense of the race. That was the second school of poetry—the meaningful school. It has held the centre of the stage throughout the historic period.

The people in our world to-day who are most boldly gifted in the poetic use of words are attempting to go back to the forms of the incantation, but without the pretense that their words have power to evoke real objects or events. They form a third "school" of poetry —the modernists, as they happen to be called, although their hearts were old when civilization began. They should be called by some name to indicate that they are interested in poetry as a thing by itself—a realization of life through imagination and language—distinct both from science and sorcery.

If this is a true account of the tendency toward pure poetry, its association with a more trivial Cult of Unintelligibility was natural and almost inevitable. The commonest function of words is to communicate practical meanings. This function has determined the whole growth and structure of language; poetic communication has been ritual or incidental. To cease communicating these meanings without also ceasing to communicate would require a rather dexterous discrimination. It would require at least that the poet should know what he is trying to do, and that he should have some sense of the special nature of his material. A poet who knew that he was trying to get rid of the practical meaning in words—their perfectly, automatic stimulation of action, or active attitude, in those who hear them—and yet preserve their power to communicate experience, would devote a great deal of attention to the *strategy of communication*. The modernists, who do not know exactly what they are trying to do, and who talk about words as though they were a material as simple in its values as dyed chalk or porcelain, have followed the opposite course. They have abandoned meanings and at the same time ignored the strategy of communication, as though these two things were one and the same. It is against this obtuseness of theirs, this foolish confusion, that I have attempted to initiate a gentle rebellion of the reader in these two essays on the Cult of Unintelligibility and the Tendency toward Pure Poetry.

III

POETS TALKING TO THEMSELVES

In the two preceding essays I assumed that poetry, and indeed all writing, is a communicative act. That is the usual assumption. "The difficulty of literature," said Stevenson, "is not to . . . affect your reader, but to affect him precisely as you wish." And since words are in their common nature instruments of communication, this seems plausible. Yet most poets would resist any such sweeping assumption, and John Stuart Mill even proposed to distinguish poetry from eloquence as speech not meant to be heard, but "overheard." In these days when critics loudly acclaim a poem like Hart Crane's *The Bridge* as one of the greatest of our generation, and quite incidentally remark that they do not know what the poet is talking about, it seems to me this question needs looking into.

Hart Crane himself once showed me a poem which began with a quotation in Latin, a language which I am sad to say I learned at a time when I had small interest in learning. I sat down and puzzled for a while, and then in some humiliation pointed to a word I did not understand and asked Hart Crane to translate it.

"I don't know what it means," he said, "I don't understand the language at all."

Tossing me this casual information, he continued an animated conversation with the red-lipped girl who had brought us together, and I continued to puzzle over his poem. After struggling a while with the English parts of it, I returned finally to the Latin as more communicative.

To spare the reader a like struggle, I will quote here a much-admired poem which according to its admirers is "far from being one of Mr. Crane's more difficult compositions."

AT MELVILLE'S TOMB

Often beneath the wave, wide from this ledge
The dice of drowned men's bones he saw bequeath
An embassy. Their numbers as he watched,
Beat on the dusty shore and were obscured.

And wrecks passed without sound of bells,
The calyx of death's bounty giving back
A scattered chapter, livid hieroglyph,
The portent wound in corridors of shells.

Then in the circuit calm of one vast coil,
Its lashings charmed and malice reconciled,
Frosted eyes there were that lifted altars;
And silent answers crept across the stars.

Compass, quadrant and sextant contrive
No farther tides—High in the azure steeps
Monody shall not wake the mariner.
This fabulous shadow only the sea keeps.

The poem seems simple enough and very sincere and also in a way beautiful. But does it not tantalize you with a certain reticence? To me it is one of the most exasperating of attractive things. It gazes out of the page significantly and in my direction, and with signs of intense emotion, but will not open its lips, will not make friends—will not, as we say, "come out with it."

I do not know anybody more freely and unaffectedly communicative than Hart Crane himself. He is particularly communicative *about* his poems—so much so that it is impossible, returning to the poems after a conversation with him, to continue in the belief that poetry is essentially an act of communication. It seems in his case to be the opposite—a thing that begins whenever he stops communicating.

Hart Crane is not only generous in communication, but also—at least as regards the English parts of his poetry—swift and convincing. He can very handily dispose of any sceptic who ventures to suggest that each syllable is not rich with values both of meaning and experience. He is in fact so brilliant in this process that he always proves beyond a glimmer of doubt not only that his poetry when explained by him can be understood by anybody, but also that when not explained by him it can be understood by nobody. Consider, for instance, that stanza about the calyx of death's bounty giving back. He explained that once in a letter to Harriet Monroe as follows:

"This calyx refers in a double ironic sense both to a cornucopia and the vortex made by a sinking vessel. As soon as the water has closed over a ship this whirlpool sends up broken spars, wreckage, etc., which can be alluded to as livid *hieroglyphs,* making a *scattered chapter* so far as any complete record of the recent ship and her crew is concerned. In fact, about as much definite knowledge might come from all this as any onc might gain from the roar of his own veins, which is easily heard (haven't you ever done it?) by holding a shell close to one's ear."

No one will deny that these lines with their exegesis reveal in the author a genuine and rare poetic mind and feeling. It is equally certain that without exegesis they reveal little or nothing at all. But this fact does not disturb Hart Crane in the least. *It does not even occur to his mind.* He is not defending his skill in communicating experience. He is defending his integrity in the art of talking to himself in public.

If any reader proud of his sensitiveness to poetry feels inclined to boast that he did understand about the calyx of death's bounty giving back, I suggest that he now cover up with a sheet of paper the paragraph following this one, and write down on the paper his understanding of Mr. Crane's first stanza—the one in which the dice of drowned men's bones bequeath an embassy. After he has done that, let him remove the paper, and see how near he has come to Mr. Crane's own explanation of its values.

"Dice bequeath an embassy, in the first place, by being ground (in this connection only, of course) in little cubes from the bones of drowned men by the action of the sea, and are finally thrown up on the sand, having 'numbers' but no identification. These being the bones of dead men who never completed their voyage, it seems legitimate to refer to them as the only surviving evidence of certain messages undelivered, mute evidence of certain things, experiences that the dead mariners might have had to deliver. Dice as a symbol of chance and circumstance is also implied."

Here again we have obviously to do with a sincere poetic mind and feeling. All that was lacking—absolutely all that was lacking—in these four lines of poetry was this ten or twelve lines of communication. Hart Crane may never grow up to the point of embodying his communication in his poetry, but he will deserve mention in the history of literature for having so specifically disproven the hard saying of Pascal that "People would never traverse the sea . . . for the mere purpose of seeing, without the hope of ever communicating what they have seen."

I had the pleasure not long ago of hearing James Joyce read—or rather recite, for he can no longer see the letters—a few pages from his *Anna Livia Plurabelle,* and discussing with him its unintelligibility. I wonder if he will object if I employ the memory of that conversation in order to prove, by the example of a brilliant genius, that literature is not of necessity a communicative act. Our meeting had resulted from the publication by me of the two preceding essays in which I maintained that the literary tendency called "modernist" is in reality a confusion of two tendencies: a tendency to give up interpreting experience, with a tendency to cease even communicating it intelligibly. Not long after publishing these essays I happened to be in Paris, and I dropped in to see my friend Sylvia Beach, who runs the charming and historic little book-store called "Shakespeare & Co." in the rue de l'Odeon. Sylvia Beach is the heroical woman who first published James Joyce's *Ulysses,* and is a great defender of the Cult of Unintelligibility at which I had been smiling. Instead of the glance of deprecation which I had expected, however, she came forward with a most jovial greeting, and her first words were: "Joyce likes your essay in *Harper's* so much—I wonder if you would have time to take tea with him while you are in Paris." I had time, of course, and I found out that Joyce not only liked my essay, but thought it was "sound criticism"—a word which I have saved carefully and carry round with me for the confounding of his embattled disciples.

Some other words of his in that conversation I saved, because they led me to this step beyond the position taken in that essay—they led me to think that it is erroneous in the first place to *define* literature as communication. Joyce seems a simple, earnest and very quiet person—poised and gently indignant about his blindness—an intellectual and yet not a thinking type, a family man too, and like all great men from Napoleon up not excessively masculine. He began our conversation by saying something that would seem to contradict my thesis about modernism flatly. He told me how glad he was that, even though I found so much of him unintelligible, I had at least enjoyed his humor.

"It would be terrible"—he said—"to think that I had done all that work and not given you any pleasure at all. I spent six hundred hours making that little book I sent you. Six hundred hours, and what a waste if it had brought you no pleasure at all! For certainly the motive of an artist—of all artists, whether they are conscious of it or not—is to give pleasure to others."

"I am very much surprised to hear you say that," I said.

"But it is true, isn't it?" he answered earnestly.

And then he told me that into the prose of the little book in question—*Anna Livia Plurabelle*—he had woven the names of five hundred rivers. The book in a certain sense is, or is about, a river. Indeed I now remember that Joyce told me before reciting a passage from it that either two people, or a rock and a tree, or the principles of organic and inorganic nature, are talking to each other across a river. One of his learned commentators has since issued a paper to the effect that it is the two sexes, male and female, which are talking across this river; another maintains that it is two washerwomen; but I believe only what Joyce told me. As he spoke the lines I watched him, and saw how much every syllable weighed and carried to his mind and feeling, and since I could not myself understand the syllables and therefore could not think and feel what he was thinking and feeling, my mind wandered a little from the music and I thought what a wonderfully different thing an intense artist is—or a man in the mood of artistic rapture—from an ordinary practical-minded adult. An artist is a man consecrated to the child's attitude toward values, and yet translated by his consecration into a world in which childhood is the sovereign thing and growing up a mere unfortunate incidental necessity.

Joyce was reciting his lines for me—to "give pleasure" to me—lines on which he had worked six hundred hours and woven into them the names of five hundred rivers. And yet I did not hear one river. I have examined them patiently since and have not yet found but three-and-a-half rivers. Moreover having had something to do with inductive and deductive logic, I know that if it took six hundred hours to weave those rivers into that prose, it will take something like six hundred thousand to weave them out. I cannot help asking myself how many people will do this work, and how much fun they will have doing it. If Joyce's artistic motive really is to give pleasure to others, it seems fair to say that he has wasted about five hundred of those six hundred hours burying the names of those rivers where people who might happen to want them wouldn't be able to find them.

Of course Joyce is deceiving himself when he says that his principal motive is to give pleasure to others. And Joyce is, like so many Irishmen, more recklessly sentimental than most of us, and so not unpractised in deceiving himself. He told me, I remember, that he liked to think how some far day, way off in Thibet or Somaliland, some lad or lass in reading that little book would be pleased to come upon the name of his or her own home river. And while that seemed a sweet whiff of a thought, it also seemed a highly incidental one, and I could not help thinking that if the pleasure of that actual lad or lass had entered into the author's motivation, he might have provided some little key or pirate's chart of some kind which would enable them to dig up their river without doing all that unnecessary hard labor. I do not know whether I said this or not, but to something that I said Joyce answered in exactly these words:

"The demand that I make of my reader is that he should devote his whole life to reading my works."

He smiled as he said that—smiled, and then repeated it.

And my answer was: "You absolutely insist on giving them all that pleasure!"

But I did not make my answer of course, because I

did not think of it until some time later when I was jotting these things down to remember. I only thought what I have often thought before, both in reading Joyce and in reading the encomiums written by his disciples, that the first and very principal thing to say about them all is that their minds are untrained and incoherent. They do not know how to think.

Joyce thinks he is writing his present extremely unintelligible prose because, whereas *Ulysses* gave us a day in the life of a man, his present work gives us the night.

"In writing of the night"—he told me—"I really could not, I felt I could not, use words in their ordinary connections. Used that way they do not express how things are in the night, in the different stages—conscious, then semi-conscious, then unconscious. I found that it could not be done with words in their ordinary relations and connections. When morning comes of course everything will be clear again. I'll give them back their language. They really needn't worry and scold so much. I'll give them back their English language. I'm not destroying it for good!"

It was impossible not to be charmed by the mild high delicate voice and the gentle smile with which this grandiose reassurance was offered. I almost hope that it may not be fulfilled, for I think it would be something of a descent from Olympus if Joyce came back and began really to talk to us again. At any rate I do not for one moment believe that the idea of writing about the night is anything more than an interior pretext upon Joyce's part for amusing himself with words in the way he chooses. The tendency appears often enough—and with no such pat reason—in *Ulysses.* Moreover, it seems obvious to me that an author who sincerely desired to convey to a reader the experience of falling asleep—through the various stages, conscious, semi-conscious, unconscious—would not begin by taking the names of five hundred rivers and burying them so deep in a polyglottical cryptogram that the poor reader would have to stay up fourteen nights in succession with seventeen foreign-language dictionaries, six encyclopædias, seven pounds of coffee, an Atlas, and a World Almanac, in order to dig up a half dozen of them.

Joyce may be trying utterly and absolutely to give *himself* to a series of experiences which he connects in some way with the process of falling asleep—to give himself to them and to the words which revive and enrich them for him—although of that too I am sceptical. But he is not devoting a moment's attention to the very complex and delicate problem of the strategy by which he might possibly contrive to communicate *some* of these experiences to somebody else—of that I am sure. His character as a stylist in this recent work does not lie in any loose semblance to the operations of a drowsing mind, nor yet in the scope of his linguistic researches. It lies in the fact that he is doing an intellectual and imaginative labor gigantic in its proportions, obdurate in its persistence, with no practical end in view whatever, not even that of communicating his experience, but solely to perfect himself in the art of playing by himself in public.

II

Practical and downright people can hardly help suspecting that there is something of a hoax about this whole cult of uncommunicative writing. And the suspicion is not confined to those remote from it, either. I have heard two personal friends of E. E. Cummings debating as to whether his prosodical and punctuational gymnastics have not been a joke at the expense of the critics of poetry. One of them thinks Cummings will some day come out and announce that he has been joking; the other insists with fervent and faithful admiration that he is really as crazy as he seems. Motives are rarely simple even in practical people, and in people who cast loose from the ruts not only of custom but of practicality, as the poets must, motives are often extremely complex. Even though a certain ironical jocularity, or a priggish or commercial shrewdness or shrewdness in the pursuit of fame, does play its part in some of these perpetrations, that does not explain them. I remember Joyce's telling me that he thought it necessary to issue his present work one small volume at a time, with a preface by one of his friends, because it was a little too "difficult" to be absorbed by the general reader all at once and without help. I asked him if he did not find that prefatory intrusion by an alien hand distasteful on æsthetic grounds. I said: "Why don't you put into your creation itself whatever hints to the reader you deem an indispensable minimum?"

His answer was a shrewd one: "You know people never value anything unless they have to steal it. Even an alley cat would rather snake an old bone out o' the garbage can than come up and eat a nicely prepared chop from your saucer."

But it would be easy to exaggerate the significance of a remark like that. People in whom deep and important responses are sentimental always surprise you with flashes of shrewd and hard wit. They have to. It is thus they survive. But nothing could be wider of the mark than to attribute to James Joyce a steady or prevailing attitude of sly foxy understanding toward his readers. His attitude toward his readers is to assume their existence for the purpose of setting him off upon the adventure of poetic speech, but within that adventure to ignore their separate existence utterly—to lose sight, indeed, of any distinction between himself and others, to become, like a little child, the very centre and circumference of the universe.

Those who feel sure they are being put upon by sophisticated rogues of poetry in these days should remember that this same Cult of Unintelligibility with its accompaniment of verbal and grammatical concoction swept over the literary world once before, and that our gentle Shakespeare in ripe years was a member in good standing of it. In some of his later plays, "A Winter's Tale" for instance, Shakespeare talks—and what is worse, he makes his characters talk—a private cerebral gibberish that goes often almost as far from verbal communication as the most extravagant perpetrations of the modernists. The tendency represented in those plays flourished long, moreover, and spread over Europe and reached a most Joycean climax in the writings of one of the most gifted of Spanish poets, Luis de Gongora, whose *Estilo Culto* became the literary sensation of a decade that in many other ways corresponds to ours, although preceding it by three hundred years. It is not likely that Shakespeare in going to these extremes of lexical experimentation altered the fundamental social attitude in which all his great poetry was composed. It is simpler to think that he experienced a shift of interest. That fascination with the ways and tastes of words which had obsessed him all his life long grew upon him here; he gave free rein to it; he played in his mind with the beings of words more than with the things denoted by them, and a quite fantastic and tantalizing obscurity resulted. But the result was not the motive. Shakespeare was probably not playing any more exclusively in his own mind in this mad dialogue than elsewhere; he was playing with different things. The error is to assume in either case that poetic creation is essentially and of necessity communicative.

It seems to me, however, equally erroneous to jump to the opposite extreme, and assert that the motive and the fact of communication plays no part at all in poetry—and even in modern poetry of the extreme type. It is not true, as Robert Graves and Laura Riding assert, that the modernists publish their poems merely in order to give them an impersonal identity. They could do that by pinning them up nicely on the inside of the barn door. The poems are made out of speech; they are made out of communication; they imply some sort of public-in-the-abstract even when they tell nothing, and it is a quite natural and simple act to put them before a public. But it is also true that they are not addressed to, or composed for, a public, and that if a public should during the process of their composition march into the chamber and preposterously attempt to respond, the poet would be shocked and injured immeasurably, or he would be deaf and he would not hear. He is speaking before people but he is not speaking to them. They are the occasion, not the cause, the pretext, not the purpose, of his speech.

I am not going to pretend that I can explain how this equivocal attitude that is both social and egocentric arises. I only affirm that it does arise and is the usual attitude of enraptured artists, whether they happen to be working with speech which is an instrument of communication or not. The two things are there together—the implying of a public and the ignoring of it. The dispute between philosophers of æsthetics as to whether art is "expression" or communication is a mere reflection of this complex mental fact. The dispute will continue, I suppose, until philosophers die, and then some scientific investigator will give us a little light on the real problem—how and why and in what ways these two attitudes combine.

Meanwhile we can convince ourselves of the reality of their combination, and make it fit into a simple and natural picture of human nature, by pointing out how almost universal it is among young children. Jean Piaget—whose four volumes devoted to child life are one of the real contributions to knowledge in our times—has found this two-fold attitude so characteristic of children's speech that he has felt compelled to invent a special term, "collective monologue," to distinguish it on the one hand from monologue and on the other from conversation.

When children are together, M. Piaget tells us, "they

seem to talk to each other a great deal more than we do about what they are doing, but for the most part they are only talking to themselves. . . . Each one sticks to his own idea and is satisfied. . . . He believes that some one is listening to him, and that is all he wants. . . . He does not succeed in making his audience listen, because, as a matter of fact, he is not really addressing himself to it. He is not speaking to any one. He is talking aloud to himself in front of others. . . . The audience is there simply as a stimulus. . . . The words have no social function. . . . Nothing could be harder to understand than the note-books we have filled with the conversation of Pie and Lev. Without full commentaries, taken down at the same time as the children's remarks, they would be incomprehensible. Everything is indicated by allusion, by pronouns and demonstrative articles . . . which can mean anything in turn, regardless of the demands of clarity or even of intelligibility. . . . In a word the child hardly ever even asks himself whether he has been understood. For him, that goes without saying, for he does not think about others when he talks. He utters a 'collective monologue.' . . . To put it quite simply, we may say that the adult thinks socially even when he is alone, and the child under seven thinks egocentrically, even in the society of others."

M. Piaget collects specimens of children's talk the way a naturalist collects butterflies, and he has estimated that 45 per cent of the spontaneous talk among themselves of average children of seven to eight years is egocentric. It is devoid of the motive of communication. And the reason for this is not that the child has conceived other people and rejected them out of his world, but that he has not clearly conceived what it is to be another person. He identifies the whole world with his own experience. A child cannot explain anything or even tell a story intelligibly, because he cannot realize that others do not know the story. The story is known; the "telling" is merely something that he does to it. M. Piaget has demonstrated this fact with a series of interesting experiments, but any one who is familiar with young children can confirm it, and will realize how much the question we are discussing may be illumined by comparing the enraptured poet to the child. The child's whole attitude toward the matter of communication, says M. Piaget in his chapter on "Understanding Between Children," arises from his "belief that he is the centre of the universe"—and I merely borrowed these words in attempting to describe what I take to be the attitude of Joyce toward his readers.

"This way of behaving," M. Piaget tells us, "reappears in certain men and women of a puerile disposition (certain hysterical subjects, if hysteria be described as the survival of infantile characteristics) who are in the habit of thinking aloud as though they were talking to themselves, but are also conscious of their audience."

I think this is a narrow saying, and that M. Piaget has not happened to reflect to how great an extent art depends upon a survival of infantile characteristics. Even the most mature of artists, the thinking singer, must have within his control the attitudes of childhood. He must have a child's excited interest in the mere being of things, a child's perceptive freedom, his freedom from habitual attitudes of action, the feeling of a child and a savage that words form a part, and indeed a rich, crude and substantial part, of things. And he must have, too, this gift of returning in rapture to that infantile egocentrism, which is not egocentrism after all because the circumference as well as the centre is ego, because, as M. Piaget says, "the whole content of the infant's consciousness is projected into reality (both into things and into others), which amounts to a complete absence of the consciousness of self." Without realizing it, M. Piaget has enriched the understanding of the lyric rapture with his severely scientific studies of childhood, in a way that all the literary critics who have expatiated upon this theme in their learned essays for so many years have been unable to do.

And if we return to the "modernist" poets with this richer understanding of all poets, we shall realize that what first and essentially characterizes them is not their unintelligibility, but their preoccupation with pure poetry. Their unintelligibility is accidental. It is a result of the fact that they are cultivating life without criticising it—just as their intelligibility when they were criticising life was to some extent accidental. In both cases their singing was often only "overheard." But a criticism of life when it is overheard is understood, because it involves that part of the value of words which is a common social possession, their practical meaning. But an individual experience stored away in words like some sacred unique object or the fragrance of it in a reliquary—the experience itself having been perhaps more than half or even wholly composed of the emotional flavors of words—that is often impossible to overhear. The pure poet—unless he has in him a vein of rather adult vanity or social kindliness to bring him down out of his collective monologue, and make him while telling it tell us also somewhat *about* it—will very easily, if he tries to experiment and develop his art, become an unintelligible poet. It is the abandonment of interpretation, not of communication, that is fundamental in the modern tendency.

III

In order to explain the flourishing of this tendency, however—the veritable international conquest of power by the Cult of Unintelligibility—we must do more than show why poets write uncommunicative poems. That is the easiest and most gracious part of the task. We must also explain why grown-up and supposedly intellectual and judicious critics peruse these poems that they cannot understand a word of, and praise them extravagantly without a blush. Not long ago T. S. Eliot issued a thin volume containing twelve pages of poetry called *Ash Wednesday,* and sold a considerable edition of it at five dollars a volume. Here is a half page of this rather expensive poetry:

> "If the lost word is lost, if the spent word is spent
> If the unheard, unspoken
> Word is unspoken, unheard;
> Still is the unspoken word, the Word unheard,
> The Word without a word, the Word within
> The world and for the world;
> And the light shone in darkness and
> Against the Word the unstilled world still whirled
> About the centre of the silent Word.
>
> O my people, what have I done unto thee."

To this oily puddle of emotional noises the New York *Nation* promptly consecrated the whole first page of its book section, and its critic of poetry, Eda Lou Walton, who thinks that Eliot is "given over . . . to classic purity of form and idea," registered an austere and reverent admiration for a poem of whose content, either as meaning or experience, she fairly demonstrated that she had not the ghost of an apprehension. I cite *The Nation,* not because its greeting of this book was exceptional, but on the contrary because it would be naturally among the last to have its intelligence overwhelmed by a price of five dollars and the eagerness of a small genteel circle of pious prigs and book-collectors, who get more of what they want out of a poem in proportion to the number of uncut leaves. *The Nation* has had some sense of humor and proportion and held up a standard of brains and reality in this country for a long time, and yet even *The Nation* feels compelled to join the conspiracy of confusion and write down solemn twaddle about the classicalness of words which convey no definite experience whatever but a sound.

The New Republic has been in the conspiracy almost from the beginning. Was it not indeed with the help of *The New Republic* that Ivor Winters and Allen Tate and Hart Crane first formed their mutual-admiration society and periodically discovered that they were, each in his due order, the most significant of the younger poets now writing in America?

Even so thoughtful a critic as Edmund Wilson remarked recently of T. S. Eliot: "He succeeds in conveying his meaning, in communicating his emotion, in spite of all his learned or mysterious allusions, and whether we understand them or not." He does not convey that part of his meaning which lies in the allusions we do not understand—nor of his emotion either—and this seems to be no inconsiderable part of both. Two of the most intelligent readers of literature we have, I suppose, are Joseph Wood Krutch and I. A. Richards. Mr. Krutch was not long ago explaining to me at length that Eliot's poem "The Waste Land," if studied carefully, will be found to consist of a series of contrasts between scenes out of the past and our modern scene, woefully sighing for the former, bitterly disparaging the latter. I had asked Mr. Krutch for help in apprehending the poem. Returning with this much help, but still baffled, I turned to I. A. Richards, who has an appreciation of the poem at the back of his *Principles of Literary Criticism,* and received this additional assistance: "Mr. Eliot is neither sighing after vanished glories, nor holding contemporary experience up to scorn." I. A. Richards is of the opinion that in *The Waste Land* Mr. Eliot has performed this "considerable service" for our generation—he has effected a "complete severance between his poetry and *all* beliefs." Another connoisseur of poetry and a poet, Merrill Moore, writes me that "*The Waste Land* is a powerful, connected, deeply religious poem, the crux of which is in 'What the Thunder said,' Da (etc.). . . ." If these three skilled and sympathetic readers have directly opposed views both of the meaning of the poem and the emotions conveyed by it, I think we may be sceptical of a fourth who assures us that the meaning and the emotion are conveyed to him although he does not know what the poet is alluding to.

The critics have various ways of explaining their rapture about literature they cannot understand. Mark Van Doren goes so far as to invent a new psychic substance to explain it—a substance which is intellectual and to be found in the head, and yet flows along "somewhere down below" such superficial things as thought and idea and understanding. In eulogizing Hart Crane's volume *White Buildings* from which I have quoted a poem, Mark Van Doren begins by confessing quite frankly that he could not understand this volume when he first read it, and then still more frankly adding that he cannot understand it now either. But nevertheless he admires and enjoys it, and insists that it is "intellectual" rather than emotional poetry. "Mr. Crane can hardly be said to think," he concedes, but nevertheless "he plays in the depths of the head." The question just what Mr. Crane plays with in that remote quarter—a thing which is not feeling and yet does not consist of thinking and cannot be understood—Mark Van Doren answers as follows: "Not with ideas as such, for they take shape only on the surface of thought, on the level where they can be expressed, but with the intellectual lava that flows, sluggishly, irresistibly somewhere down below." Taking this formula as a guide, we should feel that unintelligible poetry is at least deep, and that in order to get at this cranial substratum we should have to dig down under whatever ideas do happen to be suggested by the words in the poem. Turning to Allen Tate, however, another of the eulogizers of Hart Crane, we learn that "The poetical meaning is a direct intuition, realized prior to an explicit knowledge of the subject-matter of the poem." Here the value seems to lie not in a molten lava that lies underneath the poem, but in a rather more gaseous substance that merely clings over the surface of it. The idea is not to delve under what the poet is talking about, but read so fast that what he is talking about can't catch you.

T. S. Eliot seems to think that this process can move a little more slowly, and that a poem's subject-matter need not be regarded as inimical, provided you hold your rational faculties in suspense. "The reader," he says, "has to allow the images to fall into his memory successively without questioning the reasonableness of each at the moment; so that at the end a total effect is produced." Coming from one who was leading us into a poetical era to be described as "classical," and to be characterized by a "higher and clearer conception of Reason, and a more severe and serene control of the emotions by Reason," this formula for reading a poem he greatly admires seems a little disconcerting. But at any rate it is not sharply out of accord with the formula of Allen Tate. They both make us feel at least that it is awfully easy to read poetry—all you have to do is suspend your intelligence and "let her go." But no sooner have you reached this happy conclusion than along comes another High Priest of the modernist criticism, Ivor Winters—another admiring reader of Hart Crane—and tells us that poetry is a "moral discipline," and that you cannot get the real meat of the thing, the "subjective act," until after you have not only read the poem through, and studied it, and got an "explicit knowledge of its subject-matter," but also gone and talked it over with your friends. "By the 'subjective act' I mean . . . the non-paraphrasable part of the poetic language, or rather the poem as a whole, after one has done talking about it." And Mr. Winters is supported in this more arduous view by Herbert Read, who regards "a non-logical progression in poetry as a result of thinking raised to a more than ordinary intensity."[1]

These professional critics are all eclipsed, however, by C. K. Ogden, who tells us, in a preface to Joyce's latest instalment, *Tales Told of Shem and Shaun,* that in order to adjust our minds to the values of this new kind of literature, what we have to do is learn to talk Eskimo. Joyce, it seems, does not know Eskimo—and neither, I infer, does C. K. Ogden—but Joyce has conscious "affiliations with his Norse ancestors" and Ogden seems to think that the only way to outwit his unintelligibility is to go "still farther north" and learn a still more difficult language. This geographical approach to literature will become easier of course for warm-blooded natures after Mr. Wilkins has opened a route under the ice. Meantime Mr. Ogden already knows this much about Eskimo—he knows that Stefansson knows the language, and has told him that he "regards it as the most difficult but at the same time the most efficient language as yet evolved by man." It has twenty-seven case forms, nine each in the singular, dual and plural, and it doesn't bother with primitive little equipment like affixes and suffixes, having at its disposal "164 infixes" with which "over one thousand forms can be made out for one noun alone." *Iglu* means "house," but *"iglupakulia"* means "the big house which he built for himself and still possesses and which is no

[1]Not a quotation but a paraphrase in *The Symposium,* vol. I, no. 3, p. 320.

longer as good as formerly." It is obvious that Joyce would have no terrors for an Eskimo. The trouble is that the Eskimos are not greatly interested in modern literature. Another trouble is that there are only "about a dozen linguists" who know their language, or that particular dialect, at least, which Ogden recommends. Still another trouble is that, according to what Stefansson told Ogden, "it was only after six years of constant study and practice that he attained proficiency in its use." In view of these facts, Ogden concludes, "at least a decade may be necessary before Mr. Joyce's 'word-ballet' yields its secret even to an adjusted mind."

To this it might seem reasonable to add that, inasmuch as Joyce himself does not understand Eskimo or use any of the words out of this language, and the reader has spent this first decade merely in order to get into a proper geographical position and overcome his nervousness in the presence of infixes—it might seem reasonable to grant him a couple more decades to be devoted to the study of the actual Joyce. Indeed I for my part think that after going way up north and talking Eskimo for ten years in order to get into the right longitude and lexitude for approaching "Mr. Joyce's symbolic condensation," it would show unseemly and unscholarly haste to dash right down to the Tropic of Cancer and plunge into Joyce himself, as though there were no degrees of latitude or stages in the concentration of a symbol. Surely a mind properly consecrated to the process of adjustment would not ignore those "Norse ancestors" from whom Joyce really did borrow some words. I would suggest a very gradual southerly movement, about ten degrees to the decade. That would bring you to Paris in time to be buried with an uncut first edition of *Work in Progress* on your chest and the proud joy in your bones that you died with an adjusted mind.

Just how much, and at what, my canny and learned friend Ogden is smiling in his preface to *Shem and Shaun,* I will not try to determine. Suffice it to say that he locates the values of unintelligible literature somewhere up in the Arctic Circle beyond the reach of the non-Eskimo reader. Mark Van Doren locates them in a warmer region but one still more inaccessible to the average citizen—a molten lava lying "somewhere down below." Allen Tate locates them in a first whiff that comes off the words before the mind ever begins to operate; T. S. Eliot in a last whiff after prolonged suspension of the rational faculties; Ivor Winters in a "subjective act" that can be performed only after the mind has done its worst; Herbert Read in a thinking so intense that it transcends logic. To these opinions we may add that of Marcel Brion that it is necessary to "break through the too narrow restraints of time and space," and of Robert Macalmon that it is necessary "to 'trance' oneself into a state of word intoxication, flitting-concept inebriation in order to enjoy this work to the full." Nor must we neglect the more copious, if not altogether soul-clarifying, advice of Edmund Wilson that "in order to understand what Joyce is doing" in certain parts of *Ulysses,* "one must conceive a set of Symbolistic poems, themselves involving characters whose minds are represented Symbolistically, depending not from the sensibility of the poet speaking in his own person, but from the poet's imagination playing a rôle absolutely impersonal and always imposing upon itself all the Naturalistic restrictions in regard to the story it is telling at the same time that it allows itself to exercise all the Symbolistic privileges in regard to the way it tells it."

Where these Doctors of Unintelligibility disagree to that extent, it seems foolhardy for a simple soul who has wasted a large part of his life in the improvement of his understanding to rush in and try to say anything. However, the principal thing I want to say is that they do disagree. They disagree so completely as to what they are getting out of unintelligible literature —what it is, and where it is, and how they get it—that we are practically driven to the conclusion they do not get it at all. They bring it with them. Just as the poet uses a listener, or the idea of a listener, as a mere pretext for speech, so the listener uses the poetry as a pretext—oftener perhaps, does not use it at all, but merely makes its existence a pretext—for some poem of his own, some inward dwelling upon experience which has a value for him. There is no communication and no demand for communication on either side. But there is an *illusion of communication.* Both the poet and the critic assume that something passes between them, and being highly egocentric in the mood and during the time which they devote to art, they each go away satisfied from the encounter, and they resent as obtuse or unsensitive or "decadent" or "conventional" or "democratic" or "psychological," or otherwise extremely contemptible and unregenerate, the simple questioning of an intelligent mind: "What has actually passed between them?" and the simple answer: "Nothing."

That this is the true fact of the matter may be illustrated by the example of one of these critics—one who has been rash enough to come right out and tell us what it was that he got out of a piece of unintelligible literature.

"There will be many interpretations of *Anna Livia Plurabelle* . . .," says Padraic Colum in his preface to that work. "To myself there comes the recollection of a feeling I had when, as a child, the first time in Dublin I crossed a bridge with an elder of mine beside me. I imagine other children's minds would have been occupied with such thoughts as occupied mine then. The city—who named it? The pavements—who laid them down? The statues—what had the men done that they should claim that men should look upon them now and that men should have looked upon them in one's father's and one's father's father's time? . . . The mystery of beginnings filled the mind. And, combining with the questions that came, there were things that had to be noted—the elder one walked beside . . . the apple one bought and ate and the penny one paid for it, the beggar-woman on the bridge, etc., etc. . . ."

It is clear that this reader has had a pleasure connected in some loose way with Joyce's little book. He talks indeed as though he were holding the book in his hand. But if there is any more compact or causal relation between this sentimental reminiscence of Padraic Colum's and Joyce's six hundred hours of labor burying the names of rivers and other admirable but not unusual objects in the actual contents of the book, I am unable to find it.

Here again we must turn to childhood—and to M.

Piaget who first brought all the patience of science to the study of childhood—for an understanding of what happens in this world of art. It is "only from the age of seven or eight," he tells us, "that there can be any talk of genuine understanding between children. Till then the egocentric factors of verbal expression . . . are all too important. . . . Words spoken are not thought of from the point of view of the person spoken to, and the latter, instead of taking them at their face value, selects them according to his own interest, and distorts them in favor of previously formed conceptions. . . . Each child, whether he is trying to explain his own thoughts or to understand those of others, is shut up in his own point of view. . . . Each imagines he is understanding and listening to the others even when he is doing nothing of the kind. . . . One of the facts which point most definitely to the egocentric character of the explanations of children is the large proportion of cases in which the explainer completely forgets to name the objects which he is explaining. . . . In this connection it should be noted that the listener adopts exactly the complementary attitude: he always thinks he has understood everything. However obscure the explanation, he is always satisfied."

It needs hardly a word more to make clear the part played by the admiring critic in promoting the Cult of Unintelligibility. His part too is a childlike one. If he is a child under seven or eight years, he may actually believe that he understands, and go round puffing out his cheeks and telling us with a swagger that the new methods of writing are merely "direct and vivid," and that all the talk about not being able to understand them comes from "trying to judge them by standards other than their own, etc., etc." I am quoting from John Dos Passos, but I might be quoting from any one of a hundred men of alert fancy who mistake a stimulation of their own gifts for communication from another. As they grow a little older, a little less "shut up in their own point of view"—I mean, of course, only in their approach to a work of art—these critics begin to admit that they do not *understand* unintelligible writing. But still clinging to the idea that communication has occurred, they cast solemnly about for some mysterious formula like direct intuition in advance of understanding, or cumulative effect after not understanding, or "subjective act" or "molten lava," or almost anything to make verbal and grammatical understanding seem unnecessary to communication. At a still later stage on the way to maturity, the critic begins in a half-hearted way to *try* to understand what the poet is talking about, but still reverently feels in his failure that there is something the matter with *him,* if only the fact that he was not born in the Arctic Circle.

It seems to me that we should be tolerant when poets are too childlike, knowing that to be childlike is an intrinsic part of their creative gift. But for infantilism in critics I do not see that there is a word of defense or apology possible to be spoken. It is hard enough to put up with the moral importance of critics even when they bring to bear in their judgments the most mature psychological and social intelligence available in their time. When they are so little developed, so shut up in their own view-point, that they do not know the difference between receiving a communication and making up a fairy-story, and so little trained in elementary perception of fact that they go right on attributing all sorts of novel and occult attributes to a poet who has himself convincingly explained that his poetry is like all other poetry except that he does not make clear what he is talking about, I do not see what to do with the whole tribe but bundle them into a well-rotted ship and shove them out to sea. We should no doubt long ago have adopted this mode of mitigating the plague of unintelligibility, were it not for the fact that a majority of these critics are poets too. That leaves us nothing to do, I am afraid, but smile patiently and turn to the books of science and wait for better days.

IV

DIVISION OF LABOR IN LITERATURE

Some critics have objected to my use of the term "modernist," and they would be right if I used it otherwise than as a handy label to denote certain poets. In this use it has the great advantage of meaning nothing else but those poets. Certainly no wise man will take seriously the names of any schools of art in these days when the only art we cultivate with universal energy is that of advertising our wares.

If you take a glance back over English history, it is surprising to see how the rise and fall of schools or movements in poetry has been gaining speed. The first movement, that of the pagan alliterative minstrels, lasted longer than history can remember. The next one, that of the Christian legendarists with a leaning towards rhyme, lasted six centuries. The romantic movement under French influence held the centre of the stage for two or three centuries more. The new realism identified with Chaucer's name, and the proletarian poetry invented by Piers Plowman, divided the attention for another two hundred years. In the sixteenth century there were perhaps two schools of poetry. In the seventeenth, three. In the eighteenth, four. I am making it far more precise than it was—but the nineteenth century saw five full-sized poetical epochs. And the twentieth, unless my count fails me, has already given birth to six. In fact, in Moscow—which is affirmed by some to give us an image of our own future—I once attended an evening meeting of the Poets' Union, and listened to the reading of original manuscripts representing fifteen separate and distinct schools of twentieth-century poetry. I was carried home unconscious in the gray light of dawn, and I do not remember what any of that poetry was about, but I had the presence of mind to bring away a handbill, and here is the list of those fifteen different schools of soviet poetry: Symbolist, Imagist, Acmeist, Moscow Parnassiens, Father Damiens, Neo-Classics, Constructivists, Imago-Constructivists, Proletarian poets, Peasant poets, Futurists, Presentists, Nichevoki, Petersburg Parnassiens, and Acoitists. *Nichevoki* means "advocates of nothing," and the *Acoitists* were a school of poets who renounced all physical contact between the sexes. There was only one member of this school, a beardless youth with a prophetic gleam in his eye—prophetic, I should say, of a large family of children.

History is moving faster and faster all the time. Machinery and education are speeding up history the way moving pictures speed up the blossoming of a flower. And they are speeding it up in a geometrical progression. The faster it goes, the faster its rate of acceleration. It seems a mere mathematical inference from the above figures that in another two thousand years schools of poetry will be popping off with the rapidity of bullets coming out of a machine gun. By that time it would seem inevitable that critical opinion will arm itself with some scientific terms and distinctions, more deeply valid and more clearly defined than the names of these successive schools of poetry.

It is in this somewhat millennial mood that I wish to approach the problem of the causes of the modern tendency. Not only would the word "modernism" be a nuisance here, but the words classicism and romanticism also, for even these solidly established abstractions are mere labels for certain particular groups of poets, and no guide to the causes of things.

"The word *classicus,*" as Sainte-Beuve tells us, "was used in a figurative sense by Aulus Gellius, and applied to writers: a writer of worth and distinction, *classicus assiduusque scriptor,* a writer who is of account, has real property, and is not lost in the proletariat crowd." In short it meant *classy,* and naturally became identified with "law and order," and with the idea of restraint. It is so easy to believe in law and order and to restrain oneself, at least from anything bordering on incitements to riot, when one has a little real property and is not lost in the proletariat crowd. It also became identified with a kind of objectivity or self-effacement, not because the classes are less interested in themselves than the proletariat, but because being well fixed they do not *have* to think about themselves, and are thus able to regard protrusions of the ego or protests in behalf of liberty or individuality as slightly vulgar. And finally it became identified with a decorous consideration for conventions and for what is somewhat naïvely called "society as a whole," not because the classes are more interested in society or social organization, but because they are well pleased and protected by the existing ones. Thus a certain loose association of traits, due not to hereditary character but to the influences of social status, became ticketed as *classical.* Robert Graves regards these traits as so mystically inherent in their class origin that speaking of the "dependence of English prosody on the political outcome of the present class warfare," he voices the belief that "A Red victory would bring with it . . . a renewal of the native prosody in a fairly pure form, as the White domination of the eighteenth century made for pure Classicism." He made this statement in 1928 when the red victory in Russia was already secure and it had become clear as daylight that the "proletariat crowd," once seizing the power, were far more vigorous about law and order, about discipline, about being objective, about suppressing the individual and about having a mind only to the whole of society, than their predecessors, the people of worth, distinction and real property, had ever dreamed of being. Art and literature in soviet Russia are submitting to the grip of a state regulation and regulation by party manifesto and administrative ordering of social opinion, that makes the days of Louis XIV look like a romantic revival. That shows the folly of resting in mere literary terminologies not based on a discrimination of the causal relations of things.

As for the word *romantic,* that too has a kind of class origin, having at first designated the vernacular—that is, 'domestic slave'—languages related to Latin, and so the kind of tales told in these languages. Nor is this origin inappropriate to its use as a label for all those who contributed to the vigorous reblossoming of poetry at the turn of the eighteenth century. But after tagging this vast and variegated multitude as an adjective, it obviously can do nothing as an abstract noun but save people the labor of stating in definite language what they are talking about. In Irving Babbitt's "Rousseau and Romanticism" I have counted upwards of one hundred and twenty different meanings attributed to the words classic or romantic or the distinction between them. It is such a fine book that I think it would make an excellent monument to leave upon the burial place of these Gold Dust Twins of criticism. They have done most of the work of the literary mind for now many years. Despairing of their further labors in the sphere of criticism, Rebecca West has suggested that they be brought inside the individual—that is, turned over to psychology—and employed to designate two different phases of the creative process. I venture to assert that psychology will decline the too generous offer with thanks.

In order to understand the tendency in modern poetry which lies deeper than any of its names, the tendency to cease telling us anything about life, it is necessary to go back to the sixteenth century, I think, and reconstruct the whole story from there. Most poetic readers would agree with Havelock Ellis that speech was "never more alive than in the sixteenth century," and they would agree that those times will not return. Rabelais and Shakespeare and their companions seem like a race of giants who inhabited the earth in times long past. There is an outpouring imperious sovereignty of utterance in them, not even to be asked of the modern species. This is usually explained by the fact that they were for the first time writing in the vernacular; theirs was not only a new literature, but literature in a new language. I think that is less than half the explanation.

Those men lived on the brink of the division of labor. Not only does all art begin in those days to divide itself from handicraft—or rather all crafts begin to lose the character of arts—because of the introduction of the factory system, but throughout society there begins that increasing division of labor in all fields which has brought "crippling of both mind and body," as Karl Marx says, but which has brought also the colossal achievements of modern civilization. And in this process no element is more stupendous in its results, more fundamental and necessary to the whole, although it has been so little observed or ever commented upon, than the division between science and poetic literature. This inexorable process was but beginning in the sixteenth century, and that is a principal reason why they wrote then as perhaps no man ever will again. They experienced the stimulus of that birth of real knowledge which has created our modern world, but without feeling pushed aside by it—without losing the naïve conviction which emerged with them out of the Middle Ages, countersigned by Aristotle, that poetry itself is knowledge, and that knowledge can go no higher than the poet raises it. "Amongst all those rare ornaments of the mind of Man," says Drummond of Hawthornden, "*Poesie* hath had a most eminent place and been in high esteem, not only at one time and in one climate, but during all times and through those parts of the world where any ray of humanity and civility hath shined. So that she hath not unworthily deserved the name of Mistress of human life, the height of eloquence, the quintessence of knowledge. . . ." This was not a quaint hyperbole, but a very general attitude among men of letters in that "sixteenth century"—which, by the way, extends a good way into the seventeenth. It had not occurred to them then that any knowledge was either too large or too technical to be grasped by the poet if he wished to descend to it. Chaucer had been an astronomer, and Kepler was even then proving the Copernican hypothesis, not only by mathematical calculations, but by such arguments as this: "In the first place, lest perchance a blind man might deny it to you, of all the bodies in the universe the most excellent is the sun, whose whole essence is nothing else than the purest light, than which there is no greater star; which singly and alone is the producer, conserver and warmer of all things; it is a fountain of light, rich in fruitful heat, most fair, limpid and pure to the sight. . . . Since, therefore, it does not befit the first mover to be diffused throughout an orbit, but rather to proceed from one certain principle, and as it were, point, no part of the world, and no star, accounts itself worthy of such a great honor. . . ." How different it was to live an intellectual life in those times before science and poetry had parted company, I think few people realize.

Sir William Osler began his famous address on assuming the presidency of the Classical Association at Oxford in 1919 by regretting that the meeting was not being held in 1519, when they might have had the pleasure of listening to "a real Oxford scholar-physician," Linacre, teacher of Greek and founder of the Royal College of Physicians. Doctor Osler's address is famous because of the opinion he expressed that science needs the humanities and the humanities need science, and their "unhappy divorce . . . should never have taken place." But he himself in apologizing for not being a modern Linacre—although indeed he came amazingly near it—gave the reason why this division of labor occurred and why it was inevitable. "In those happy days," he said, "to know Hippocrates and Galen was to know disease and be qualified to practise." That is not the whole reason, for knowledge grows intensively as well as extensively, and as it delves deeper it divides not only the laborers but the commodity also, and poets and scientists cease even to speak and write the same language. This too was pointed out by Doctor Osler, and although his address was ostensibly a plea for the union of science and poetic literature, it was in fact a demonstration that scientific progress had compelled their divorce.

He need not have gone back so far, however, as 1519—not so far indeed as 1619—to find science and poetry still married together in the same mind and the same book, unconscious of any incompatibility in their ways. He did find them, indeed, in Sir Thomas Browne's *Religio Medici,* his favorite book, and in Robert Burton's colossal and curious *Anatomy of Melancholy,* a veritable memorial museum of that unrecoverable age in the history of man's mind. Even Francis Bacon himself, the herald of scientific method, could turn with no sense of a change in pursuit or profession from puttering with bubbles in an alembic to studying out the hidden meanings of fables from antiquity. It was only as the achievements of Gilbert and Harvey and Galileo and Descartes and Newton and Robert Boyle became known to the educated world that science began both to seem, and so far as concerns astronomy and physics and chemistry and anatomy at least, to be, a pursuit and a profession wholly distinct from literature.

In 1645 "divers worthy persons, inquisitive into natural philosophy and other parts of human learning and particularly of what has been called *New Philosophy* or *Experimental Philosophy*" agreed to meet once a week and each to read a paper or give a demonstration. They became the Royal Society, and it was not long before the Royal Society adopted resolutions on the style in which the reports of its members ought to be delivered—resolutions which effectively and forever drove poetry out of the books of natural science. "They have exacted from all their members," says Thomas Sprat, writing the history of the Society in 1667, "a close naked natural way of speaking, positive expressions, clear senses . . . bringing all things as near the mathematical plainness as they can. . . ." And Sprat accompanies this piece of great good news with a triumphant outcry against the "trick of Metaphors," which he thinks "may be plac'd amonst those *general mischiefs,* such as the *dissension* of Christian Princes, the *want of practice* in Religion, and the like, which have been so long spoken against that men are become insensible about them. . . ."

In the century to follow, poetry will be driven as ruthlessly out of the books devoted to political and economic science. Thomas Hobbes in his *Leviathan* is already warning the public against "Metaphors, Tropes and other Rhetoricall figures" instead of "words proper." "For though it be lawfull to say, (for example) in common speech, *the way goeth or leadeth hither or thither, the Proverb sayes this or that* (whereas wayes cannot go, nor Proverbs speak;) yet in reckoning, and seeking of truth, such speeches are not to be admitted." Thus Hobbes laid down the law against poetry in English political science, although he was himself among other things a poet, and although the very title of his book is a metaphor, and his prose style so well set out with tropes and rhetorical figures of speech and so little confined to "words proper," as to constitute another great monument of the days before this division of labor was really complete. From Hobbes' *Leviathan* through Mandeville's *Fable of the Bees,* to the solid prose labors of Adam Smith, is but another story of the gradual banishment of poetry from the pursuit of knowledge.

In the nineteenth century it is the "Science of Life" which ponderously separates itself from the general body of literature. Erasmus Darwin wrote what he knew about evolution in verse; Charles Darwin not only wrote practical language but confessed when he had done that the ardors of a life devoted to science had made it impossible for him even to keep an ear open to the arts. H. G. Wells, wishing to bring this science back a little way on its path, to make it accessible at least to readers of literature, is compelled to associate himself in a co-operative enterprise with two men who, not distracted by the poetry, have specialized in the knowledge, of life. And he describes this maturest form of the division of labor by saying: "The senior partner is the least well-equipped scientifically. His share has been mainly literary. . . ." Thus not only the word *poetry,* but the word *literature* itself, would seem to be losing all its old association with the enterprise of reliable knowledge.[1]

And throughout the twentieth century the same division has been defining itself with the same fateful rigor in all discourse about mental attributes and the nature and behavior of men. Here the men-of-letters and the professors of literature, fighting their last battle, will for a short time still persuade themselves that wisdom is something else besides completed and rightly applied knowledge, but in the end they too will surrender to that necessary condition of all human progress —co-operation through the division of labor.

These three centuries, then, since Shakespeare and the Elizabethans, have seen the division between science and poetic literature advance gradually throughout the whole universe of human discourse. It is obvious that this development is fundamental if we wish to give an account of the literary tendencies of those centuries in terms of cause. That does not mean, of course, that this development is the sole cause of everything that has occurred. It has brought other things after it, or come with them—industrial capitalism, the machine age, finance capital, democracy, sex equality, proletarian revolution, the World War. And there is always the dance of the chromosomes to remember. It would be metaphysics to exalt any one of these causes as prime mover above all the others. It hardly needs

[1]Compare this use of the word *literary* with that of Thomas Thomson, writing the history of the Royal Society in 1812: "The only account of a Literary Society which can be at all valuable or interesting, is a detail of the efforts they have made to increase the stock of knowledge, and to promote the various branches of science to which they have directed their attention."

more than to be said, however, that the separation of all the sciences out of her body one after another in the course of three centuries, has played a major part in determining the evolution of literature during those centuries. Professor Whitehead in his book on *Science and the Modern World* has touched this subject, but he imagines it is only the results of scientific study —the kind of knowledge acquired—which has affected the poets. Thus he is able to say that "so far as the mass of literature is concerned science might never have been heard of," and to imagine that what has affected literature in certain sensitive points is only the "mechanistic" view of the world at which science seemed to have arrived. I am afraid Professor Whitehead has no adequate idea of the egotism of poets. What troubles them, and what affects them, whether they notice it or not, is not that science proposes a "mechanistic" as opposed to an "organismic" formulation of knowledge, or anything else that science proposes. What troubles them is that this knowledge, whichever way it is formulated and whatever it may be, is formulated by scientists and not poets. It is science and not poetry. It is too complex and highly specialized to be mixed up with poetry, or find poetry a help either in its discovery or the expounding of it to adult minds. Into whatsoever field it advances it reduces poetry from her high throne as the "mistress of life" and the "quintessence of knowledge," to the position in relation to knowledge of a mere datum, or at best an object-lesson or method of teaching by means of imaginative experience what was discovered by other means and is known in other terms. And it advances inexorably into all fields.

It is because poetry has never been studied from the standpoint of this, the central event in her whole history, that there appears no intelligible order whatever in that history, and we find plausible such books as that of E. E. Kellett, in which the major changes in her character throughout history are described as a mere "Whirligig of Taste." I want to describe those changes in English poetry—in briefest outline, and with an eye mainly to explaining their end-term, the modernist poets—as they appear from this vital point of understanding.

Milton still believed with unwavering mind that poetry is the highest science, its riches to be attained "by labor and intent study, which I take to be my portion in this life," and by "devout prayer to that eternal Spirit who can enrich with all utterance and knowledge, and sends out his Seraphim with the hallowed fire of his altar, to touch and purify the lips of whom he pleases: to this must be added industrious and select reading, steady observation, insight into all seemly and generous arts and affairs." Theology protected Milton from feeling the division that was far advancing in his life-time, or submitting to its effects; he remained, by the special grace of God, an Elizabethan. The first strong sign in English literature of the separate existence of science is to be found in the so-called "metaphysical poets." They were metaphysical only in that their most delicate raptures concerned thoughts rather than things. They were intrigued by science, by the astonishing things coming to pass at the hands of people who devoted themselves not to learning but to thinking. They seem to have felt towards thinking as towards an exciting adventure somewhat like discovering America, and they made poetry out of thoughts. That is to say, they made words reproduce thoughts, not with an eye single to the meaning as a scientist would, but with an eye to putting forth the whole inward being of a thought as a thing to be enjoyed for its own sake. You might describe the transition from the true Elizabethans to the metaphysical poets as a transition from poetry as an assumption of knowledge to poetry as a serious playing with ideas. And from playing with ideas in England it was a short step to toying with conceits in Italy and France, and from toying with conceits in Italy and France they were soon taking the words apart and putting them together in new ways in Spain. Thus the first reaction of poetry to the birth of science from her loins—the turning of so many eyes away in admiration to this new portent—was to accept and then even begin to over-emphasize, as though in a pet, her own resulting lightness and inconsequence.

This mood did not of course give a real equilibrium and could not last long. Poetry finally regained her self-esteem by discovering that she had never really had anything much to do with truth, least of all in its vulgar and mean form as natural science, that a refined intellectual pleasure is her essential preoccupation. She came to rest in a feeling of the elegance and acknowledged social superiority of this preoccupation. Within twenty years of Milton's mighty asseveration that the eternal Spirit could enrich and touch the poet's lips with all knowledge, John Dryden was declaring that "Delight is the chief, if not the only, end of poesy," and that "the court" is "the best and surest judge of writing." Another contemporary of Milton, Thomas Hobbes, introduces his translation of Homer to the readers of poetry—who, he remarks in a parenthesis, "are commonly Persons of the best Quality"—with the assertion that "the work of an Heroique Poet is no more but to furnish an ingenuous Reader (when his leisure abounds) with the diversion of an honest and delightful Story, whether true or feigned." Hobbes did not of course forget that this honest story might inculcate the moral virtues; the reader must not imagine that the idea of poetry as a learning died suddenly a complete death, and that of poetry as an elegant pleasure as suddenly rose in its place. The history is one mainly of emphasis. The element of "delight" was not ignored by the Elizabethans, nor the element of "instruction" forgotten by their successors. The emphasis finally arrived at by those poets who set the fashion for the period we call classical, is most neatly intimated in the saying of Alexander Pope that in poetry,

"Blunt truths more mischief than nice falsehoods do."

It is somewhat more crudely stated by George Granville, Lord Lansdowne, in his *Essay upon Unnatural Flights in Poetry:*

"Important Truths still let your Fables hold,
And moral misteries with art unfold;
Ladies and Beaux to please is all the task,
But the sharp Critick will instruction ask."

Compare this with Sir Philip Sidney a hundred years before, making his noble boast: "So that the ending end of all earthly learning, being vertuous action, those skils that most serve to bring forth that, have a most just title to be Princes over all the rest: wherein if we can shew, the Poet is worthy to have it before any other competitor. . . ." And compare Edmund Spenser—"our sage and serious Spenser," as Milton called him, "whom I dare to name a better teacher than Scotus or Aquinas"—speaking of poetry as "no art, but a divine gift and heavenly instinct not to be gotten by labour and learning, but adorned with both; and poured into the wit by a certain ἐνθουσιασμος and celestial inspiration." You will see what a wide difference an emphasis of this kind can make.

It is commonly assumed that for some mysterious reason deep organic passions disappeared out of the literary world for these generations called "classical," or were brought under restraint by men who loved order and moderation with a purely intellectual love. The fact is that these men were driven by the deepest and most fixed of human passions, the desire for invidious distinction. No longer able to find it as the Elizabethans had in the glorious position of poetry in the hierarchy of the sciences, human and divine, they sought it in the elegant association of poetry with the leisure hours of the people of quality. To this end, and driven by this unrestrained passion, they endowed poetry with those virtues which are supposed to distinguish these people of quality from the common herd. And those virtues—"the Vertues of an Heroic Poem, and indeed of all writings published," to quote the inimitably perspicuous Hobbes again, "are comprehended all in the one word Discretion." The whole proceeding might well be described as an effort of the literati, after having lost that exclusive superiority so long secured to them by the Latin language, to recapture it by building up a style in the vernacular that no downright and plain man with something important on his mind would use.

It was here that the phrase "polite letters" came in and played its part, and the phrase "belles lettres" came in also, and the phrase "good taste." And the word *wit* from having meant intelligence came to mean a ready tongue, and the word *virtuoso* from meaning a man of intellectual power came to mean a man of æsthetic talent, and the ideal of the *Savant* was replaced by that of the *Beau Esprit,* and the ideal of propriety and the obeying of established rules acquired the same prominence in literature that it possesses in the court or the drawing-room, where as "fine manners" it is an indispensable means of making hereditary leisure conspicuous. If poetry was not the quintessence of knowledge, it was at least the quintessence of refinement, and the proper intellectual recreation of a gentleman. And to this could be added the comforting reflection that even the Royal Society knew nothing except about the external world, and that after all "the proper study of mankind is man." In this study "wit" could still disport itself, even if not wisdom, and the poet still boast of "Reason" and of a "natural sense" that is better than systemized knowledge.

As to that boast of "Reason" which still deludes so many, I think it is time to remark that a poem which gives pleasure by an elegant dignity and restraint of diction is not one whit more reasonable than one which gives pleasure by sending a barbaric yawp over the roofs of the world. Reason has nothing whatever to do with the case. The confusion of the ideal of "Reason" with this cultivation of the social position of poetry, is due to the insecurity of that social position. In the first place, natural science was steadily throughout these two centuries improving its status. Even in 1665 Joseph Glanville complimented the Royal Society on having so "redeemed the credit of philosophy" that it would soon be accounted "none of the meanest breeding to be acquainted with the laws of nature and the universe." In the second place poets had no title to their position; they were mere fashionable appurtenances of the lordly life, about as secure to perpetuity as the lace collar or silk breeches that it pleased the Lord to wear. Boileau unconsciously immortalized the humiliating inner truth of this phase in the history of poetry—and also gave a good glimpse of the kind of "Reason" which prevailed through it. In his *Art of Poetry* which was translated by William Soames with the help of John Dryden and set the pace for the whole "classical era" in England, he advises poets *not* to make their art a trade or sell themselves for gold, and then to the question what they *shall* do to keep from starving, replies in all suave solemnity:

> "What can we fear, when Virtue, Arts and Sence,
> Receive the Stars' propitious influence;
> When a sharp-sighted Prince, by early Grants
> Rewards your Merits, and prevents your Wants?
> Sing then his Glory, Celebrate his Fame,
> Your noblest Theme is his immortal Name."

In this insecure position it is not surprising if poetry, besides looking down upon science and gently ridiculing its labors, also looked up to it, and showed a disposition to lick its boots and imitate its virtues, and pretend to be of a parallel nature. This phenomenon has appeared elsewhere—most notably perhaps in Zola's celebration of the "experimental novel." But in Zola's time science was in a more fact-gathering phase, and his boast to be himself a kind of doctor of research in the front rank of the advance of science, led not to a display of "Reason" but of "realism." In the period called "classic," science was in a more mathematical or pattern-making phase, and it was a natural emulation for poetry to make a great matter of patterns too, and to call this pattern-making and this cult of cool elegance and restraint, except in praise of Princes, by the name of Reason.[1]

Such was the equilibrium attained by English poetry after the first shock of its separation from science. It became, as one might expect, a more trivial thing, but by dint of imitating science, and by bolstering itself up with a high and mighty priggishness, and making a severe enterprise of good breeding and a nice behavior, it managed to save its face. As science pressed forward, however, assuming the form of an almost passionate

[1]It seems clear to me that the two types of creative mind, the one which loves to make patterns and the one which loves better the materials of which they are made—are to be found in both science and poetry. It is often remarked that the mathematical scientist is like a poet, and prophets of confusion are not wanting to tell us that he is a poet. He is interested in fitting the conceptions of things together in a vast logically consistent design, mending or modelling them often solely that they may fall beautifully into their place. The poet makes his designs of the experience of things, and his consistencies are not necessarily logical, and it is not helpful to confuse these two makers of designs. There is a similar analogy between the fact-gathering scientist and the poet who is more interested in the colors of experience than the patterns he makes of them, but it is equally erroneous to confuse "facts" in the scientific sense with the sheer qualities of experience as they interest a poet.

love of "Reason," and a frenzy to apply "Reason" not only to astronomical and physical problems but to the problems of society and education—a proceeding which would most certainly and unceremoniously cast down those people of quality from that secure position in which they were enjoying the refined delights of poetry—the rôle of feeding out these delights to these particular people became a too precarious and too obviously trivial trade for a great poet.

A great poet happened to be born—two great poets happened to be born—and they signalized their arrival by revolting explosively against the foundation of this whole prevailing mode of speech, the division of labor between poetry and truth. Reason, we now hear, is a mere limitation of the energic principle and father of all truth, imagination or spiritual sensation, which will ultimately triumph over Reason and in a second coming of Christ or Poetry save this world from deadness and from doom. "God's prophets are the poets who have the courage to take their own imaginings for truth." That is the "Art of Poetry" according to William Blake. And Wordsworth is little behind him in this embattled re-entry into the lost realms of knowledge. Not only is the poet alive to nature, according to Wordsworth, but nature is alive to the poet and by him only and his diligent sympathy to be reached unto and understood. If poetry is not perhaps "the quintessence," it is nevertheless the "breath and finer spirit of all knowledge; it is the impassioned expression in the countenance of all science." "Its object is truth, not individual and local but general and operative; not standing on external testimony but carried alive into the heart by passion; truth which is its own testimony, which gives competence and confidence to the tribunal to which it appeals, and receives them from the same tribunal. Poetry is the image of man and nature." It is this great and conscious declaration of war on the division of labor between poetry and science—this heroic attempt, by mysticism or by metaphysics, to return to the attitude of the Elizabethans that inaugurates the new era which we call "romantic" in English poetry. Shelley, a thousand miles from Wordsworth in every other motive and conviction of his mind, is at one with him in this. He is at one with him, and goes beyond him and beyond even his Elizabethan forebear, Sir Philip Sidney, who kept at least to the path of a sensible plausibility in his *Defense of Poesie.*

"Poetry," cried Shelley, "is indeed something divine. It is at once the centre and circumference of knowledge; it is that which comprehends all science, and that to which all science must be referred. It is at the same time the root and blossom of all other systems of thought; it is that from which all spring, and that which adorns all; and that which, if blighted, denies the fruit and the seed, and withholds from the barren world the nourishment and the succession of the scions of the tree of life." Is it possible to deny that in this reassumption of the scope and grandeur of an art of knowledge, this challenging of science to mortal combat for the whole universe, instead of sitting content with the petty superiority of good breeding and a special entrée as polite letters among the people of quality, lies much of the essence of the so-called Romantic Revival in English poetry? It was an effort to recapture the great speech of the Elizabethans by denying and destroying that very system of divided labors which has brought us down from it.

Shelley's revolt is unique in this, however, that he was irreligious and that he studied science and loved it. If he carried science and poetry both up into the flying clouds of his eloquence and confused them, it was only because his own mind and his own ardent hopes of humanity relied on and contained them both. He might have been quite happy to think of poetry as a winged herald and forerunner toward those great ends of joy and love and justice toward which he believed true science was to bring the race of man. This makes Shelley a modern poet in a sense that neither Blake nor Wordsworth is. And Keats—if I may speak out of a mere personal feeling of his mind—had a better sense of the underlying facts of the matter than any of them. Perhaps because he had set out to study medicine and turned from that to poetry, he felt without much thinking the depth of the cleft between this art and the art of acquiring or expounding knowledge. He was a man of keen and steady revolutionary convictions which he knew how to express with dramatic force and a hard humor, but you can read his great poems from end to end without ever hearing the echo of them. They were something else than poetry. I know it is now the fashion for the unbelievably virtuous people who preside over the growth of English literature, having denounced Keats as a mere sensualist for a hundred years, to try to make it up to him in the only way they know how, by attributing to him the very essence of the interior flame that keeps pure the soul of a Sunday

School teacher. For this they make all they can of the confused idealism of his ungrown mind, the influence of his elders, the cry from his divided heart, "Beauty is truth, truth beauty." But I believe the steady and real thing in his heart was a consciousness of the division, and that when once, seized by a strong passion for knowledge, he expressed the thought that poetry may be "not so fine a thing as philosophy—for the same reason that an eagle is not so fine a thing as a truth," he said something right out of himself wiser than what others were teaching him. To me at least he seems to belong, with his pure poetry and his matter-of-fact mind and his *trouble* about the relations between poetry and truth, even more than Shelley, to our own age.

For of course the revolt of Wordsworth and Blake and Shelley, and their great attempt to recapture the kingdom of knowledge, failed. The movement both of poems and theories of poetry since then has been a gradual retreat, a reluctant acceptance of the steadily advancing division of labor, a search for some independent function and prestige for poetry to replace in a democratic society that post of caterer of elegant delights which had kept up her complacence in the days of gentlemen and ladies. Browning, of course, and Emerson, stood by the banner of Wordsworth, and Walt Whitman believed with Blake that in some mysterious way too subtle for the books of logic, poetry arrives at, and is, if not indeed the "centre and circumference," and not even perhaps the "breath and finer spirit," yet at least the "tuft and final applause of science." In Tennyson an exquisite pure-lyric poet was buried and half lost in the big black hat and sombre cloak of the

Village Preacher that a Wordsworthian tradition demanded he should be. Matthew Arnold prolonged the tradition with a sly compromise, dodging the words truth and knowledge altogether, and calling poetry a "criticism of life." In that dry slogan—distasteful to both sides, as a compromise upon essentials always is—the cognitive poets, so far as concerns a belief in their own mission at least, are clearly in the decline. Thomas Hardy keeps but a faint-hearted pretense in *The Dynasts* to make any criticism of those Napoleonic wars of which his poem treats. Certain "Impersonated Abstractions or Intelligences, called spirits," hover over the drama and make temperamental comments from time to time, but Hardy himself warns us that they are to be taken "for what they may be worth as contrivances of the fancy merely. Their doctrines are but tentative, and are advanced with little eye to . . . lift the burden of mystery of this unintelligible world." During Hardy's life a great part of the mystery was lifted from that particular episode by a study of the natural and economic forces underlying it. But he knows nothing of that; he regards it all as a "calamity . . . artificially brought about." He is a poet, and the attempt really to understand history has become an affair of the prose thinkers. The formulæ of modern historic research would indeed fit awkwardly in the singing lips of those impersonated abstractions or intelligences called spirits. In those shadowy beings, uncertain of their function, uncertain of their thoughts, the Wordsworthian revolt, the grandiloquent attempt of poetry to recapture her place in the kingdom of knowledge, is approaching its end. Stephen Benét in his epic of our American Civil War makes no effort of understanding whatever—seems indeed to take for the moral of his tale, a renunciation of understanding, of all purposive attitude, of all judgment.

> "Say neither . . .
> It is deadly magic and accursed,
> Nor 'it is blest,' but simply it is here."

Robert Bridges, in his *Testament of Beauty,* comes down to the desperate expedient of fitting pedestrian text-book instruction—the language of the foot-note—into the metrical forms of the Iliad and the Odyssey. And Alfred Noyes clings to the last flapping shred of the pretensions of poetry to have something to do in the sphere of cognition by writing ecstatical gossip about the soul life of the men of science whom he acknowledges to be the "Torch-Bearers." That is the end of the life-story of poetry as "quintessence of knowledge."

Since the middle of the century poetry has lived most vividly in those who regarded themselves, not primarily as sages or priests or teachers, but as artists. The pre-Raphaelites abandoned themselves to a painting of the colors of emotions—of flesh and angels and emotions. And the definition of poetry as emotional language, formulated by John Stuart Mill, began rapidly to obliterate all memory of a day when poetry had been identified with truth. Swinburne, as though set in motion by the definition, poured out a liquid stream of language like tide running out through a channel, a liquid in which not knowledge only is lost, but frequently the meaning too, and in which a bold man may cast loose and swim far out borne rapidly until he is lost utterly to the solid earth, as Swinburne himself loved to do, or with a like abandon loved to tell everybody he did, on sunny days in the blue ocean. George Meredith made poetry of happy passion in "Love in the Valley," and of unhappy pain in "Modern Love," and though he was very intellectual, he had nothing to say to us about either one of them that we have been able to remember, except that there they were. John Masefield does a certain perfunctory preaching, but happily it burdens him as little as it does any of the readers of his strong unintellectual tales of action and emotion. Edna St. Vincent Millay has almost recaptured the language of the Elizabethans, but only to clothe therein her feelings and her fearless will to have them. Carl Sandburg is a kind of successor to Walt Whitman, but not the kind that looks back to him as he looked back to Jesus, comrades in a prophetic mission, "journeying up and down, till we make our ineffaceable mark upon time and the diverse eras." Carl Sandburg has rather left it to the Marxians—the socialists or the communists or the I. W. W., and without even quite assuming the task of deciding which—to look after that ineffaceable mark upon time and the diverse eras. Robert Frost has built him a little rustic philosophy with which he thinks to lift poetry back to her place among the ways of knowledge. "I have wanted of late years," he says in an essay on *Education by Poetry,* "to go further and further in making metaphor the whole of thinking. . . . The metaphor whose manage we are best taught in poetry—that is all there is of thinking." But his philosophy consists mainly of not asking himself the most obvious question: What is the difference between poetic and scientific comparison? Why, if metaphor is all there is, and it is best taught in poetry—why did science ever appear upon the scene at all? We do not go to Robert Frost for education. We go to him for the almost uneducated simplicity—the almost indolent simplicity—with which he communicates to us a kind of experience not elsewhere accessible and which we like to touch. Archibald MacLeish has a philosophy too, or a long dark poem at least about relativity, in which he seems to want to rescue some last little remnant of the universe, if it is only Einstein himself, from Einstein's understanding. "Something inviolate"—and I suppose he wants to keep it so for poetry. But to what end I cannot see, for he says elsewhere in the same volume that

> "A poem should not mean
> But be."

That at any rate is what a majority of poems do in this modern era—they do not mean but be. Edwin Arlington Robinson compares with Robert Browning much as Carl Sandburg does with Whitman—except that in his case we are gladder to be spared the homiletic element, the sentimental theological philosophy of optimism. The "imagists" made a stir with their vague and trite program only because underlying it, and implied in their very name, was the timely assertion that poetry need not do any more than paint a picture. And so it is in varying degrees with all the standard poets of this day. Although they are not conscious, any more than

Keats was, of the break with an antique tradition, they are taking their place more and more among the artists rather than the priests and teachers of mankind.

And we need not be surprised if beside these "standard" poets—poets, I mean, who have moved into the new position gradually, and not completely, and without giving the sense of an abrupt outrageous change—we find a group of extremists, excitedly modern, making a veritable crusade and consecrated glorious life work of the art of telling us nothing in their poems. These "modernists" are in truth merely an extreme manifestation of the position of all poetry in our time, the retreat before science. But that is not the whole explanation of them. They are so extreme, and so ingenious about it, for historic reasons of their own. They belong to a different tradition. They derive from a different source. They do not look back, or carry our minds back, to John Keats, who wrote pure poetry but struggled to believe it was identical with truth. Their direct forebear and mind's ancestor—although they are separated from him by a long journey both in time and space—is Edgar Allan Poe, who first among modern poets boldly accepted the total separation of poetry from truth.

"It has been assumed," Poe wrote in one of nis astonishing little essays, "tacitly and avowedly, directly and indirectly, that the ultimate object of all poetry is truth. . . . We have taken it into our heads that to write a poem simply for the poem's sake, and to acknowledge such to have been our design, would be to confess ourselves radically wanting in the true poetic dignity and force:—but the simple fact is, that . . . .

there neither exists nor *can* exist any work more thoroughly dignified—more supremely noble than this very poem—the poem *per se*—this poem which is a poem and nothing more. . . ."

In that cool declaration of independence—declaration of the dignity of poetry without truth, the *nobility* of poetry in a new society where nobility meant intrinsic worth, and not titles and land or the glamour to be gained by hanging around people who possess them—in that is to be found the key, I believe, to the unique and crucial position Poe has come to occupy, with his few frail lyrics, in the history of poetry both English and French. For Baudelaire was enraptured with Poe and transported and translated him, essays and poems and all, into France, where he came to appear a kind of fountain source of the whole modern tendency.

In France there had been no such revolt and rallying of poets to regain the world as had occurred in England. It is significant that the French revolution, so often held responsible for what is called the romantic revival in English poetry, produced no glimmer of such a revival in France. What happened in France at the same time—and, if my view is right, in the same connection—was the conscious attempt of André Chénier to combine poetry with science, to overcome this division of labor by himself studying science and writing with his own hand as poetry a whole series of volumes titled with the names of gods, but which we in our matter-of-fact way should describe as the Outline of History, the Outline of Geography, the Outline of Biology, the A B C of Astronomy, the Elements of Chemistry, the Foundations of Economics, and the General Principles of Political Science. . . . Only a few fragments of these labors of a Herculean Lucretius were ever composed, and they were neither poetry nor science but only a kind of rhymed oratorical eloquence. That in order to make poetry of the law of gravitation, Chénier felt obliged to give it an occult influence upon his own soul—exactly the kind of pre-scientific astrological influence which the accurate study of gravitation had displaced—may serve to suggest the inevitability of his failure. "Just the same, there was something there," as he himself said, tapping his head meditatively when sentenced to the guillotine. It has been a matter of dispute among French critics whether André Chénier was the last of the "classics" or the precursor of the "romantics." He does indeed occupy a unique position in the history of poetry, and may prove to have been the precursor of something that lay far beyond them both. His effort, at any rate, occupies the place in French literature that is occupied in England by the revolt of the poets against science, their effort to reassert, as poets and by divine right, their sovereignty in the realms of knowledge.

When France came to her break with the refined tradition, she had this gigantic undertaking behind her, the fragments of it lying in her hands. Her "romantic movement" was, therefore, in the main not a revolt against the division of labor but an acceptance of it—a heroic assertion of the importance of literature as an art, and as one capable of commanding prestige on its own merits, and without imitating rationality or putting on the fine manners of a lordly class. They talked about "truth" and "nature" in 1830, but what they meant by truth here was reality and not knowledge about it. Their central tendency was toward realism, or the mere painting of experience, and they emphasized those aspects in which the artist's experience is unique and so escapes from among the objects of understanding. The pith of their excitement, or the most advanced point reached by it, is contained in the exclamation of Gautier: "Radiant, resplendent words, rhythm, and melody—these are poetry. Poetry proves nothing and tells nothing," and in his celebrated formula "l'art pour l'art." It was to a literature which had arrived at this mature stage in the division of labor that Poe came over the sea as a herald of something new and wonderful. I do not know what that new and wonderful thing was, unless it was a scorn for the prophets, and a very deliberate perpetration, engineered with an ice-cold purposiveness that is scientific, of ecstatical conditions sufficiently extraordinary in their beauty, or sufficiently bizarre, to raise poetry once more to a high place in life without feudal snobbery on the one hand, or on the other the pretense to prove anything or tell anything. That was the equilibrium at which poetry arrived in France in the days of Baudelaire.

And if the "symbolist" poets added any deeply new thing, it was certainly not that they made these word-conjured ecstasies symbolic of some truth, or suggestive of some generalization into which they might enter. On the contrary they delved deeper into the unique character of the individual ecstasy. All words are symbolic; it is only through a common agreement as to the signification of a whole system of symbols that communication becomes possible. These poets were trying in spite of the practical symbolism involved in the very nature of language to make words come down close to the unsymbolizable thing, the individual thing in each experience. As Edmund Wilson says in his delightfully sympathetic book, *Axel's Castle:* "Symbolism may be defined as an attempt by carefully studied means—a complicated association of ideas represented by a medley of metaphors—to communicate unique personal feelings." Mr. Wilson regards this as a swing away from the "mechanistic" tendencies of science. But unique personal feelings are no more opposed to mechanism than are the most universal social feelings. Unique personal feelings are opposed to science itself. They are what refuses to enter a generalization. They are what is left over when science has done its worst. In moving from that preoccupation with words and that taste for the indefinite which in Poe and his companions had brought poetry so near to music, towards an exact faithfulness to whatever is unique in the experience suggested by the words, a trait which has brought it nearer to painting, these poets were only taking a new and boldly brilliant step in the development of poetry as an art now totally distinct from the art of general knowledge. That some of them ran close to madness, and that one of the most audacious, Rimbaud, after touching the outside circumference of pure poetry, stepped back into the practical life and died a merchant and a man of action, are most natural results of the intensity with which they consecrated themselves to this pure art.

It is necessary thus to travel with Poe across the

water to France in order to give even a spare outline of English poetry. For our movement of the nineties, associated with the word *decadent* and the phrase *art for art's sake,* and with the names of Walter Pater and Oscar Wilde and Arthur Symons, was a kind of home-coming of this wanderer. It was a reflection in England of the complete and conscious acceptance by these French poets of the distinction between being a poet and having knowledge, their cultivation of poetry as a pure and sensitively deep trance of realization. The highest fruit of this exceptional moment in English literature—and one of the rarest jewels in all literature —is Walter Pater's formulation of the ideal of pure poetry as an ideal, not of art only, but of life. What an arduous ideal it is, to "burn always" with a "hard gem-like flame!" How much more arduous than "decorum" or to behave always like a gentleman with a proper amount of money in the bank!

An impression prevails that there was an effective moral reaction, or reaction of social intelligence, against those devotees of art for art's sake. But I think the opposite was true. There was a realization that in their preoccupation with sin, their exaggerated delight in a freedom from moral meanings, these exceedingly British young men were feeble in their own impulse and superficial. They were exemplifying the very bondage to morals which they denounced. Even Walter Pater tinged with a color of naughtiness his sublime expression of an ideal—an ideal as needful to man as any other of the many that he needs—by withdrawing it from his book at the bidding of some thin-flanked prudes of the frightened bourgeoisie. They were in bondage to morals, those men of the nineties, and they were unaware, moreover, that morals is but one kind of practical thinking. The deeper tendency, of which their sinful and delightful excitement was a mere top-ripple, is the tendency of art to acknowledge itself independent of, and irrelevant to, all practical thinking and all reliable truth, and yet to flourish and live universally and cultivate with ardor its own domain.

It is this deeper tendency—inevitably involved in the progress of human culture—that underlies the poetry of our contemporaries which we call modernist. They are a still further development—not of that movement of the nineties, which was but a belated echo in moralistic Britain of Gautier and the mood of the thirties in France—but of the consecrated effort of Poe and Baudelaire and Mallarmé and Rimbaud and all those desperately poetic Frenchmen of the last half century to explore every corner of the mind and every device of language to find values which poetry can have without pretending to have general knowledge. And it need not surprise us, if besides their prepossession with the "symbolists" in France, these pure poets should incline back toward the beginnings of the seventeenth century and find a companionship of intellect with the "metaphysical poets" of their own country. For the startling and absorbing development of psychology in our times—the invasion by science of the last citadel of humane letters—has naturally produced an effect not unlike that of its first incursion—its first birth, I should say, as an independent speech and profession. Zola could still pretend to himself that his realistic art of literature was possessed of the honors of science, that its purpose was "to solve scientifically the question of how men behave when they are in society"; he could do this because it was still possible in his time to ignore the existence of psychology. "If the experimental method leads to the knowledge of physical life," he said, "it should also lead to the knowledge of the passionate and intellectual life. From chemistry to physiology, from physiology to anthropology and to sociology. The experimental novel is the goal." With the best will in the world to deceive ourselves, we could no longer accept this construction. We know that the goal of that progression is not novels of any kind but the text-books of psychology.

We are confronted throughout the entire universe of human discourse with the division between scientific and poetic literature. Where our own parents consulted the poets for direct guidance in the unmanageable crisis of their lives, we consult the nerve-specialist or the psychoanalyst, or some technical expert in education, or household economy, or the theory of business cycles, or the economics of the class-struggle and the seizure of power. To "know the best that has been thought and said in the world" rings false to the ardent spirits of our day; we want to know what, if anything, has been found out to be true. We see that just as in the seventeenth century the Galileos and Newtons and René Descartes, eloquent men as they were, drove poetry out of the books which convey knowledge about the external world of nature, so in our time the Pavlovs and Freuds and Marxian Lenins are driving poetry out of the books which convey knowledge of man. And to them we are turning for guidance. That is why the poets have ceased to try to tell us anything about life—because they have gradually and fully been compelled to realize that *as poets* they don't know anything about life. That is not their business.

PART IV

TOWARD A SCIENCE OF LITERATURE

I

WHAT POETRY IS

I

THE conflict between science and religion was, or will be, adjudicated for intelligent people by a scientific study of religion. It has been so with magic. It will doubtless be so in the future with systems of metaphysical belief. Indeed I think the current "reconstruction in philosophy" might almost be described by saying that philosophy, having once vaingloriously set out to explain science, is now somewhat consenting to be explained by science. Undoubtedly the same thing will happen to literature, in so far as literature professes to have a validity in conflict with the findings of science. The scholarly defenders of "literary truth" will continue to hold their own in a dying fashion, until men have approached literature itself with the methods of trained observation and experiment, and learned to state in general terms what it is and how it differs from their own activities.

What *is* literature apart from science? What is the literary mind? What will it have left to do, thousands of years hence when trained investigators with statistics and laboratory findings under their bulging arms may conceivably have *some* tested and dependable word to say upon almost any problem that arises? These are the questions that demand answer, once we have penetrated the superficial commotion about romantic and classic, naturalist and humanist, tradition and experiment. And since it is quite obviously poetry, or the poetic ingredient, that makes literature deeply different from science, it is not too much to say that the central problem for those concerned about the future of literature is the problem of defining poetry.

The very idea will provoke a smile among the sophisticated, for it has become almost a commonplace these days that poetry cannot be defined. "Poetry," says Herbert Read, "is properly speaking a transcendental quality—an effulgence radiating from the sudden transformation which words assume under a particular influence—and we can no more define this quality than we can define infinity." "What is man," cries T. S. Eliot, "to decide what poetry is?" Edwin Arlington Robinson defines poetry as an "indefinable." And even Professor Snyder, whose little book, *Hypnotic Poetry,* is the latest real contribution to this subject, remarks with a sigh that he does not look with much hope "toward the general controversies over 'What is poetry?' which have been carried on since the dawn of history." This agnosticism is a new thing, and testifies, I believe, not to a deeper or finer experience of poetry among our critics, but to a dawning apprehension among them of what it means to define a thing. They are ready to give up, because they see clearly that a million definitions have failed to define, but they do not see what help this very fact can give them in the task of definition.

The world is indeed overfull of ingenious and sprightly essays which purport to tell us what poetry is, but really tell us what kind of poem the author likes, or upon what quality when reading he most fixes his attention. Poetry has been defined by estimable authorities as imitation of human life, glimpse of the divine, wine of the devil, as expression of emotion, sublime expression of truth, aspiration toward beauty, communication of pleasure, as speaking pictures, apparent pictures of unapparent natures, as reality, make-believe, as concrete, as abstract, metaphor, metre, madness, wisdom, sanity, trance,—there is almost no way in which poetry has not been defined. There is no sphere in which "the best that has been thought and said in the world" shows a more bewildering disjointedness, a more total lack of focus and complete incapacity to guide the inquiring mind, than in this sphere of the essay on poetry. Our critics perceive this, but it does not occur to them to make the most simple inference from it—namely that the word poetry is an extremely general term, and must apply to something quite ordinary and wellnigh universal. If you can find poetry in all the situations by which sane and wise men have proposed to define its essence, then you can find it almost anywhere. And the only possible way to give clear sense to a word of such wide application is to find a very general definition, one which will include all those applications and yet also significantly exclude something.

Of course there is a voluntary element in all definition. If Herbert Read wishes to confine the word poetry to a few rare and ecstatic states of his being which he also calls transcendental effulgences, nobody can stop him. Such states of being exist, and the word poetry exists. But if we can find a clear and highly general distinction which corresponds to the uses of this word, or makes intelligible at least a large proportion of its important uses not only now but throughout history, and which provides the best as well as the most natural first step towards a useful classification of literature, then I think the voluntary part of the act of definition —the arresting of this particular word and conscripting it to this purpose—can safely be left to the practical good sense of mankind.

The attempt to define poetry was put on a wrong track at the beginning, owing to the absence in early times of novels and prose dramas. For Aristotle the term poetry included all kinds of fiction writing, and thus he thought he could distinguish poetry by its subject matter—call it "imitation of life," and regard the diction of the poet as incidental. The mere fullness of experience has displaced his use of the word poetry—confused enough in his own day, it seems to me—and to cling now to the antique idea of a "poetic subject," as Matthew Arnold did, is merely to stand stuck in the mud while history passes you by. It is poetic diction that we have to define. We have to describe what happens when a man who has something to say says it poetically, and how it is that this poetic way of speaking when concentrated and developed becomes poetry instead of prose. It is absurd to say that these questions cannot be answered; they can be answered as soon as we understand our minds. It is still more absurd to be afraid to answer them as I think many lovers of poetry are, lest something be lost, as though defining a general term could exhaust or destroy the wealth and variety of the particulars.

The problem, I repeat, is to find a definition general

enough to include all these particulars. To say that poetic diction is beautiful, or true, or divine, or devilish, or passionate, or sensuous, or effulgent, or pictorial, or indeed to attribute to it any other special quality of experience, may be a good way to lead someone into it, but will not serve as a general definition, for the moment you select one of these qualities, I can show you poetic diction which exhibits the opposite. Even if you become very matter-of-fact and "in despair of giving a serious definition of poetry," say with Professor Santayana that poetry is "metrical discourse," I can find you examples of diction which is not metrical, but is so vividly metaphorical that you will have to call it poetic. When Miss Edith Sitwell, wishing to tell us that the plants in her garden are bending down with their blossoms near the earth, says that they "begin to cluck," we do not have to have metre to assure us that this is poetic. On the other hand, if you regard metre as accidental, and say, as Miss Helen Parkhurst does in her recent book called *Beauty,* that "The quintessence of poetry . . . is little else than metaphor," I can bring you examples of diction that is metrical but not metaphoric—a great part of the popular ballads, for example—and you can hardly deny that they too are poetic.

Metre and metaphor "belong together," and our definition will have to be general enough to include them both and explain their companionship. It will also have to include language that may be neither metrical nor figurative, but deliberately and as though with malice aforethought arouses our emotions. It is not poetic to shout, "Look out, there's a rattlesnake!" when there really is one, no matter how much emotion the words arouse. But to cry "Vipers and venom!" into the vacant air suggests that a poem is about to begin, if it is not perhaps already finished.

Emotion is, in fact, together with metre and metaphor, so commonly found in poetry that it too has been used as a defining term by matter-of-fact people, by people who understand that the problem is not one of ingenious invention but of adequate generalization. There are two reasons why poetry cannot be defined with the word emotion. One is that emotion is present in all alert states of being; to identify poetry with emotional speech would be almost to identify it with wide-awake speech, and that indeed is too general. The other reason is that as soon as you define emotion and really distinguish it from other elements in experience—or to the extent that you do so—it becomes easy to show that poets frequently violate an emotion and destroy it when they are interested in something else. Psychologists are not well agreed as to the nature of emotions; all men agree, however, that they belong among the inner as opposed to the outer feelings. They differ from sensations like color and sound which come directly in to us from causes in the external world. And the moment you have defined emotion even to this small extent, a glance over the field of poetry will show that poets are not at all exclusively preoccupied with it. I always like to prove this with that passage from Homer's *Iliad,* where Ajax, the great fighting man of the Greek army, their sole bulwark in the absence of Achilles, falls wounded in battle. He lies there bleeding and gasping, and the Trojans come ramping over the plain, and you would certainly think that if poetry were solely devoted to emotions, a supreme poet would not let pass this supreme chance. But just as though to disprove this too introvert definition of poetry, Homer catches sight of the blood flowing down on Ajax's thigh, and he becomes so interested in the mere color of that blood that he wanders off babbling about it as though he had never had an inward or deep feeling in his life. He babbles like a rustic—or what we call a pastoral poet. "Why, it was so darned purple," he says, in effect, "that it reminded me of those pieces of ivory—you know those girls over in Caria that dye little pieces of ivory to make ornaments for the bridles of those fine horses they have over there, awfully pretty girls, and they get it all over their arms. . . ." That single—and perhaps slightly irreverent—recollection of a great poet so preoccupied by a quality of external, or as they say, projicient, sensation, that he ignores and trangresses the feeling-tone of his own climax of tragedy, suggests the difficulty one would have in defining poetry by emotion, once one had really defined emotion.

I dwell on the impossibility of this definition, because the attempt has a certain scientific standing. John Stuart Mill made it sound very wise and technical by linking it up with the "association psychology" of his day. Ideas, according to that psychology, are associated on a basis of "resemblance," "contiguity" or "emotional congruity." And the poets, said Mill, are "those who are so constituted that emotions are the links by which their ideas, both sensuous and spiritual, are associated together." I have called Homer to witness that this definition will not hold, because it seemed well to have a big and respectable witness. But the case could be more easily proven by any of our very modern poets who have been so earnestly striving not to be romantic that they have almost a neurotic aversion to emotional congruity. When E. E. Cummings, in his delicately almost sublime poem of a cathedral at sunset, introduces the word *bloated* to describe the rose acres in the evening sky—a word sacred so far as I can testify to the memory of dead fish—this choice, or comparison, or whatever it may be, is certainly not "association by emotional congruity." Years ago, before Mr. Cummings was known as the inventor of the punctuational gymnastic, I sat with him and some others in a room where a cat was purring. In a pause of our conversation—which was a rather chilly one, he being a poet and I for the moment an editor—he suddenly exclaimed: "I have it—it's milking the cow, it's the milk scudding into the foam in the pail!" The emotional incongruity of this remark to the prevailing atmosphere was so great that everybody, as I remember, was a trifle embarrassed. But as a pure matter of auditory sensation it was so accurate that it remained in my mind—John Stuart Mill to the contrary notwithstanding—as the sure proof of a poet. It was, indeed, significant of a whole small epoch of poetry in which a meticulous and witty sensuousness has been more popular than inward feeling. With that epoch behind us, it should be obvious at least that poetry cannot be defined with the word emotion.

II

If the crucial word in our definition must be more general than the name of any element or quality in experience, then obviously it must be some such word as quality or experience itself. If I say that poetic diction has or conveys more qualities than prosaic—if I say it is more like experience, or more *of an* experience, to read it—I think everybody will agree with me, no matter what kind of poetry he likes. And that is, in fact, all that is possible and all that is necessary to say. Poetic diction suggests the qualities of experience; it does this more than prosaic diction does; it does it more than is practically necessary, or necessary to theoretic understanding. When a prosaic or practical companion would be content merely to point to something, a tree for instance to which he wishes you to attach a clothes-line, a poet will take the trouble to say "Hitch it to that old hickory," or perhaps he will say "that shaggy old hickory." He is interested in the quality of the thing, and not wholly focussed upon its use. And when, in the absence of things, a poet wishes to remind you of them, he again goes farther than is necessary for mere purposes of identification. He speaks of old trees, even when he is not talking about any particular ones, as "knotty, knarry, barren," because he likes to remember trees. And when he is talking about a whole woodsful of these abstract trees he calls it "some branchy bunchy bushybowered wood," because he wants to feel as though it were here. Even indeed when there are no trees in question, and no "thing" in question at all—only the poetry itself, as in these days seems often the case—the poet is still trying to convey the quality of an experience. And to make us clearly, or intensely, or richly, or vividly conscious of this quality is the whole of his effort. It is an effort, as Miss Edith Sitwell very accurately affirms, to *heighten consciousness.* Pure poetry is the pure effort to heighten consciousness; it is poetry spoken when a practical person would have nothing at all to say.

Prose, on the other hand, is merely the practical way of talking. It names things with the ordinary names through which we have become adapted to them, and indicated their important relations, and learned to use them, and it regulates our attitudes toward them with no more suggestion of their quality than is necessary for identification. It does not matter in the least whether the things in question are real or imaginary; it matters only how they are spoken of. There is not a purer example of naked prose style in English than that of Jonathan Swift in his extravagantly fanciful account of *Gulliver's Travels.* Indeed it is the complete absence of poetic realization from these tales—the fact that they are told in the perfected language of an inventory of goods or a text-book of information—which gives them their uniquely veridical flavor. Usually in literature fanciful events are recounted poetically, and therefore this extreme prose style induces an attitude of belief which, in view of the incredibility of the events, gives us a feeling like realization. A kind of inverse poetry thus results from the very practicality of the language. But the fact remains that our most fanciful classic is written in our purest prose. And there is no conceivable way to describe this prose except to say that in telling us things, it refrains from suggesting their qualities. If a real adventure were as prosaically described, we should consider the book somewhat lacking in color—which is to say, in intimations of what things are like—and we should be quite right. For ordinarily, and except for scientific or business purposes, a good prose style must contain its ingredient of poetry. Indeed absolute prose, or language used without a hint of the concrete existence of things, is to be found only in books of logic and mathematics.

III

People who have read a few thousand of the literary definitions of poetry will realize that the one I am advocating is not unfamiliar. On the contrary it is a view which has already, without any clear consciousness of the process of generalization by which it was arrived at, begun to prevail among the more alert critics and teachers of literature. Bliss Perry in his *Study of Poetry* urges his students to "remember that poets are endeavoring to convey the 'sense' of things rather than the knowledge of things." Robert Graves says that the virtues of verse are these: "Its rhythms, rhymes and texture have an actual toxic effect on the central nervous system. In the resulting condition . . . voices are heard, images are called up, and various emotions felt of a far greater intensity than in normal life." John Drinkwater in his delightful little book about *The Lyric* describes poetry as "the sign of that which all men desire . . . intensity of life or completeness of experience." "Extreme activity of the perceptive mood," he calls it. And with a tranquil innocence of technical terminology, he speaks of "the poetic emotion, or intensity of perception." He is pointing the same way as Miss Sitwell with her "heightening" of consciousness. Hart Crane, too, in defending some of his metaphorious sins, described the whole province of the poet's art as "added consciousness and increased perceptions." Even the philosophers, who have for the most part little attended to the real nature of poetry—using the word most often as a kind of scrap-bag for any old pieces of things that would not fit into their systems—are waking up to this clear and more general conception of it. Professor Whitehead takes it quite for granted when he says: "I hold that the ultimate appeal is to naïve experience and that is why I lay such stress on the testimony of the poets." He is wrong no doubt in laying stress on their *testimony*—especially to the existence of such things as "eternality"—for testimony involves interpretation. But he is right in looking to them for a *communication of the quality* of the naïve experience. I think it may be said that the literary mind as a whole—except where it has lapsed into an agnosticism that is indolence upon this subject—is drifting toward that conception of poetry which I propose that it grasp clearly and adhere to.

The manner and the course of its drifting—in England at least—may be indicated as follows. Coleridge, although in rapture he wove, like Wordsworth and Shelley, a power of knowledge into the very definition of the poet, nevertheless did in a cooler vein contrast poetry correctly with science. "A poem," he said, "is that species of composition which is opposed to works of science as having for its immediate object pleasure, not truth." The modern drift toward wisdom has consisted of putting, first "emotion," and then afterward "experience" or "intensity of life" or "the sense of things" or "added consciousness" in place of the word *pleasure* in making this distinction. And this great step forward has been taken because our more realistic psychology has taught us that "pleasure" is an abstraction not often pursued by any, and by some anxiously avoided. The poet is no more and no less concerned with this abstraction than the scientist.

But there is a further step forward to be taken—likewise under guidance of our better psychology. Not only is the poet not seeking pleasure in the naked and abstract way that Coleridge imagined, but the scientist is not seeking a "truth" quite so embracing and akin to a total report of experience as he and the essayists of his day conceived. In order fully to grasp the definition of poetry as a communication of the qualities of things, it is necessary to realize the extent to which science is not a communication of these qualities. We are in process of realizing this, and the realization is working a deep change in our attitude toward all mental problems—a change so deep that we may now even genuinely hope to succeed where so many have failed in comprehending the nature of poetic speech.

Science does not merely refer to things in our experience and state what they "are," but interprets them and states how they are to be "conceived" in relation to other experiences, and to the interests and modes of behavior of the conceiving mind. This fact, which had become apparent to those who studied the mind itself scientifically, has been driven home to all scientific students by the recent extreme developments in theoretical and practical physics. To take a simple example, it was once hotly disputed among physicists whether light consists of waves in a disturbed fluid, or of a stream of moving particles. This hot dispute over what light "is" has now dissolved away into a common agreement to conceive light in both ways, or in either that happens to be convenient in working out a given problem. Light as an experience could obviously not "be" both waves and a stream of particles. Indeed I do not see how it could be either one or the other, for in order to see these waves or these particles you would have to have light shining on them, and it would have to be—begging the physicists' pardon—*real* light! But such remarks do not any longer disturb the physicists, because they so generally realize that the question what light "is," is not the one they are trying to answer. They are trying to find out how light should be conceived in order to generalize its important relations to other things, and enable them to predict or control its behavior.

This new understanding of science prevails so widely to-day that Clarence I. Lewis in his book on *Mind and the World Order* is able to speak of "the absurd prejudice—now happily obsolescent—that science is 'just a report of facts.'" What is not quite so widely understood—although even more important for the theory of poetry—is that long before science begins, the very language with which it begins has already accomplished a vast work of practical and theoretic interpretation. We are far from the experienced facts when we begin to talk about them. Professor Lewis has demonstrated as convincingly as Bergson, and without any ulterior motives of a mystical order, how persistently all words, and indeed all thoughts, interpret experiences from the standpoint of purposes and modes of behavior and social co-operation—so much so that it is impossible, he thinks, even to allude to an experience without so interpreting it. There is such a thing, he comforts us, as the uninterpreted *quale,* the "given-in-experience," but it is not to be communicated in language. To describe a thing as "edible" is quite obviously to interpret it for purposes of action, but to describe it as "an apple" also contains such interpretation. Even to call it "a thing" is false to the sheer "feel or quality." Trying desperately to suggest what the sheer feel or quality is, which being interpreted becomes an apple, Professor Lewis calls it "a round, ruddy, tangy-smelling somewhat," thus startling with one phrase of poetry the most strenuously prosaic volume I have read in years. It could not be otherwise, for poetry *is* the attempt to make words suggest the given-in-experience.

It is undoubtedly true that this goal is, in an absolute sense, unattainable. The given-in-experience in its purity cannot be spoken, and that is why the modernist poets, having resolutely set out to speak it, are going through such a variety of metagrammatical contortions. The life of our race has been predominantly filled with strivings or anxieties; we have been all the time trying to adapt ourselves to the environment, or it to us; and our speech reflects this preoccupation with action and adaptation. But it is equally true that we cannot get away from the given-in-experience; some lingering image of it remains with us so long as we speak, and indeed so long as our thought is conscious. And I suspect that the growth of language has been influenced by the desire to communicate sheer qualities far more than Professor Lewis or any of his colleagues in the instrumental logic have happened to imagine. It seems to me sentimental and foolish to say, as Professors Greenough and Kittredge do in their text-book on philology, that "language is poetry." The growth of language must obviously be, like the use of it, partly poetic and partly practical. That word *ruddy,* for instance, has probably survived or been revived alongside its cousin *red,* because of its value in exactly the function to which Professor Lewis devotes it. With its more colorful vowel and that hard and yet dancing *ddy* at the end, it suggests a quality of experience whose difference from red would not often matter practically, but is worth communicating for its own sake. *Tang* also is a word to some extent, I think, intrinsically poetic. Poetry at any rate is not merely a trick that we have learned to perform with a practical instrument; it has played its part in creating the instrument.

Professor Lewis, then, in his eagerness to prove that words do not communicate the given-in-experience, has proven that to some extent, when chosen and employed to that end, they do. He has done this so well as to make it plausible that if he had a sustained passion for thus restoring a sense of the given, and for building up structures out of the experiences restored—such a passion as he has for clarifying our interpretations and unfolding the relations between them—he might be as distinguished a poet as he is a logician. Indeed I do not see that his "round, ruddy, tangy-smelling apple" is greatly inferior in its kind to Chaucer's "knotty, knarry, barren trees," or Hopkins's "branchy bunchy bushy-bowered wood." It is certainly the same kind of talk.

IV

When the words *poetic* and *prosaic,* or still better *poetic* and *practical,* have been identified with this most general distinction which can be made in the uses of language, the millions of literary "definitions" of poetry fall into their true place as indications of the various things that can be done with, or made out of, poetic diction. But it remains to show that the three almost universal attributes of poetry, those with which even scientific minds have tried to define it—metre and figure and a preoccupation with emotions—stand in a particular relation to poetic diction as so defined. They each enter into the technique of suggesting the given-in-experience and heightening our consciousness of it.

Let us consider first the mystery of the poet's addiction to an essentially monotonous rhythm. I cannot think of any other art besides poetry in which so much labor has been expended in the effort to be monotonous. If you go back to the early Anglo-Saxon poetry, you find that it sounds almost like beating a drum or a tom tom—or, as Andrew Lang says, "like blows of hammers on an anvil."

"Icy in glimmer and eager for sailing."
"With weapons of warfare, weeds for the battle."
"Bold and battle grim brandished his ring-sword."

These two-stroke lines, each stroke repeating the consonant of the last, were strung together by the old bards or glee-men for hours and hours. It seems almost incredible that the most sensitive and intellectual men of the clan should have been so wilfully tedious in their public talk. They even left out the definite article most of the time in order to reduce their poetry as nearly as possible to a perfectly regular series of twin yells, grunts or shouts. In order to understand this strange thing, you have to remember that these glee-men were also jugglers and magicians, and that they danced too and banged on a stringed instrument, and that the whole performance was largely hypnotic.

The subtler poets of our day conceal the monotony of their metre by pushing it down underneath a more flowing growth of speech, decorating it with the delights not only of syncopation but of complete riot and rebellion against its iron beat. But although they rebel and riot against it, they never permit us to forget that beat completely. Verse is distinguished from prose exactly and only by the degree to which this monotonous mathematical drumming which lies in the heart of all rhythm forces itself upon our attention. As Edward Sapir has expressed it, "Verse is *rhythmically self-conscious speech*. . . . Verse rhythms come, or should come, to us; we go to the rhythms of prose." There is no other difference. And for my part I find it still incredible that intellectual and sensitive people with no unkind motive in their hearts, should expend the most intense efforts of which the mind is capable in order to force this monotony upon us along with their most lively conversation, unless they are still trying to hypnotize us.

Professor Snyder insists that in order to read poetry wisely and criticize it well, we must learn how to distinguish hypnotic poetry from the poetry that he calls "intellectualist." He is right, I think, in emphasizing these two extremes, and advising us to approach and judge them differently. And since our poets at the moment are striving so hard if not altogether successfully to be intellectual, his book becomes a plea for the appreciation of poetic rapture with which I deeply sympathize.[1] To my mind it is the people who employ metre *without* the purpose to entrance—who dress out the most cold, sober and sophisticated of adult "propositions" in irrelevant sing-song—it is they, and not the poets of rapture, who may be asked to defend theselves against a charge of "intellectual immaturity" and of playing with a childish toy. At any rate Professor Snyder realizes that his distinction is one of degree, and he does not oppose my contention that the original and basic function of the rhythmic stroke in poetry—the reason why it got there, no matter what merely delightful objective patterns certain mental types of people may choose to make out of it afterward—is that it hypnotizes the reader, or brings him a little way into that hypnoid state in which any experience that the words suggest is realized with a completeness approaching hallucination. That a mild monotonous metric stroke

[1]Professor Snyder makes one erroneous statement which I wish to correct. He says that in my *Enjoyment of Poetry,* where I first suggested that hypnosis explains the association of metre with poetry, I evinced "a certain timidity" about applying this principle, and merely left the matter to be decided by "a mature science." I was timid and disposed to await a mature science, not about the hypnotic effect of a rhythmic stroke nor its relevance to poetry, but only about whether that effect could be explained by the assumption that the nervous current proceeds in waves. About that I should still speak without a great deal of courage, although it seems on the whole more probable to me now than it did then. The difference between us is that I applied the principle to metrical poetry universally, and Professor Snyder corrects me—without denying that it may have had originally this universal application—by showing that it is possible to distinguish poetry that is hypnotic from that which is not.

is a means of lulling us into these states, is a piece of psychologic wisdom as old as the race of man. That it belongs naturally upon the lips of poets, if poetry is defined as making words suggest the experienced qualities of things, is obvious enough.

Another slight custom is so general among poets as almost to belong to the definition of their speech, and that is their use of archaic or liturgical forms of expression—the *thee's* and *thou's* and *for aye's* and *forevermore's* in English poetry, for example—which effect a separation of the poetic moment from the ordinary flux of life. They make entering a poem seem a little like going to church. Even when the poem is quite manifestly nothing but a glassful of the wine of the devil, and sparkles all through with the lewdest passions of this world, it still has often this kinship with the language of worship. It is the old kinship, never too close, between magic and religion. For these forms too are to be interpreted as a part of the baggage of the witch doctor. They are weird instruments of a wand-like nature which he lifts over us to get us transfixed and fit for the ritual slumber. They are somewhat out of fashion in these days when poetry, rather overwhelmed to see how much can be accomplished with straight talk and machinery, has been aping prose rhythms and trying to cover up all signs of its origin and true base in the practice of magic. Whether these wonder-working expressions will come back with the inevitable return to hypnotic rhythms, we shall wait to see.

Our next task is to show that a preoccupation with emotions belongs to poetry in the same special way as a disposition to put us to sleep. And this is perhaps the most difficult problem that a definition of poetry has to face, for there is nothing more indubitably associated with wakefulness than emotion. I remember that being kept awake by his own emotions was what led Professor MacDougall to his theory of emotional instincts as the very source of nervous energy and purpose. His theory is not widely accepted now—any more than any other theory of the emotions—but the agreement is universal that emotions accompany an aroused and active state of the body. In fact the assertion made by James and Lange thirty-five years ago, that emotions are merely sensations of bodily change and movement—they are how it feels to behave in certain ways—is still the underlying assumption of most attempts to locate or explain these inward elements of experience. It would seem, then, that our definition has the impossible task of reconciling two exactly opposite things, the stimulant and the sedative—or, as I like to call them, the wine and sleep—in poetry.

This impossible task will accomplish itself without the slightest effort on our part, if we but remember that poetic diction when it is metrical is employed in the absence of the external things of which it wishes to heighten our consciousness. The poet strokes us with his syllables and lulls us into a controlled slumber, in order to make us vividly aware of external impressions which we are not really having. A part of his "given-in-experience," that is to say, is not actually given—it is not there—and only in dreams or states of dreaminess or trance, can we be made vividly to perceive things which are not there. It is for the sake of this external part of experience that the poet resorts to the mesmeric arts, and literally tries to sing us to sleep.

But there is another element in every experience, an element of inward feeling, which is present when things are present, and forms a part—often indeed the intensest part—of our experience of them, but which also remains available when the things are gone. To this inward element, which we so conveniently carry round with us—and which when it has a certain degree or kind of poignancy we call emotion—the poet has naturally a different attitude. He wants to evoke this, so far as he can, in reality and not in image. He is here no mesmerist or magician, but a lexical and social engineer. And we need not be surprised if, as we surrender to the somnolent monotony of his rhythms, we find him deliberately plunging words soaked with hot feeling into our hearts, and even pounding our blood-stream with that very rhythm which seemed only to be lulling our pulses to rest. He is impelled to these opposite tactics by an identical motive, the desire to convey vivid experience. Those inward feelings are a part of experience, and so belong to his effort as ends. But they are also that part which he can really and not only imaginatively evoke with words, and so enter into his technique as a means of giving intensity to the whole. That is the reason why, in spite of so many clear facts to the contrary, wise men continue to insist that poetic diction can be defined as solely preoccupied with emotions—as though a poet were of necessity introverted and romantically shut up inside his own viscera—as though, indeed, any such one-dimensional creature of feeling could exist.[1]

[1]The fact is that the word *emotion* as commonly used by writers on æsthetics does not mean emotion at all, but means an aroused

V

When language is not metrical or wantonly emotional, we still call it poetic if it contains a luxury of surprising and rich adjectives and figurative expressions, particularly those swift figures, metonymy and metaphor, which do not help to explain like maps or illustrations, but rather obscure the meaning of the sentence in which they occur. If then we can explain these "figures of speech"—which no rhetoric or grammar-book ever has explained—with the same generalization with which we explain metrical rhythm and a preoccupation with emotions, we shall be entitled to call that generalization the beginning at least of a scientific conception of poetry.

So long as figurative speech is vaguely described as using words in "out of the ordinary" ways, calling a thing by an "unusual" name, or applying to it an adjective that is not "habitually" applied, its value to the art of heightening consciousness is obvious. The ordinary, usual and habitual slides through our brains without enough friction even to attract attention. We have heard the expression *sharp point,* for example, almost as often as *How do you do?* or *All aboard!* and that is reason enough for saying *thrilling point* or some phrase like that, if you wish to make us vividly aware of the dangerous end of a sword. However, it will not do to say *sky-scraping* or *loud-thundering* point. That might arouse a certain consciousness, but it would be of the author's dullness rather than the

but inactive consciousness. They use this word, not in order to distinguish an element in consciousness, but in order to distinguish that whole condition from an enterprising one.

sharpness of the sword. In order to heighten our consciousness of any particular experience, figurative language must depart from the ordinary in certain special ways. These ways have been imposingly classified and given alarming long Latin names by grammarians who had not the slightest idea why anyone should depart from the ordinary at all. And the names are so much like those of prehistoric animals that they have frightened a great many people away from poetry. But the acts themselves are simple enough, and quite harmless, and there are only two of them. One may, instead of calling an experience by its own proper name, call it by the name of some element within it; or one may depart from it altogether and call it by the name of some other experience that is similar. These acts might be described adequately as figures of choice and figures of comparison. Thus I may say "The sudden bulk of a man alarmed us," instead of saying "A bulky man suddenly alarmed us." That is a figure of choice, and would be called *metonymy* or *synecdoche* by the grammarians, just as fire was called "escaping phlogiston" by chemists who did not have the slightest idea why it occurred. Or I may say "A sudden mountain of a man alarmed us," and that is a figure of comparison, called *metaphor* by the grammarians. In the first case I have replaced the "ordinary" name of the man with the name of his own bulk; in the second, I have replaced it with the name of another bulky thing.

That figures of choice do heighten our consciousness of a suggested experience may be seen in the example of the "sudden bulk" of a man. And with a little reflection it may be seen how they do this. They emphasize, more sharply than the corresponding adjective would, a specific detail or quality in the experience. In actual life we always receive experiences, especially at moments of high consciousness, with some quality or detail thus dominant. We receive them with our attention focussed. Indeed, a "heightened consciousness" and a focussed attention are, in the language of many psychologists, but two aspects of the same thing. A low consciousness is a diffused one. Poetry keeps calling out the names of specific details and qualities in things, and even when possible lets these replace the general names of the things, because it is trying to arrest our attention. It was to this technique that Professor Lewis resorted in order to suggest that given-in-experience which practically interpreted becomes an apple. He abandoned the general name of the object and called it a "round ruddy tangy-smelling somewhat." He thus became a poet—but not quite, I regret to say, a pure one. For his habit of practical interpretation survived lamentably in that word *somewhat.* What has that to do with the given-in-experience? It is merely the most general interpretation Professor Lewis could think of, and really carries us still farther away from experience than would *apple* itself. With a little instruction from our modernist poets, Professor Lewis would soon learn to abandon these last survivals of the practical or prose habit. He would name his uninterpreted apple a "round, ruddy, tangy-smelling," and nothing more. And that would be a "figure of speech"—metonymy or synecdoche, or what you will—defined by the grammarians as "naming the part for the whole," "the container for the contained," "the author for the creature," "the attribute for the substance," and so forth. It should be defined as omitting (or subordinating) the practical name, which by immediately identifying an experience with a general class toward which we have established attitudes of action, reduces our consciousness to a minimum, and supplying a new name which, while suspending our tendencies toward action, selects a focus for the resulting heightened consciousness or attention.

To explain why figures of comparison inhere in the essence of poetry is a little more difficult, although the fact is most obvious of all.

> "Her paps are like fair apples in the prime,"

sings the old bard. And this seems so intrinsically and naturally to be the essence of song, that if he adds:

> "What need compare, where sweet exceeds compare?"

we find it difficult to regard this as a serious question. He is merely despairing of the essence of his art. It is, however, the most serious question that can arise for anyone who wishes to make a definition of poetry. Why does comparing a thing with something else that is not similar in any practical way heighten our consciousness of it?

In order to answer this question it will be necessary to decide why we ever become conscious of a thing in the first place. And this is especially difficult because psychologists have no very fixed attitude toward the problem of consciousness—except for a few, at least, who have been reduced by the "Behaviorists" to a fixed attitude of fright. But I think most of those who feel free to concede that we do become conscious, and that also we become *more* and *less* conscious, will agree that what makes us conscious of one thing rather than another, is usually some difficulty that it presents from the standpoint of our activities. We can dress ourselves from top to toe without once consciously perceiving a limb or a garment, provided the garments are in their proper place, and the limbs too, and all goes well. But if something obstructs the process—if an arm will not pass through the sleeve of a coat—then that situation automatically swims into our ken. Or suppose it has been dimly in our ken, it becomes more sharply so. It swims into the focus of attention. And as it does so the sleeve which our arm will not pass through becomes, let us say, a hole in the lining of our coat. As soon as we have perceived the experience in this way—and perhaps inwardly named it *torn lining*—the process of dressing is resumed with a correction, and may now go through to the end without further intrusion from the mind. I think that is a fair example of how consciousness arises, or is heightened, in practical life. And that use of the words, *torn lining,* in order to resolve a situation that was in doubt and enable us to resume an obstructed activity, is typical of the practical or prose use of words. It shows how practical words, in their simple and original function, not only do not heighten consciousness, but reduce it and get rid of it.

I do not know how you could better define consciousness in that case, than to say it was the process of resolving the experience of a coat-with-an-impenetrable-sleeve into the experience of a coat-with-a-hole-in-the-lining. It was identifying an unfamiliar experience with a familiar one for purposes of action. And as soon as this identification was accomplished and action resumed, the consciousness lapsed. It lapsed because the identification was, as we say, correct. But that is little more than saying it was the one which permitted the action to be resumed and carried successfully through; it was the practical identification. It seems then that consciousness is, arises out of, or depends upon, two things—a blockage of action, and an identification of one experience with another so that action may be resumed. That being the case, what could a person do who desired to heighten consciousness, or intensify, or preserve, or prolong, or in any other way cultivate it for its own sake—what could he do that would be more fundamental than to suggest *impractical identifications?* Poetic metaphor is the employment of words to suggest impractical identifications. You may choose this or that identification for any one of a thousand reasons, all of them very interesting but none general enough to enter into the definition of poetry. *Any* impractical identification that you can induce somebody to listen to is poetic, because it is the essence of an attentive consciousness. It is mind suspended on the brink of action.

VI

If we could observe, not only introspectively but also objectively with a microscope, the exact situation in a nervous system at the moment when it becomes conscious of something, the next step in my argument would be to describe this situation and convince the reader circumstantially that it consists of delayed action and incomplete association. We cannot observe the functioning of the nervous system through a microscope; all we can do is to observe its structure and then guess at its functioning. But it is important to note that those who have made a life work of such guessing agree with the introspective account of the matter I have given.

Psychologists first began to realize the close relation between consciousness and action toward the end of the last century. Out of a million impressions that fall continually upon our sense organs, we become aware only of a tiny few, and it seemed at first reasonable to say that these few are the ones about which we do something. In 1900 Hugo Münsterberg went so far as to maintain that an excitation of our brain centres by an incoming nerve current does not entail a conscious experience at all, unless the current passes out in the form of a motor discharge. That is, to put it crudely, we do not hear the hen cackle unless we go after the eggs. As soon as this statement was thoroughly made, however, it began to appear that exactly the opposite is true. The things we respond to with a complete muscular action—as a hand to the banister or an eye-wink to a drying eye—are just those of which we do not become conscious. It is only when one appropriate muscular response is blocked or hindered by some other, that we seem to pay any mental attention to it. And moreover the "degree" of our consciousness seems to depend upon the extent of the hindrance. Professor Montague of Columbia presented this view, and if you will forgive his rather technical language, he presented it very clearly and well:

"Perceptions are presumed to arise synchronously

with the redirection in the central nervous system of afferent currents into efferent channels. When this process of redirection is prolonged by reason of the many conflicts with the cerebral association currents, then the consciousness is prolonged, keen, and complex. When, on the other hand, by reason either of innate adjustments or of long practice, the journey through the central labyrinth is quick, smooth, and direct, then the consciousness, if present at all, is simple, faint and brief."

The next chapter in this story was written by Professor Margaret Floy Washburn of Vassar College, who published a book in 1916 in which she showed that there is an element of truth in the assertions of both Münsterberg and Montague. A perception does not become conscious unless a responsive action is *initiated,* but it also does not become conscious unless the initiated response is *obstructed.*

"Consciousness," she said, "accompanies a certain ratio of excitation to inhibition in a motor discharge, and . . . if the amount of excitation either sinks below a certain minimum, or rises above a certain maximum, consciousness is lessened."

This may sound a little abstruse, but it is merely a statement from the standpoint of a person observing your brain, of something that you yourself can observe in your own mind. A world of things is continually within range of your attention; you commonly notice only those which impel you to action or have some relation to what you are doing, and of these you vividly attend only to those whose relation to your activity is not quite fixed and sure.

If you are really intent upon gathering eggs, for instance, you will pass right by the garden without noticing the flowers. But if a hen happens to make a noise under the flowers, you will notice that. And if the noise is *something between* a cluck and a cackle, you will become very clearly conscious of it. You will turn your attention to it because it contains both excitation and inhibition. A cackle would divert you into the garden to hunt for a hidden nest; a cluck would send you on to the barn where you normally gather the eggs. And moreover your consciousness will grow "less" in proportion as one or the other of these tendencies dominates. If the sound, as it swims into the focus of your attention, becomes emphatically a cluck—and is perhaps named a cluck with some phantom motion of your throat and tongue—you will pass on to the barn and hear it no longer. If it becomes a cackle, you will turn into the garden, and there too—unless perchance it suggests *two directions* in which you might go seeking the nest—it will slide away into the fringe of your attention. When you find the nest, the hen may still be exclaiming over her achievement, but you are no longer aware of the sound. You have interpreted that given-in-experience and fully responded to it, and it is gone out of your life forever.

Such is the dependence of consciousness on a "ratio between excitation and inhibition" in a person who is gathering eggs. And if, on the other hand, a person is gathering flowers, a whole flock of hens may cluck and cackle themselves to death without his ever noticing that a sound has been made. But now let us suppose that a person is gathering neither eggs nor flowers, but, like Miss Edith Sitwell, a "heightened consciousness" of her garden—then the flowers have only to bend over hen-like on their stalky stems and they themselves will "begin to cluck." For a clucking flower—to a person properly equipped with both egg-gathering and flower-gathering possibilities of motor discharge—provides exactly that "ratio between excitation and inhibition" upon which a heightened consciousness depends.

Of course it is not only when he actually walks into his garden gathering consciousness, that a poet finds himself to be, as it were, in a state of metaphor. It is the same when he remembers or imagines a garden, or wishes to convey the realization of a garden to others. For not only external perceptions, but images and ideas, and indeed all conscious qualities, arise, if this theory is true, as a result of conflicting movements. The movements are usually minute, tentative, hardly begun, invisible to an external observer—unless in some tricks of "mind-reading" they are detected. But even so they must each one not only be aroused, but also checked and delayed, in order to give rise to any conscious experience.

"All thoughts and mental images," Professor Washburn asserts, "all the contents of consciousness, rest not simply on delayed full motor response, externally visible, but on delays in the system of tentative movements. When these systems run smoothly we have 'unconscious thought'; when delays occur we have 'sensations' and 'images.'"

That is about all that psychology has to say about the interior causes of consciousness. And even that cannot be said of course with a great and dogmatic certainty.

It is a good circumstantial and faithful guess in a field where the appeal to observation is limited. It accords well, however, with the views of those who are making the most valuable use of psychology, the Freudian physicians. For them the failure of a motor conflict to produce, or sustain, the consciousness in which it might be resolved, is almost the definition of functional disease in the nervous system. It accords with that operational or instrumental logic which views science itself, not as a mere "report of facts" but as a solution of problems in adaptation and behavior. Indeed, before ever Hugo Münsterberg started the discussion I have recounted with his "action theory" of consciousness, John Dewey had anticipated the outcome of it. "The sensation or conscious stimulus," he said in 1896, "is not a thing or existence by itself; it is that phase of a co-ordination requiring attention because, by reason of the conflict within the co-ordination, it is uncertain how to complete it. . . . It is the holding of the movement at a certain stage which creates the sensation, which throws it into relief."

The importance of this theory for our attempt at a psychology of poetry lies not only in the explanation of metaphor, but in the possibility it offers of describing the poet, or the poetic-minded person, from the standpoint of an external observer. If this person, as we assume, is not seeking some defined end under the drive of specific needs or tendencies, but is seeking a heightened consciousness for its own sake, he would be committed, not only to a continual series of impractical associations as the poets indubitably are, but also to a continual series of interrupted motions. He would be—however inwardly and invisibly—in exactly the condition which biologists describe, when writing the life-story of the lower organisms, as "general motility." The phrase belongs to Professor Jennings, who cites this account of the condition as it appears in the flatworm:

"Sometimes individuals are found which for a brief period (two or three hours) seem in much more active condition than usual. They move about rapidly, but do not conduct themselves like the excited individuals. As they move they keep the anterior end raised and wave it continually from side to side as if searching. Specimens in this condition react to almost all mechanical stimuli, whether weak or strong, by the positive reaction, turning toward the point stimulated. Experimentation failed to show that this condition was due to hunger."

In my opinion this tiny organism is the prototype of the poet, and the organic condition here described is the one with which every attempt to explain poetry should begin. It is a condition of search, and the search is for nothing more specific than increased or intensified experience. When this motive, or mode of behavior, is seen at the source of life as well as in the highest manifestations of mind through language, the full generality of our definition of poetry begins to appear. Poetic speech is not so much an art as a natural material in which artists may work. And the material is life itself, in so far as words can assist in making it conscious or communicating it.

II

ART AND BIOLOGY

It has always seemed to me that the question about poetry and art is at bottom a biological question, a question as to the nature of life in general. Accordingly in my *Enjoyment of Poetry,* although I knew then even a little less than I do now about biology, I made bold to assert that the distinction I was drawing between the trance of realization and the impulse to adjustment was to be found in the very origins of life. I developed this idea a little more carefully later in an essay on *The Will to Live,* and Professor C. Judson Herrick has done me the honor—and my present argument the inestimable service—to endorse that essay and quote it in his studies of the nervous system. As I cannot afford to do without this solid and unexpected prop from the laboratories, I am going to reproduce here the passage from my essay which he quotes in his *Neurological Foundations of Animal Behavior.*

"We shall find not only that experience as such is welcome to life, but that life of its own accord goes in search of experience. That 'general motility' which Jennings has to add to the specific reactions, in writing the biography of lower organisms, will, if separately dwelt upon, supply a standpoint from which life can be viewed as fruitfully as from the standpoint of adaptation to stimuli. We are not merely trying to adapt ourselves in order to stay alive, but we are trying even more energetically to live. Everything we do and think is not a reaction; a great deal of it is action. The 'Behaviorist' is not so much to be condemned for his refusal to observe or consider 'states of consciousness,' as for his totally inadequate view of what he does observe and consider. The interaction of organism and environment is for him carefully divided into reflex arcs, all operating in one direction. A stimulus to the end-organ, a commotion in the central-nervous system, then a response in the muscles—that is the whole story of life in his laboratory. But life interflows with reality in full circles. We do things not only because we have a sensation, but also in order to make a sensation. And so do the most elementary organisms. Any rubber ball can react, but it requires life to act. And life does act. It seeks experience."

"Experience," Professor Herrick adds in his own words, "is not something to which the organism is passively subjected. In response to stimulation it reaches out actively to meet the exciting agent; but it does more than this, it is constantly seeking new contacts. . . . The evolutionary factor here is more than self-preservation; it is self-realization and fulfilment."

Whether it is *self*-realization may depend upon a variety and a complexity of things, but that living matter has a tendency toward realization as well as adaptation—a character of striving, without specific ends or narrow discrimination of pain and pleasure, to extend and intensify its experience—seems quite indubitable. To attribute to elementary organisms a "will to live" or an "instinct of self-preservation" in the negative sense of a wish to avoid death is not legitimate, for that "will" or "instinct" is merely a generalization by the scientist of many specific tendencies to behavior in concrete situations. But a will to live in the sense of an affirmative reaching out after life's experience is an actual and concrete action, or tendency to act, of all the instincts; the generalization here is not made by the scientist but by the abounding energies of the organism. I do not see how anybody can stroll through an aquarium after feeding time, or walk down Broadway after dinner, without seeing before his eyes this most elementary fact.

This fact is, indeed, usually conceded incidentally—or implied by some by-remark or footnote or parenthesis—in books which treat of organic life with any thoroughness. William James took a rather mischievous pleasure in reminding his readers that they like the smell of a skunk—until it gets too strong. "Every one," he said, "who has a wound or hurt anywhere, a sore tooth, e.g., will ever and anon press it just to bring out the pain. If we are near a new sort of stink, we must sniff it again just to verify once more how bad it is."

Professor MacDougall, in his *Social Psychology,* says almost the same thing about emotions:

"The intrinsic feeling-tone of the emotions seems to follow the same rule as that of the sensations, namely, that with increase of intensity of the emotion pleasant tends to give way to unpleasant feeling-tone; so that, while at moderate intensities some are pleasant and others unpleasant, at the highest intensity all alike become unpleasant or painful; and, perhaps, at the lowest intensity all are pleasant."

"Thus fear, at low intensity, does but add a pleasurable zest to any pursuit, as we see especially clearly in children, sportsmen, and adventurous spirits generally; whereas at high intensity it is the most horrible of all experiences."

Such is the nature of man. And Margaret Floy Washburn in her book on *The Animal Mind* gives an identical testimony about the amœba. After specifying the causes of his negative reactions, she says: "The significance of the positive reaction is harder to determine. It seems to be given in response not to a special kind of stimulus, but to a mechanical or food stimulus [that is, to any perceptible stimulus] of slight intensity."

These remarks, which I have picked up casually and to which I could easily add others, imply that almost anything which happens along with a quality sharp enough to arouse consciousness is likely to be greeted by a robust organism with the positive reaction. The organism is "interested," that is to say, in experience as such. I suspect that most of what has been entered under the head of "instinct of curiosity" is in no wise a desire to investigate and know, but a desire to taste of and to live through—a "love of trying it," as the Russian word for curiosity more wisely says.

II

I think one reason why this more affirmative view of life does not prevail among biologists is that the sciences of life are still young enough to imagine that they can explain *why* everything behaves as it does. Chemists and physicists have pretty well ceased to delude themselves about this. They realize more clearly—or they reflect more often—that their explanations merely tell us in highly general terms *how* things behave. When they ask the question *why* in regard to some event, and answer with a learned *because,* all they are doing is showing this event to be a particular example of more general rules already discovered as to *how* things behave.

Now of course if the behavior of living matter could be shown to be but a particular example of rules already discovered as to the behavior of matter in general, the biologists would have a right to use the words *why* and *because* continually in this same sense. And indeed the greatest discovery in biology—the evolution of life and the rôle played by natural selection—did make it seem as though the entire account of living matter might be given in "mechanical" terms. Living organisms have such and such attributes and behave thus and so, according to Darwin's theory, because this makes them fit to survive, and by a simple dying in the struggle of those who were unfit to survive, these traits and behaviors have been perpetuated and developed. Almost all biologists—although refusing to decorate with the word "vitalism" the mere limits of their knowledge—are now ready to concede that this account of the process is inadequate. But nevertheless the habit of assuming that any attribute or mode of behavior is "explained" when it is shown to be useful to some life purpose, and that it cannot be explained otherwise, survives in their minds. It is really a pre-Darwinian habit, a habit of thinking in terms of final causes. So long as the theory of natural selection was believed adequate, it removed final causes from biology—and that was perhaps its greatest service—but now that it is *believed* inadequate and yet *tacitly taken for granted* as an ultimate principle of explanation, it may be said to have given final causes a new lease of life.

If an amœba wiggles, all that is necessary in order to be "scientific" is to insist that the wiggle fulfils a useful purpose of which the amœba knows nothing—that it is directed toward the "universal goal of animal behavior, namely, to dominate more completely the environment." If a puppy gambols or a young lamb skips, to be scientific is to assert that these happy creatures are merely preparing their muscular and nervous co-ordinations for the future struggle. If a child romps and pries into everywhere, he too is seeking adjustment, is "impelled by his developing needs." If grown-up people throng into side-shows and anatomical museums, they are "resolving complexes" and "compensating for infantile frustrations." If they are to be found at concerts and art-galleries, it is because beauty "reconciles their conflicting impulses," or shows them "a reality that is greater than the real." In short it rarely occurs to us since Darwin discovered that wonderful theory of natural selection, and performed with it the Herculean labor of cleansing deific mysteries out of the study of evolution, that after all it may still be true and not altogether a naïve remark that

"Dogs delight to bark and bite
For 'tis their nature to."

No doubt it is unfair to attribute the too glib tendency of our times to take practical justification for causal explanation entirely to the prestige of the principle of natural selection. It is a part of the temper of the age. The union of a theological past with a high pressure of business interests and an environment of mechanical contrivances in the present, doubtless has something to do with it. When a strong-hearted poet like Conrad Aiken tells us that it "must be because beauty is useful to him, performs some vital function in his life," that this "absurd tickling of the soul" seems important to man, and proposes to mend all our critical confusion with the formula that out of "psychic frustrations . . . we have evolved the universal language of healing which we call art," I think we may fairly conclude that this negative attitude toward life is embedded in the very structure of our overgrown capitalistic civilization. When men are sick, all life itself is but a healing; and I should regard a general acceptance of this criterion in criticism as a proof that the whole world is sick.

III

My thesis that healthy creatures have an interest in living and not merely in avoiding death, can be supported not only by picking up *obiter dicta* from the general psychologists, but still better by examining the attempts of the more physiological psychologists to decide what the terms pleasant and unpleasant mean, or what conditions in the body correspond to these feelings. One of the most interesting of such attempts is that of Floyd Henry Allport, who suggests that unpleasant feelings arise in consciousness as a result of the discharge of a nerve impulse through the sympathetic division of the autonomic nervous system, which prepares our vital organs for retreat and defense. It is a feeling of the response in those organs to the discharge. Pleasantness is a feeling of the condition in the vital organs enervated by a discharge through the cranio-sacral division, which prepares us for the functions of nutrition and sex. Professor Allport makes this scheme very plausible indeed, but when he gets it all finished, he finds himself obliged to add: "A certain exception must be made to the statement that cranio-sacral impulses underlie pleasant emotional states generally. There are several sources of pleasant affectivity, such as bodily exercise and habit, excitement of games, elation, and mirth, which possess no discoverable relation to the cranio-sacral functions. . . . These pleasant states appear to be due to afferent impulses from reactions carried out by unimpeded cerebro-spinal impulses." Here again *pleasant* is a more general thing than *unpleasant*—a mere matter of being unimpeded in the exercise of life.

In another place Professor Allport says: "Our theory . . . offers a good basis for distinguishing physiologically between pains which are unpleasant and those which are not. It is well known that light pains on the skin are far from unpleasant. Unpleasant pains are severe ones; their efferent impulses are powerful enough to break through into the sympathetic." And here once more the *unpleasantness* of severe pains is explained, but the *far-from-unpleasantness*—that is to say, the *pleasantness*—of mild ones, remains as much a mystery as ever.

It seems to me that Professor Allport could pull his

speculation together better by saying that the source of unpleasant feeling may be physiologically identified, and also the source of some feelings that may be described as pleasant in a narrow sense, but over and above that and in a larger sense conscious life itself is pleasant—so long as it is not *too* unpleasant! Such a formula would also resolve a conflict in the statements of James and MacDougall that I quoted above. For according to MacDougall's way of putting it, the painful emotions when enjoyed at a low intensity are *pleasant*. According to James it is the very *unpleasantness* that intrigues us, it is not because it is good, but "to verify how bad it is," that we must forever venture in this way with our senses. The truth in both these views is that beyond good and bad—or not primarily concerned at least to "unperplex bliss from its neighbor pain"—there is that "positive reaction," not to the mechanical or food stimulus, but to stimulus in general.

Professor Herrick sums up his similar opinion in this way: "The simplest view seems to the writer to be that the normal activity of the body within physiological limits is intrinsically pleasurable, so far as it comes to consciousness at all. There is a simple joy of living for its own sake." And again: "The normal discharge, then, of definitely elaborated nervous circuits . . . is pleasurable, in so far as the reaction comes into consciousness at all. . . . Conversely, the impediment to such discharge, no matter what the occasion, results in a stasis in the nerve centres, the summation of stimuli and the development of a situation of unrelieved nervous tension which is unpleasant until the tension is relieved by the appropriate adaptive reaction."

Instead of the word "normal" in this statement I should want to read some word like robust or adequate, for I have known organisms to plunge with alacrity into a large unpleasantness for sheer delight in the fact that, whatever else it may be, it is not normal. But I doubt if Professor Herrick would stick very hard here for any particular idiom. The point is that conscious experience is itself pleasant, and more of it is more pleasant, until or unless some factors enter in to make it unpleasant. If this is true, it certainly constitutes the foundation upon which all discussion of æsthetics—if not also of morals, politics and therapeutics,—ought to rest.

In fact, in order to pass from Professor Herrick's statement about pleasure to an understanding of art in its elementary and most general character, we need only remark that he has left it entirely to chance whether those precious discharges "come to consciousness at all" or not. Art does not leave that critical matter to chance. Art is a deliberate effort to bring them to consciousness. Professor Herrick, because he is not an artist, but the one opposite thing that is equally alive in these days, a scientist, is content with his remark that the "activity of the body within physiological limits" is pleasurable, and the "discharge" too is O.K., so to speak, and whether it happens to come to consciousness or not, so long as there is no impediment, no stasis in the nerve centres, no tension, and we get the "appropriate adaptive reaction." But the artist has to remember that the very thing, and the only thing, which will bring this "activity of the body" to consciousness, and make it hang there in vivid being, is that same impediment, that stasis in the nerve centres, that condition of tension involving a delay or failure of the appropriate reaction. That is the essential difference between Professor Herrick and an artist. And that is the essential and most general definition of the technique of art. It must arouse a reaction and yet impede it, creating a tension in our nervous systems sufficient and rightly calculated to make us completely aware that we are living something—and no matter what.

It seems to me that if all the arts, and not only poetry, were approached by those who wish to judge or understand them with this more affirmative view of life itself, a great deal of solemn and preachy discourse which stands up like a wall between art and the enjoyment of it, might be cut down. If we find in some work of art a "reconciliation of our conflicting impulses," then besides being art it is for us a kind of medicine. If we find in it a translation of reality into something greater than the real, then besides being art it is a very charming and dangerous miracle, a thing very much like what magic set out to be. A thousand of these specific values may be found in various works of art, as in poetry, but the value proper to all art is the universal value of an increased consciousness. It is because of this that to all simple minds the antithesis between "fine art" and the practical or "useful" arts is both obvious and very deep. John Dewey would obliterate this distinction. He would resolve the present confusion in æsthetic criticism by getting rid of the "sharp division between means and ends, fruitions and instrumentalities, assumed by current thought." But current thought has arrived at that wisdom by an arduous path of pain and rebellion that it will never retrace. Such a change in criticism is impossible, not only because the artists themselves are in revolt against the tyranny of the practical, or because with religious contemplation fading in our blood they alone can redeem us from that tyranny. It is impossible for a deeper reason—a reason which John Dewey's functional psychology and logic have made so clear—that there is an antithesis in the very nature of things between vivid consciousness and fluent action. This is the very antithesis he is trying to deny. A utensil can only through some ceremonial effort, or when imported from far times or countries, become the source of heightened consciousness, because we flow from a utensil smoothly into the action for which it was designed. Was it not designed to make that action as nearly as possible unconscious? Who can make lyrics of the handle in his hand? But it is quite otherwise with the picture of a handle, or the picture of a utensil, or the picture of any other thing toward which in its reality we have a prepared response. The picture, like the metaphors of the poets, contains that which excites the response and that also which inhibits it. All fine art is to some extent, and will forever be—and no invention or sophistication can ever quite deliver us from this —an "imitation of nature." But it is an imitation of nature in other material than hers, in a different modality or dimension, deliberately inadequate, and with its inadequacy enhanced by wilful distortions and intrusions of incompleteness. And its purpose is not to divert us when we are tired of real experience with the trick of mimicry, but to enable us at the height of energy to withhold the act and become aware of our experience.

PART V

THE FUTURE OF LITERATURE

I

ARE POETRY AND DRAMA DYING?

THERE is an idea abroad that poetry has seen its day. Not only does a prosy prophet like H. L. Mencken tell us that writing poetry is "chiefly a function of intellectual immaturity," but a critic like Edmund Wilson, a skilled lover of poems, believes it likely that "for some reason or other, verse as a technique of literary expression, is being abandoned by humanity altogether." And the same dismal rumor is abroad about prose fiction. The death of the novel was predicted by an eminent critic not long ago, and several elderly readers have since avowed that what they call the novel is already dead. Joseph Wood Krutch has recently announced "the death of tragedy," and Houston Peterson now comes forward with the news that comedy also is on the rails. "The time may soon come," he gaily predicts, "when drama will be written only for the unsophisticated by the unsophisticated." Among the literary critics, too, some advancing shadow has fallen. About twenty-five years ago two of the most eminent of them, Anatole France and Jules Lemaître, declared, the one that he was incapable of criticism, the other that criticism is a "chimera." And since that day there has been such a flight over the land of "theories of criticism" as to suggest still more ominously that some doom is near. Among English teachers too, and professors of this or that literature, a kind of anxious turmoil has arisen, a mood of self-scrutiny and solemn protestation of dignity such as might be expected of a corpse if it could speak. Professor B. H. Bode, addressing an Association of English Teachers, introduces his remarks by declaring, with a most thoughtful courtesy toward his audience, that he will refrain from raising the question whether there is such a thing as an English teacher—such a "subject," at least, as English. From all these signs it is evident that literature is passing through some sort of mortal or near-mortal crisis, and I think it behooves us to find out if we can—if only for the sake of the record—what literature is, or what it was.

Literature seems to be an art like music or painting, and yet unlike music or painting this art merges into the more practical business of acquiring and conveying information. You can pass by a series of gradual steps from a lyric of Sappho to a cook-book or a school Algebra, and never be able to say at any point: here literature ends, here information begins. When a man plays a tune or paints a picture, we assume that he is cherishing or communicating an experience. We do not at least instinctively suspect him of trying to educate us or tell us how to behave. Poets cherish and communicate experiences, just as painters and musicians do, but the material in which they do this happens to be words, and words are also the standard instruments with which advice is given and knowledge about experience conveyed. Hence the reader of literature never quite knows what he is doing—whether he is enjoying a treat or getting an education or both. The writer too is often uncertain about this. He may steadfastly abjure "propaganda" and detest tales with a moral, and declare himself absolutely uncontaminated with a grain of wisdom—indeed he may even renounce communication itself, and resolve never to cast so much as a look in the direction of those who may listen to him—and nevertheless when he sees them listening in large numbers and with mouths automatically open, he will hardly resist the temptation to drop just a hint as to what they ought to know or be doing. It is almost inseparable from the nature of speech to do this. Literature at large, therefore, is a mixture of poetry, or words used to cherish and communicate experience, with practical and scientific talk in which words are used to interpret experience or convey knowledge about it. All arts contain to some small extent this mixture—it is indeed difficult to communicate anything without communicating some attitude of knowingness towards it—but in literature the two things are so closely bound up together that they are commonly identified and talked about in one lump. Matthew Arnold defined literature as "all knowledge that reaches us through books," without ever reflecting that he was excluding pure poetry at one extreme and including mail-order catalogues and telegraph manuals at the other.

Once we realize that poetry and the poetic element in literature is made out of the immediate qualities of experience, and that the knowledge *about* experience which comes to us from books is literature only if it comes mingled with these qualities or conveyed by them—then we are in a position to distinguish literature from science and from directions for playing ping-pong or oiling a Ford motor, and arrive at some considered judgment of what is happening to it in this extraordinary age. Literature is becoming more and more deeply differentiated from science; it is becoming differentiated from science in wider and wider spheres. Science is steadily and sharply advancing into all those fields in which the art of poetry and poetic prose has flourished. And science advances by driving poetry out—by ignoring the experienced qualities of things, abjuring them, denying them, in all possible ways getting them out of the way of a conception of things which brings out their relation to other things and to our purposes. This has long been obvious in the sphere of physics. Indeed science in this sphere may almost be said to have begun in the arrant assertion of Democritus that the whole world of immediate experience is unreal, a mere delusion with which by common consent or convention we agree to be deluded. "According to convention," said Democritus, "there is a sweet and a bitter, a hot and a cold, and according to convention there is a color—in reality there are atoms and the void." And this arrant assertion was revived by Galileo and became the foundation of modern physics. It is quite obvious that the poet, and indeed the literary mind in general, cannot get along without sweet and bitter, hot and cold, and still less without color. In this sphere therefore the opposition between knowledge *about* things and acquaintance *with* them—between science and poetic literature—was quickly perceived and accepted, and but for a few philosophers who tried vainly to delve down under the distinction, nobody made any great commotion about it. That this same opposition between the actual experience and the valid conception arises to some extent in every sphere into which science extends its technique, has not been perceived, it seems to me, and far from being accepted, it is the very thing about which without any clear perception of it all the commotion is being made.

It may be valid, and also, in certain situations, important, to describe the passion of Mr. C—— for Miss L—— as a transfer of the mother-fixation, or as a conditioned reflex, or in any other way in which a mature psychology may some day describe it. But it will not enable Mr. C——, whose full name for all you can learn in the medical journals might be Catullus, to communicate his experience of that passion to Miss L—— or to anybody else. Poetry can no better get along with "transferences" and "conditioned reflexes" than it can with atoms and the void. Nor can it any better get along with "economic interpretations"—to take another example of contemporary importance. It may or may not be that the proper way to engineer a revolution is to conceive it as a "conflict between the social forms of production and the relations in which production is carried on." It would seem from the success of Lenin that that is a fairly practical way to conceive it. But it is certainly impossible within the limits of that conception to *experience* a revolution, or in those terms to *communicate* the experience to others.

And so in every sphere of life into which science advances, no matter how tentatively and with a groping instrument, in some form or other the distinction is immediately set up between the various ways in which things may be experienced and the valid conception of them in their practically important relations. What had been "literature"—an amateur commixion of experience with interpretation—falls apart into a more universally reliable interpretation on the one hand and a more individual and abandoned experience on the other. It is this grand specialization of function, marching inexorably forward over the whole field of human interest, which is causing such a turmoil in the literary citadel, and producing these wild rumors of the decline of poetry, and the decay of fiction, and the death of drama, and the evaporation of criticism, and the superannuation of the English teacher, and the non-existence of the professor of literature. Let us see if there is not a little exaggeration in these rumors, and just what actual changes they portend.

Joseph Wood Krutch feels that not only tragedy is impossible in this modern world, but that life itself has come down to an inglorious meanness owing to the ravages of scientific knowledge upon our young happy illusions, that leaves us no choice but to drink the cup of a comparatively painless despair. I find this painless despair of Mr. Krutch's a most brilliant and even a bracing concoction, but I am quite unable to believe it is a product of the mixture of scientific knowledge with life. Life seems too frail in such a story, and scientific knowledge too grandiose. "In the course of a few centuries," Joseph Krutch tells us, man's "knowledge, and hence the universe of which he finds himself an inhabitant, has been completely revolutionized, but his instincts and his emotions have remained, relatively at least, unchanged." Now it is important to remember that, except in a fantastic figure, the universe, like man's instincts and emotions, has remained relatively unchanged. Astronomy has not yet swerved the earth a hair's breadth out of her course. And moreover those instincts were born of the universe and not any conception of it, and the two were getting along together in a brilliant amicability long before either young happy illusions or scientific knowledge ever came in and began to play about the picture at all.

It is true that a more accurate knowledge of the universe entails great readjustments of emotional habit, but the depth of these readjustments is universally exaggerated by people who make a business of ideas. It is exaggerated by Mr. Krutch to an extent which makes him seem at times totally evaporated up out of the real world. "Biology and psychology . . .," he tells us, "explain away the awe of emotional experience just as earlier science explained away the awe of conventional piety." But earlier science explained away the entities to which that piety was attached; biology and psychology have done nothing but give to familiar and warm entities some new names indicating the relations in which they are to be found. When Joseph Krutch tells us that love has need of Aphrodite, or the "Platonic Ladder," or some religion or philosophy to "hypostasize" a justification for it in the structure of the universe, we are tempted to wonder whether he has lost or merely forgotten his youth. Of all things love has the least need of Aphrodite or any ladder. Let him read Edna Millay's sonnets beginning "This beast that rends me in the sight of all," or "Night is my sister and how deep in love," or "Not in a silver casket cool with pearls," or

> "Now by this moon, before this moon shall wane
> I shall be dead or I shall be with you!"

He will find love burning in a mind quite well informed of "complexes" and "ductless glands," and not in the least inclined to deny the part they play.

The truth is that Mr. Krutch is not talking about life, but about literature. A knowledge of how the different parts of the world are importantly joined together can cast no blight on life for those who strongly love it. But a feeling that the language in which this knowledge is conveyed is the sole language of *reality*—that can indeed cast a blight on the high spirits of a man of letters. It is not true that "lyric flight" is impossible "in a world of metabolism and hormones, repressions and complexes." It is just in this world that all lyric flights have taken place. But it is true that lyric flight is impossible in a *language* of metabolism and hormones, repressions and complexes. Mr. Krutch's opinion that there is no choice between this language and the language of unreality is the error which lies at the bottom of his whole airy castle of despair. "The world of poetry," he says, ". . . . represents the world as man would like to have it, while science represents the world as he gradually comes to discover it." It would be truer to say that poetry represents the world as man discovers it and will always discover it, science as he must view it in order to make it over as he would like to have it. These two ways of representing the world were formerly all mixed up together; now they stand apart. And what deeply troubles Mr. Krutch—and is confused by him with the superficial problem of adjusting life to new knowledge—is the problem of adjusting literature to the separate existence of knowledge as such. If some enterprising Freudian—going a little beyond the "id" and the "super-ego"—should one day verily discover, or verily convince Mr. Krutch, that love is universally caused and controlled by an arrow shot from the bow of a small pink baby with wings not big enough to lift a squab from the nest, he would find this scientific knowledge quite as hostile to the enterprise of conveying what love is in its immediacy as complexes or ductless glands.

The "death of tragedy," it is needless to say, rests upon the same frail basis as the "death of love." If it is true, as Joseph Krutch believes, that the Greek dramatists and Shakespeare stand high above anything else the world ever produced in sublime tragedy, a mere calculation of probabilities would explain the absence of any similar prodigy within three hundred years of Shakespeare's death. At any rate Shakespeare did not use Aphrodite, or the Platonic ladder, or any religion or philosophy whatsoever, to "hypostasize" a justification for his heroic characters or their emotions in the structure of the universe. That is exactly what Shakespeare did not do. What he did do was to use a sovereign language, a language which in cleaving to the qualities of things seemed also to be giving the best knowledge about them. The dividing in two of that language is what makes Joseph Krutch think the world of tragedy is lost.

It is this, too, which brings Houston Peterson to the extremer opinion that drama itself is becoming unacceptable to sophisticated people. "Drama," he tells us in his *Melody of Chaos,* "has traditionally served to portray a more or less clear-cut conflict between individuals, values or forces; but when a single personality is seen as utterly diverse, an ordinary 'dramatic' conflict appears absurdly simple and misleading." Dr. Peterson would surely not maintain that clear-cut conflicts between individuals, values and forces have ceased in this modern world, diseased though it be with the "mania psychologica." The conflicts are here, and the personalities are as single as they were before. The *mania psychologica* consists of a natural interest in a developing technique for understanding those personalities and conflicts in their relations. This process is a different thing from dramatic art. It cannot in the old simple ways combine with it. Its language is not the same. It has a different motive and requires a different education. Eugene O'Neill's lamentable attempt in *Dynamo* to combine a vivid play with some sort of psycho-analytic or machine-age propædeutic suggests the real difficulty with which the drama is confronted. Personalities and conflicts as conceived by science—and therefore by purposeful people who want to do something with or about them—will not coalesce with personalities and conflicts as felt, or seen, or represented to perception. To the ambitious playwright this presents indeed a problem—or a thousand problems—but it does not mean that life is any less dramatic, or the drama any less compelling as an art. It is not sophisticated people who will no longer enjoy personalities in conflict on the stage, but people who are unsophisticated enough to think that science tells us what these things in their intrinsic being *are*.

As for the approaching doom of poetry—that fashionable rumor, too, I think, is based in large part on the same misunderstanding. It is easy for H. L.

Mencken to dismiss poetry as a "function of intellectual immaturity," because he is himself not too mature intellectually to feel at home with the average farm-hand from the Ozark mountains in the opinion that poets are people who go round with their heads in the clouds, having no interest in real life. The essential character of poetic language, he tells us, is "its bold flouting of what every reflective adult knows to be the truth." Mencken seems at times, with his brilliant mind, to make efforts to stay in the boob class lest his sparring with the boobs should cease to entertain us. His argument as to the infantile character of poetry actually rests upon the assumption that it is impossible to escape from reality and write maudlin fiction in practical language. The contrary is true. The poet even when he writes maudlin fiction dresses it in the colors of reality. There is fact in his diction even when there is none in his theme. Plato denounced poetry—or at least one-half of Plato denounced poetry—for its bold flouting of what every reflective adult knows to be the truth, and Aristotle replied that poetry is more true than history. It should have been obvious right there—and would have, if the world had not taken just that moment to fall asleep—that poetry is neither truth nor lies, but a way of telling them both. The only question there can be about truth and poetry is a question about the relation of this way of telling to the things told. Does it cleave to the reality of those things or doesn't it? And the answer to that question depends upon whether you have a naïve or a sophisticated view of science.

The identification of poetic diction with unreality is

a natural counterpart of the naïve assumption of science that its function is to tell us what reality "is." In proportion as science has grown mature, however—and grown even godlike in its power to perform miracles upon reality—the men of science have more and more clearly realized that their theories do not tell us what reality is, but only how we must conceive it if we wish to perform these miracles. This realization had gone so far in 1901 that the French mathematical physicist Henri Poincaré exactly reversed that grandiose declaration of Democritus in which his science began. "The void," he said—or to quote him more accurately, "our idea of space"—is nothing but a "convenient convention." "Euclidean geometry itself is only a sort of convention of language"—and he ridiculed, too, the idea that an "atom" is a fact. I quote Poincaré, not because he occupies a supreme or ultimate position in the criticism of science—no such position has been attained—but because his exact reversal of the saying of Democritus so neatly epitomizes one of the greatest steps ever taken by the human race on the road to intellectual maturity. His books were but a distinguished incident in a gradual realization among physicists that the relation of their formulæ to "reality" is a complex and somewhat remote one, and that the sheer experiences—the sweets and bitters, hots and colds, with a knowledge of the relations between them and how they may be handled—is about all the reality man will ever grasp. They express this—and also perhaps a little of their chagrin—by calling these experienced qualities the "brute fact," but they might just as well, since they are determined to be emotional about it, call them the angelic fact. They are at any rate what is "given." It seems to me that this realization has become so general in mathematical physics, only because this science has gone so far, and that in other sciences when they become mature we shall realize how deep is the gulf between the "reality" of a thing and the formula by which we practically or theoretically "understand" it.

Now the idea that poetry is dying out, belongs with the idea that scientific formulæ convey or describe "reality," and that poetic figures and images delude and scatter us up into a realm of fancy or ideality—a feathery somewhere which no solid man would inhabit. It was natural for Francis Bacon, who believed that science consists in "the contemplation of things as they are," to give poetry this rather dubious praise that it "doth raise and erect the mind, by submitting the shows of things to the desires of mind." But in our time, when the most up-to-date apostle of scientific method can only avow that it will give us "a picture of nature which is in the highest degree convenient, but not necessarily in any ultimate sense real," it is absurd to cling to this naïve and totally erroneous conception of poetry and the motives of the poet.

It does not matter to my argument whether you accept this extreme assertion—which I quote from Frederick Barry—or whether you declare that the picture is proven in some sense real by its convenience. It is proven real only in its portrayal of the important and fixed relations among the qualities of nature. As for the qualities themselves, they do not for the most part appear in the picture at all, and when they do they are quite likely to take the form of "convenient fictions." It is the endeavor to fill in and rectify these qualities—not to escape from reality—that makes the poet's picture different. In the scientist's picture a bite of sugar may be described, let us say, as $C_{12} H_{22} O_{11}$, and since that indicates enduring and orderly relations between the sugar and many other things, it is a most convenient picture. The poet refuses for the sake of convenience to forget that the sugar is sweet. The poet is impractical, not because he is more than other creative men decoyed by dreams, but because he is interested in getting acquainted with things rather than in getting adjusted to them. And he is unscientific for the same reason—because whereas science seeks convenience at the expense of reality, he seeks at the expense of convenience the most assured reality there is, the qualities that things have, or may have, in experience.

An excellent way to convince yourself that realness is the essence of poetic language is to read all the examples by which Professor Lowes, in his *Convention and Revolt in Poetry,* tries to prove that its essence is illusion:

"Lie still and deep,
Sad soul, *until the sea-wave washes*
The rim o' the sun."

"All in the hot and copper sky,
The *bloody* Sun, at noon,
Right up above the mast did stand,
No bigger than the Moon."

"*Large* and smoky red the sun's *cold disk* drops,
Clipped by naked hills, on violet-shaded snow."

"I wept as I remember'd how often you and I
Had tired the sun with talking and sent him down the sky."

"Part of a moon was falling down the west,
Dragging the whole sky with it to the hills."

"Like a four-sided wedge
The Custom House Tower
Pokes at the low, flat sky,
Pushing it farther and farther up."

Is not each one of these examples a particularly reckless abandonment of the convenient conception—the conception of things in their important relations—through sheer loyalty to the actual reality of them as they come to us? Suppose that instead of saying

"... the sea-wave washes
The rim o' the sun,"

I say

"The sun goes down."

That, too, according to Professor Lowes, is poetry because it is an "accepted illusion." In *reality,* he would say, the sun stands still and the earth moves. He would have said that, at least, a few years ago when he published his book. Now, however, he will find that those who are interested only in the relations of things—and to whom he attributes an interest in whatever "is"—have decided that this too is an illusion. The sun does not stand still any more than the earth does. The proper way to express their relation is by a mathematical formula that does not regard either one of them as fixed. But in that formula the last shred of "reality," except in so far as the bare statement of a single isolated relation may be real, is gone. It is evaporated in the high thin air. And the only way you can ever get it back, or get back to it, is to climb humbly down the same ladder you went up until you arrive at the immediate presentation:

"... the sea-wave washes
The rim o' the sun."

The scientist comes back down that ladder only once in a while, and because he has to. The poet comes down continually and because he loves what he finds at the bottom of it. He loves real experience.

The differentiation of these two ways of talking, growing ever deeper and spreading into new fields, gives rise to a great problem for poets. But to imagine that it will ever extinguish the poet's art is like imagining that man will give up life itself for a convenient conception of it.

II

IS THE NOVEL AT A DEAD END?

If poetry itself is immortal, we need not greatly worry about the novel, which is a kind of mongrel child of poetry and prose, a species most admirably adapted for survival in this practically scientific world. The English novel, or the possibility of it, was born in the eighteenth century in the discovery of Daniel Defoe that lies could be told more convincingly in prose than poetry. Up to that time it had been usually assumed by those interested in the narrative aspects of literature that poetry and "feigned history" were one and the same thing. It had been assumed, that is, that any one who wished to tell a made-up story and give his readers a feeling of its actually happening—no matter whether it was more true or less true than history—would use all the arts inherited by the poet from the magician, the arts of rapture and hypnosis and the heightened consciousness. Only those high tales of chivalry which people associated more with history than fiction, and those strings of episodes from low life which they took as mere humorous amusement, were as a matter of course told in practical language. The epoch-making discovery of Daniel Foe, who called himself Defoe as the first step in a brilliant career of putting things over on the public, was that if the arts of the poet are abandoned absolutely, and the most fantastic things related in the most matter-of-fact and circumstantial of practical language, the very language of commerce and the Royal Society, an attitude of temporary belief is engendered more stable and more easy to play upon than that mixture of suggestibility and excitement in which from prehistoric times it had been customary for story-tellers to make their tales seem real. A novel differs from a narrative poem—wherever it does differ—in that a belief that the thing happened is substituted for a heightened sense of its happening. And this substitution is capable of overwhelming success in narrative forms, because it sets free from distractions that practical tendency of our natures, that "restless desire to arrive at the final solution," which Coleridge so justly contrasted with the "pleasurable activity of the mind excited by the attractions of the journey itself." It gives us one of the great benefits of poetry, the concentration of our being upon experiences not our own, without demanding as poetry does the suspension of our habit of practicality, our going forever forward towards a goal. We can read a novel in the same fundamental attitude in which we acquire information or do business, but poetry demands an abrupt change. It demands that we be at the same time idle and energetically alive.

It is for this reason, I think, that we are inclined to deprecate in novels a too poetic language, and we find a certain appropriate merit in the cumbersome locutions of Dostoyevsky, or the style of Theodore Dreiser, which moves forward like a large but immature lumber-wagon loaded to the ricks with laboriously collected and most conscientiously specified and authenticated downright indubitable matters of fact. Or we are carried away by the astute device of Ernest

Hemingway, who does not write novels in his own person at all, but in that of an invented character less poetic and less intellectual than he, and less familiar with the riches of the English language, a resolute low-brow of the prize-fighting or bull-fighting variety —a part of Ernest Hemingway, to be sure, but not, by the grace of God, the whole—and one who in a long story, especially when he makes the mistake of trying to describe a landscape, may become a rather tiresome companion, and in certain moments of intense and not altogether simple passion even grows as irritating as would a young man with an affectation of baby-talk. All these ways of writing—among which we must also number the felicitously uncouth translations of most Russian novels—promote in the narrative a quality which we describe indifferently as "honesty" or *"vraisemblance"*—two things not accurately identical!—or as a sense of the "destiny" and "inevitability" of the movement. I do not mean to say that this quality is incompatible with the poet's trance—for in many true-seeming novels passages of rapturous poetry are embedded—but merely that it is more easy to be had. Especially in an environment of business and of intellectual endeavor, an attitude of practical although temporary belief, an information-acquiring attitude, is far more accessible and easy to keep up than the attitude of tranced imaginative realization. For this reason the novel is an art-form appropriate to our age. It effects, in the narrative sphere at least, a kind of compromise between the moods of poetry and prose.

To imagine that this excellent invention will disappear from the earth before civilized man disappears, seems to me the most outlandish of all dismal dreams about the future of literature. Novels are too easy to read, and they are too easy to write, for any danger of extinction to approach them. It is an almost universal opinion, however, that this literary form like others is passing through some kind of sea-change at the present moment. Grant Overton tells us it is the plot which has "decayed"—has been decaying indeed throughout the entire history of fiction—and particularly the significant plot, the plot that used to demonstrate something, if only God, freedom and immortality. Sherlock Bronson Gass believes it is the "critical intent that the 'new' novel . . . has foregone." Grant C. Knight thinks that the new novelists have not so much "foregone" this intent as lost the power of it. They suffer, he says, from "the enervation of the period"—an enervation otherwise manifested, we may note, by little trips to the north and south pole, round the world flights in airplanes, mushroom growth of sky-scrapers, monthly explosions of the visible universe at the hands of the Higher Physics. . . . At any rate, Professor Knight, who seems to have read all novels, finds the modern novelists enervated, and says they have "lost the hope" of improving mankind. "Dickens helped better the conditions of the London poor; . . . *Uncle Tom's Cabin* was good anti-slavery propaganda; but the novelists of 1930 look askance at purposeful novels and the young critics sniff at Upton Sinclair." Virginia Woolf maintains that the new novelists have neither lost nor foregone anything, but have merely decided not to interrupt their proper business of writing "books" with wholly irrelevant intents and enterprises.

Of the novels of her immediate predecessors she says: "Sometimes I wonder if we are right to call them books at all. For they leave one with so strange a feeling of incompleteness and dissatisfaction. In order to complete them it seems necessary to do something—to join a society, or, more desperately, write a cheque. . . . The Edwardians were never interested in . . . the book itself. They were interested in something outside." Storm Jameson feels, on the contrary, that there is "a blind spot, a dead end, in the Georgian novelists." And she locates the cause of this condition neither in a foregone intent, nor a lost hope, nor a return to their proper creative business, but in the fact that they do not know enough. "Now it is not in any way required of a novelist that he should know, actually know, anything about the scientific achievements of his age," she tells us. "But it is required of a great novelist that he should be awake to the spirit that is producing these achievements. . . . As much as the modern scientist knows of life, he, in his own terms (which are not theirs), will know."

I cite these various opinions because I could not myself even successfully pretend to be an authority in this field. I notice, however, that the opinions all have the same drift; they imply a tendency among novelists identical with the one I have been describing among poets. It is a tendency to renounce, or at least to relax, the claim to be a sage, a critic of life, a counsellor, a man who comes "before the great ones of society, much as the son of Imlah came before the throned kings of Judah and Israel; and who speaks truth as deep, with a power as prophet-like and as vital"—to quote Charlotte Brontë's famous tribute to Thackeray—a tendency to relax that claim, and take a place, whether with pride or humiliation, among the artists, leaving the vital truth-speaking business to others. The others to whom the novelists are leaving this vital business are, as Storm Jameson perceives, the scientists. But I am afraid her hope that a great novelist may be born who will know as much about life as the scientists, but know it "in other terms," is destined to a complete disappointment. The two ways of knowing to which she alludes are the skilled or professional way, and the unskilled or amateur way. And the reason why our novelists seem to know less than their forbears is that the professional way of knowing has entered their field. They actually know more than their forbears, for there is so much more known, but they do not know enough more, and cannot in the old amateur way learn enough, to compete with the professionals. Henry James used to say that nothing excited him more than "a psychological reason," and I think that is a large part of what excites everybody in a good novel. But for psychological reasons—in a pure form, or with a vital need to understand them—we do not go to Henry James, who made novels sound like psychology, but to William James, who made psychology sound like a novel—or to the successors of William James, who do not even take the trouble, or command the talent, to make it sound so. Or we *shall* go, let us say, to the successors of these successors of William James—for I am not contending that psychologists really know very much, but merely that the function of knowing is splitting off from the function of communicating experience, and that this explains the current changes in the novel as well as in poetry. Virginia Woolf, with her haughty zeal for the novel that is "self-contained"—the pure novel—merely carries to an extreme, as the modernist poets do, the present position of her whole profession. There is hardly one of them who could be imagined saying, as Dostoyevsky did of *The Brothers Karamazov:* "I consider my task (the refutation of anarchism) a civic exploit."

To be sure, Theodore Dreiser has recently sued a motion-picture company for eliminating the "indictment of society" contained in his *American Tragedy*. And I suppose that for people who want to find it, the indictment is there. It is there if society is there. But Dreiser's indictment is so loosely drawn, so irresponsibly thought out, so little possessed of direction or linked up to any plan, prospect or motion of the mind toward mending any definite thing, that his great novels merely rise up one after the other and stand there like mum giants, incapable of pointing, incapable even of casting their shadows in a single direction. Dreiser is neither an "Edwardian" nor a "Georgian" novelist—nor either a Coolidgean or a Hooverian, I am glad to say—but just a man who has been writing powerful novels for the last quarter of a century. He represents perhaps better than the modernists the present predicament of the literary mind. He has not learned their trick of being arrant about not having wisdom. He feels ashamed about it. When he was asked by *The Bookman* a while ago to join a little orgy of "personal statements . . . on life and their own work" by America's leading authors, this is what he said:

"I can make no comment on my work or my life that holds either interest or import for me. Nor can I imagine any explanation or interpretation of any life, my own included, that would be either true—or important, if true. Life is to me too much a welter and play of inscrutable forces to permit, in my case at least, any significant comment. One may paint for one's own entertainment, and that of others—perhaps. As I see him the utterly infinitesimal individual weaves among the mysteries a floss-like and wholly meaningless course—if course it be. In short I catch no meaning from all I have seen, and pass quite as I came, confused and dismayed."

I happened to see Dreiser not long after that paragraph was published. He was piling brush on a bonfire in the late afternoon of a hot autumn day—looking, I must say, more like a Stone Age giant than a literary mind. As he stood there heavily wiping the sweat off his face, I told him how much I admired the solid eloquence of his statement. It boomed out among the others like the voice of the earth itself. I quoted the last sentence to prove it.

"Well," he said, "there's one word I left out. I left out the word ashamed—confused, ashamed and dismayed."

It is very important, in the first place, if you want to understand Dreiser, to put that word back in. In the second place it is important to remember that Dreiser, with all his talk about "chemisms," has a passionate antagonism toward any pushing to extremes of a genuinely scientific attitude. He will defend with mad heat such a belief as that if ever he meets a certain early acquaintance, a most ominous personage, at some street-crossing or while passing through a railroad station, a dire calamity in his own life will inevitably follow. Dreiser got rid of his religion, or tried to, but he did not accept, or enter into, the scientific method of understanding—the scientific conception of what it is to understand. He did not join the march of science. He merely borrowed from it a few dolorous phrases with which to decorate and make more torturing the incapacity of his literary mind for any participation in the *growth* of knowledge. And so he stands there, just as all serious-hearted literature in this era stands, unable to "imagine any explanation . . . that would be either true—or important, if true." He stands there confused, ashamed and dismayed. But just accidentally, and almost, as it were, surreptitiously—the way a person in bad company will perform a good act—he steps over to Soviet Russia, and there he finds that a body of men of science, the State Planning Commission, having actually drawn up his "indictment of society," detailed and documented it, and also made blueprints of the reconstructions necessary and possible to be carried out, have furthermore set the teeth in it and started it to work. And there he feels, in spite of himself, affirmative and enthusiastic. And he comes back to America and toils hard to explain how reasonable that is, and moreover sets his big shoulder under many similar though smaller efforts of intelligence toward decent justice. In this equivocal way Dreiser's literary mind accommodates itself to the separate existence of science.

Sinclair Lewis is more definite in his indictments of

society than Dreiser, and his need of accommodation to this situation is therefore more immediate and pressing. He accomplishes it, as H. G. Wells does, by the method of co-operation, by calling upon the experts in knowledge for assistance. In a foreword to *Arrowsmith* he generously acknowledges his debt to Doctor Paul DeKruif "not only for most of the bacteriological and medical material in this tale but equally for his help in the planning of the fable itself—for his realization of the characters as living people, for his philosophy as a scientist." That foreword alone makes *Arrowsmith* an outstanding event in the history of the novel, but that is only an extreme instance of the manner in which Sinclair Lewis always contrives, when his indictment of society runs deep, to outwit the division of labor between literature and science. He calls in the experts. So far, moreover, his indictment of society has not run too deep. Perhaps a still more significant novel than *Arrowsmith* is the one that Sinclair Lewis has *not* written, after so long studying the ground for it and consulting so many experts, about labor and the revolutionary movement. I do not know how he would state the reasons why this novel hangs fire so long, or seems quite incapable of being born, but I think I know what the reasons are. The socialist movement differs from all other popular movements or associations of its nature throughout history in that it is a scientific undertaking. It is based upon a searching analysis of the economic process and of the economic causes of historic change. Whether its theory is valid or not may still be considered a question, but it is far too maturely scientific a question to be weightily attacked by a novelist or dealt with in a novel. Sinclair Lewis wants to say something important and something of his own, and he is clear-headed enough to see that in this field he cannot do so without taking sides on the scientific theories of Marx and Lenin. He is clear-headed enough to know too that a novelist is not a scientific thinker. He has the choice, therefore, of ignoring the maturest achievements of the human mind in the proposed field, in which case his novel will be rejected by solid people as carrying a message of no weight, or accepting wholesale either the Marxian theory or the bourgeois theories opposed to it, in which case his novel will carry a weighty message, to be sure, but the message will not be his own, and he will be sniffed at by the critics, as Upton Sinclair is, for writing "propaganda novels." It is nothing but the existence of a mature scientific theory *in process of application* in the proposed field, which makes it impossible for him as a literary man to enter there with his own forceful comment.

As to Upton Sinclair, I think it is important to state that he is a brilliant educator, one of the ablest and most effective in the world to-day, and the world is not so well educated that anybody can afford to sniff at that. But it may also be said in behalf of the sniffing critics that education is a somewhat different thing, or has been in the literary past at least, from great creative art. The critics sniff at Upton Sinclair not only because they dislike his message, and not at all because they dislike novels with a message or fail to realize that these have been the greatest novels in the past, but because the message in this case is not from Upton Sinclair but from Karl Marx. Sinclair has not, except in *The Jungle* at least, discovered or conceived a new thing or a new way of looking at things. His message, moreover, is one which in its own proper nature has shaken off that integument of poetry in which throughout so long a period it had been cloudily enveloped, in order to become a clear, sure and reliable guide of action. To reclothe this theory for the benefit of immature minds in the prosy poetry of a novel, however valuable a task it may be and however skilfully performed, is a very different thing from delivering in the form of a novel one's own individual view and solution of some problem of contemporary or universal life.

The peculiar and somewhat isolated position of Upton Sinclair among Western novelists, is thus in another way characteristic of the present predicament of the literary mind. His novels are anything but isolated in Soviet Russia, where all writers are officially regarded "primarily as practitioners," and where literature is judged as a "war weapon of the proletariat." I quote these phrases from Panferov, whose recent novel *Brousky* has sold upwards of five hundred thousand copies, and who declares that "its theme is as follows: innumerable natural resources are lost because of our unpardonable ignorance." In that vast country—I beg to remind the sniffing critics—Upton Sinclair is regarded as one of the few great novelists of the world.

However, I am reserving the subject of literature under the soviets—or rather literature and the Marxian science—for treatment in another volume. Here I merely want to point out that the essentially instructive novels of men like Sinclair and Panferov, and the purely experiential novels of Virginia Woolf, are equally characteristic of the "dead end" at which this literary form may seem to have arrived. For that dead end is nothing but the sharpening of the division between these two functions—between the propagation of knowledge and the communication of experience. It is the same dead end at which poetry and tragedy and comedy have arrived, and it raises the same problem, the problem of the future relations between poetry and truth.

III

THE REALM OF LITERARY TRUTH

THE division of labor—and let us say also of play—between poets and scientists, and the cleavage of the two commodities they make, does not any more mean the end of poetry than of science. But it does mean a loss to poetry that science cannot feel. For a sense of the presence of universal truth was one of poetry's sublime ingredients. Science *is* this ingredient and wants no other.

There is a motion among literary men to-day to try to mend this loss. Conrad Aiken is studying psychopathology and talking about the grandeur of Dante and Lucretius. Aldous Huxley is advising poets to think up a new "method of dealing with abstractions" so that science may again become the "subject matter" of poems. He thinks the reason why this has not happened is that "a poet in whose mind ideas are a personal moving force does not happen to have appeared." A strange statement, to which he is led because he does not make clear to himself what he means by science becoming the subject matter of poetry. He makes no distinction between Lucretius who taught science in poetic language, and John Donne who did not teach but took scientific ideas as experiences, as material out of which commingled with his emotions to make poems. The distinction is absolutely vital. It is doubtless true, as Huxley says, that Einstein—or Yeats, if he understood Einstein—could "write the most impassioned lyrics about relativity and the pleasures of pure mathematics." Edna Millay has written an impassioned, though to me not wholly convincing, sonnet about the pleasures of pure mathematics, and Archibald McLeish has made that troubled poem about relativity. But these achievements do not bring us one step toward reviving the times of Lucretius and Empedocles. Those were times when poets could hope to convey in the same breath a lively sense of the world and the most technical knowledge about it. In order to be a modern Lucretius, you would have to write lyrics, not about Einstein's theory, but about motion in terms of Einstein's theory. And that is impossible because motion cannot be experienced except from some standpoint, and Einstein's theory is a device for talking about motion independently of all standpoints. No conceivable creatures—not even Shelley's wild-eyed charioteers who

> "lean forth and drink
> With eager lips the wind of their own speed,"

could write in Einstein's language the poetry of motion—not any more than they could write epithalamiums in the language of Freud or John B. Watson, or compose hymns of revolution in the terminology of Karl Marx. It is idle to deny this opposition, or imagine that poets can recapture the realms of science by merely going there, or by thinking up a new "method of dealing with abstractions." Poetry is compelled by its very nature to yield up to science the task of interpreting experience, of finding out what we call truth, of giving men reliable guidance in the conduct of their lives. The boast of Matthew Arnold that "More and more mankind will discover that we have to turn to poetry to interpret life for us . . .," that "Poetry is nothing less than the most perfect speech of man, that in which he comes nearest to being able to utter truth," was but a last cry of defiance from the dwindling men of letters to the new leader of the herd.

There is no one to repeat Arnold's gallant cry to-day. In its place we have Sacheverell Sitwell talking blandly of the "nearly cancelled rôle of the poet," and we have the noble and morose growl of Julien Benda, indignant because poets are *not* interpreting life for us, because literature has ceased to utter truth and given itself over wantonly to the "pure feeling of things." M. Benda laments ferociously the disappearance of what he calls intellect from modern literature, but he is himself too literary in his training to ask himself the most obvious questions: Why has intellect disappeared from literature? Where has it gone? He seems to imagine that intellect in disappearing from literature has disappeared from the world. He makes furious mock of those who assert that art "must present things *in their reality,* and not in the *distorted forms in which the intellect represents them.*" In scorn of them he cries: "Let us recall that this distortion of things by intellect —which is merely the capacity of man to make the sensory world intelligible—was considered in the seventeenth century, when Descartes first made it known, as one of the great honors to which the human species could lay claim." Are we to infer that in our time the species has ceased to strive after the honors of Descartes, that the movement initiated by Descartes and by

Bacon and Galileo is declining and coming to an end? Surely the very opposite thing is happening—the distortion of things by intellect in order to make the sensory world intelligible, and make it moreover serviceable—has gone so far and flourished so fantastically, that even the *minimum of immediacy essential to poetic literature* is incompatible with its further growth. Intellectual interpretation is still an honor, a far greater one now than in the time of Descartes, but the honor is indeed remote from the man of letters. Science has withdrawn intellect from literature. It has divided truth from immediacy. And the event is inexorable, inherent in the development of science. It is not a degeneration of French society, but a specialization of human functions against which M. Benda is protesting with so savage a moral indignation. His arrant and absolute demand that art should again become "an attempt to comprehend life" would be, if it came from a scientist, a demand that art give place to science. Coming from a man of letters it is a demand that scientific progress cease, and that we return to those amateur times when the comprehension of life and the communication of its qualities were not yet distinguished. In short, M. Benda's fine and ferocious tirade is merely a last phase of the literary man's battle against the advance of science into his domain. No longer able to resist the enemy, he turns frantically upon his own colleagues and attacks them.

It is the function of science to comprehend and criticize life; poetry is our living of it vividly and together. Only after that extreme statement is made can we correctly apprehend, as qualifications of it, the various intellectual possibilities that lie open to poetry and to poetic literature in an age of science. I for my part am much in accord with M. Benda in his wish that poets might continue—or begin again—to use their brains. Indeed I think my own poetry has suffered from the too controlling sense I have had of this inherent divergence of two functions. When I want to comprehend life I want to comprehend it as those do whose purpose is control; I do not want to beguile myself by some mixture of semi-comprehension with an imposing presentation of its colors. When on the other hand the colors of life engage me deeply I do not often have the impulse to wind a saying around them, to build an ulterior meaning into them, to make some symbol or signal or semaphore out of them, as though they had not their value in themselves. Thus although intellectual and a poet, I am not an intellectual poet—not yet at least—but one of those whom M. Benda would denounce with terrible force, although unjustly, as tainted with the "greed of immediacy." I say unjustly because I would gladly find a way of escape from this dividedness and put myself into a book of poetry as a whole man, or at least two halves of a man pulled together in some manner that is not too obviously a make-shift. I approach the problem, therefore, of bringing truth back into poetic literature, or at least deciding what are the boundaries of the realm of literary truth, with the best will in the world to make them wide.

I remark first that the man of letters has as good a right to make large guesses about things totally unknown as the man of science. He has still a sovereign freedom in the vast kingdom of our ignorance. Here he can mix poetry and opinion with the old beautiful and sublime caprice, here stake his claim to "truth which is its own testimony," here still insist that he is not a ballad-monger but a seer and a sage. One has only to remember how many are the questions upon which scientific authorities disagree in order to realize how vast this realm is in which the poet can still feel welling up the old sovereign and preposterous conviction, in which "intellect" can still robe itself in asseverations and expatiate and plume itself and put on a great spectacle of the discovery of truth, without fear of being suddenly brought low by a verified and well-aimed fact from the door of some laboratory or from behind some pile of statistics. The realm is vast—and yet it is steadily dwindling. Emerson would look foolish enough coming forward in our times with his solemn annunciation of a "Law of Compensation." We are too familiar with valid laws and the manner in which their validity is established. To his assertion that "labor is watched over" by this mystic law, we should reply by pointing to the statute law and to a pile of documents called "compensation statistics." For all his high art in the poetry of ideas, Emerson would be put down as a crank or a mountebank if he came out on our bookstalls with his grave essay on "Compensation,"—and yet that is a fair example of what is called "literary truth," a fair operation of that faculty which Emerson, like other men of letters in the nineteenth century, called "intellect" in conscious opposition to the activities of the mind in science.

Not only are the fields dwindling in which a man of letters can display this proud faculty with complacence, but even in these fields he can hardly help sometimes reflecting—so great is the prestige of science—that if they are still free to him, it is not because he has conquered them but because they are unconquered. It may be that they are unconquered because they are still unconquerable by the methods of true knowledge; it may be because they have not yet seemed in comparison to others worth conquering. These two causes alone determine the outposts of science. A "literary truth," may therefore be defined—provisionally at least—as a truth which is either uncertain or comparatively unimportant.

One of the most delightful of literary truths to me, and one apt in this connection because of its "mathematical" form, is this *Meditation* of Pascal:

"I lay it down as a fact that, if all men knew what others say of them, there would not be four friends in the world."

It seems a little absurd to bring such a delightfully swift and helpful remark into relation with the problems of verified knowledge. And yet if you will but imagine a world in which flood-prevention or the curbing of a bubonic plague happened to depend upon our determining the reliability of that small statistic, you will concede that we should know before long to a close approximation of exactitude how many friends would be left in the world under the proposed circumstances. We should have experts plotting curves all day long of the decline of friendships, both in number and elasticity to stresses, tensional, tortional and transverse, under a controlled increase in publicity for all frank and delightfully malicious conversations. I am disposed to think the curve would fall abruptly to a depth almost as appalling as that contemplated by Pascal, but then rise again very gradually in such a way as to indicate that if the publicity were absolute the friendships would multiply enormously and show an elasticity almost as appalling. At any rate the tests will never be made because the labor too far exceeds the reward. And for that sole reason Pascal's apothegm bids fair to remain a literary truth throughout all time to come. Another literary truth, and one which survived long not because it was relatively unimportant, but because it flourished in a field unconquered by science, is the saying—almost as classic in literature as the *Meditations* themselves—that Pascal "plumbed the depths of man's moral nature." Pascal flayed and tortured himself to death and died morbidly torturing those dearest to him, through a perversion of impulse which a glimmer of the clinical knowledge of man's moral nature availed of in good season would probably have relieved. The statement that Pascal "plumbed the depths of man's moral nature" still survives in wide circles as a literary truth. You will hear it repeated by people who in a crisis similar to those Pascal blundered and bled his way through, would not turn to him for counsel but to an alienist. Nevertheless it survives only because these people, at least in their character as readers of literature, have not yet been reached by the advance of scientific knowledge.

There is of course a gift of imaginative sympathy, necessary above all to the clinical psychologist, to put him in possession of the data for a skilled application of his science. And this may to some extent be cultivated by reading the literary works of men preeminently endowed with it. There are other things besides knowledge. There is that gift which Morris Cohen calls "sound judgment," or the ability to "guess what is relevant and decisive" in situations not capable of minute analysis. It is true, as he says, that "in practice the statesman, the business man, and even the physician, may often find the remark of a novelist like Balzac of greater help than long chapters from the most scientific psychology." But this does not alter the truth I am proving, for my proof rests upon no adulation of science, and no schematic disjunction of it from any man's good sense, but quite the opposite, upon the assumption that science even in its most imposing forms is nothing but an *undistracted* effort to get knowledge or apply it. Lenin was a supreme example of that "sound judgment" which Morris Cohen perceives to be so vital in the social sciences, but Lenin's judgment was sound in the highest degree only because he had mastered to the last detail and without admixture of poetry all that any science had to say about his specialty of engineering revolution. As science extends and deepens its domain, those cases in which the soundest judgment can be rendered by a man cultivating the mere art of letters will grow steadily fewer. That is the inexorable fact.

In 1863, in a letter to Renan, the French chemist Berthelot first clearly confronted this question of the realm of literary truth. He drew a distinction between "positive and universal science which imposes itself upon us by its own certitude," and those "poetic aperçus of a particular and individual order" to which he gave the quaint name of "ideal science." He defended the rights of this ideal science, identifying them with the right to liberty, but at the same time he asserted that positive science "declines no problem," and that the ideal science must be recognized to possess less certainty, and indeed no certainty at all and no probability, except as it rests "upon the same methods that make the force and certainty of positive science." The realm of these "poetic aperçus," and therewith the liberty of them, has greatly dwindled since that day. It has so dwindled that for us the scheme of Berthelot can no longer solve the problem. An intellectual poet cannot find to-day in this "ideal science" either the scope or force of conviction that his nature demands. Here he must be ever in a mood of circumspection, ever ready to retreat before the advancing columns of those whose devotion to truth is pure of the poetic motive.

There is another way, however, in which a poet can be intellectual—another way, perhaps, of defining "literary truth." Instead of offering for belief ideas too unimportant or too difficult of verification to have been really established as true, literature can offer ideas not for belief but for enjoyment. Ideas, we must remember, are not only "about" experience; they are also experiences, and so loved by poetic minds for their own sakes and regardless of their meaning's truth. We seldom realize—especially we pious Anglo-Saxons—how much the pleasure of a reading man consists in mere adventuring among selomn judgments which he does not dream of acting upon or accepting. He explores the books of wisdom as others explore Africa, not seeking tame maxims and pieces of serviceable counsel, but seeking strange, gorgeous or impressive scenery peopled with alien and undomesticable ideas. Who can resist the maxim of Vauvenargues, "To accomplish anything worth while, a man must always live as if he were never going to die," or refrain from reciting with Thomas à Kempis, "Know for certain that thou must lead a dying life"? Goethe remarks in praise of Shakespeare: "It would be hard to find a poet each of whose works was more thoroughly pervaded by a definite and effective idea than his." And he adds in illustration: "*Antony And Cleopatra* expresses with a thousand tongues the idea that pleasure and action are ever incompatible." What is it that this idea, which is not even the second cousin of a truth, can add to the play for a thinking mind like Goethe's? It has, he would say, a "literary validity." Even "superstition," he remarks elsewhere, "does not harm the poet, for he knows how to make its half-truths, to which he gives only a literary validity, count in manifold ways for good." What is this literary validity which may be possessed by a superstition, and by such an idea as that pleasure and action are ever incompatible? Can it mean anything but that the idea falls happily and with a ring of genuine appropriateness into its place? It is finely savored and well set out to be enjoyed. If the statement seems extreme, it is only because the distinction here is not absolute, but is one of degree. There is a progressive relaxation of the interest in validity all the way from a report of Paul Heyl on *Gravitational Anisotropy in Crystals* to a book like Herbert Read's *The Sense of Glory,* in reading which no gentleman, I am sure, would have the crudity to ask the author what the Sense of Glory really is.

The French are so much less embarrassed than the English in the presence of a naked pleasure, that they find it quite natural to take this view of literary truth. In introducing his famous history of French Literature, Gustav Lanson remarks: "Literature has this superior excellence, that it accustoms us to take pleasure in ideas. It causes man to find in the exercise of his thought at once his joy, his repose and his renewal. . . ." Not a word here of truth. M. Lanson does add, to be sure, that literature is "in the most noble sense of the word a popularization of philosophy," but that I take to be his comment upon philosophy rather than a retraction of what he has said about literature. Of all Englishmen it was of course only John Keats who penetrated to the pith of this matter with his startling description of the quality which makes for success in literature as *Negative Capability.* "I mean . . ." he said, "when a man is capable of being in uncertainties, mysteries, doubts, without any irritable reaching after fact or reason. Coleridge, for instance, would let go by a fine isolated verisimilitude caught from the Penetralium of mystery, from being incapable of remaining content with half-knowledge. This pursued through volumes would perhaps take us no further than this, that with a great poet the sense of Beauty overcomes every other consideration, or rather obliterates all consideration."

Literature, then, as a thing distinct from science, may be a pure communication of experience; it may interpret experience in spheres as yet untouched by science; it may offer interpretations as intellectual things to be enjoyed and without a tense regard to their validity. . . . To which we must add that in these spirited activities, serious and yet set free from the tether of verification, new ideas and suggestions of infinite value to science may be born.

To my mind, however,—and I think most deep lovers of literature will agree,—for the creation of big masterpieces this is not enough. If the integral and solid deep element of truth-speaking is gone out of poetry, something is gone that must be searched after and brought back, if it can be, and at whatever cost. There is no comfort in the suggestion of I. A. Richards that the poet can still control our destiny—as does the campaign orator—by working up "emotional attitudes" which we will then meekly go forth and carry into action without the pretense on either side that he has spoken truth.[1] With all respect to Mr. Richards's great merits, I think his plan for saving the race from moral and political chaos by uprooting emotions from the authentic objects to which nature had attached them, cultivating them in the library, and passing them round in little verbal capsules guaranteed to make people virtuous without troubling their intelligence, is merely the most fantastic and last effort of poetic literature to save its dignity in isolation from scientific knowledge. There is no hope of any renaissance in this.

For that hope we must turn to the possible results of a clear consciousness of the situation upon the part of poets. André Chénier could not remarry poetry with science, because he did not understand what had divided

[1]In his book on *Practical Criticism,* pp. 185–6, Mr. Richards himself unintentionally brings the poet and the campaigner at a General Election into the same not very flattering category. I have criticized his books at length in a Note beginning on p. 297.

them, or what each in its isolation is. And Conrad Aiken fails for a like reason. At least he does not seem to know what poems are, or even what he thinks they are. In one place he describes the poet's function as to "compensate" with imaginings for impulses frustrated in the world of real experience; in another, to "translate in . . . form of literary art the consciousness of modern man"; in a third, to choose a "lofty promontory from which to view the world of [one's] experience"; and in a fourth, he says that poetry is "the most successful of the modes" by which man has "adjusted himself" to new experience. With these four contrary winds of purpose blowing in his head at once, it is no wonder Conrad Aiken finds himself confessing of his own metaphysical legend of *John Deth:* "My meaning was, and has largely remained, obscure to me." With all respect for Houston Peterson's persuasive volume, I do not believe it is the bewilderment of a modern world illumined by science that is reflected in Aiken's "Melody of Chaos"; it is the bewilderment of a modern poet reading science and trying to get it back into poetry without a plan.

It may be true, as Conrad Aiken says, that poetry is "once more slowly and painfully learning to think." I hope so, but I do not see the signs of it. I find the germs of a new literary era, not in poetry at all, but in a more humble tendency that has come among us without blare of trumpet or invocation of Lucretius—the tendency of men of letters to lend their pens to the agreeable communication of scientific knowledge. The whole aspect of our book-shelves and reading tables is changed already by this process. A text-book of science is no longer a vile, dog-eared and detested relic of school-days—best used even then as a missile—and now tossed up into the attic with the broken furniture and the half-worn shoes. It is an honorable and renowned volume, praised for its charm, and fast crowding along the shelf once monopolized by the Meditations, the Maxims, the Book of Apothegms or Collection of Essays, first series, second series and third. In America we used to have an imposing array of "literary" magazines—*The Atlantic Monthly, The North American Review, The Century, Scribner's, Harpers, The Forum.*—*The Century* is dead; *The Atlantic Monthly* has descended from its pedestal; *The North American Review* has followed *The Atlantic; Harpers* will accept nothing until you prove that it is not too "literary"; *Scribner's* is given over to "contemporary themes," and *The Forum* to "controversy." Of all that stately galaxy, only the poor *Bookman* totters along under the sagging banner of "literary truth." And even *The Bookman* forgetfully admits that this truth is not after all true—that "literature is primarily literature, a means of refined and intellectual pleasure." This change is no part of the jazz movement, or the reflection of a temporary taste for rapid and shallow stimulation. It is a part of the quick resistance of thoughtful people to the continuance of an activity that has become frivolous.

It has two aspects. It appears as a tendency of the man of letters to delve in the findings of science, or even to associate himself with scientists in order to give the world along with the pleasures of gracious writing some technical and dependable knowledge. The fact that H. G. Wells, who has always insisted that the writer ought to class himself, "not with the artists but with the teachers and the priests and prophets," finds himself compelled in fulfilling his high purpose to humble his brilliant pen to a task of co-operation with technically trained specialists in producing a book of reliable knowledge about "life," becomes especially significant when you remember that for Matthew Arnold, less than fifty years ago, criticism of "life" was a phrase adequate to define the poet's function.

And this tendency on the literary side is supplemented by a tendency on the part of scientists to emerge from their dim laboratories and unventilated textbooks, and take a little exercise in the air of social communication—a tendency of which Sir James Jeans's book *The Universe Around Us* may serve as an example, because it is a book in which not only verified knowledge, but so far as possible the process by which it was verified, a glimpse of the scientist's experience, is made accessible, and made dramatic and beautiful to any person of intellectual tastes. The ablest literary men are serving an apprenticeship in science; the ablest scientists are serving an apprenticeship in the art of friendly communication. And the process is almost as important to science as it is to literature, for science is becoming so specialized in its own labors that the investigators in one field can hardly communicate in their technical language with those in another. For the purpose of understanding each other—if not indeed, sometimes, themselves—they must learn to express their findings in a somewhat literary language.

It is out of this language spoken by those who have dwelt with scientific knowledge—friends of its validity and of the cool scepticism in which it hangs suspended —and yet whose tongues and eye-balls have not grown too dry to taste and see the heaviness of sweet and bitter, the reality of color, that I look for a renaissance of truth-speaking poetry. I do not mean that works of poetry are to be text-books. To speak honestly, even Lucretius failed of a sustained poetical success in that genre. Nor do I mean that poets are to curb their whims and tack their poems carefully together on a last supplied by "Reason" or the latest discovery in the clinic or the laboratory. They will have to be spontaneous and have liberty. If they cannot be spontaneous after reading science scientifically, and knowing truth in her own terms, then my hope is utopian. But I believe that when they understand what science is, and what its division from poetry is, so that they can clearly know when they are doing one thing and when the other, when and in what manner they are combining the two, this will be possible. Knowledge is not hostile to spontaneity when it is clear and complete, not any more than the light of day is, which makes the world larger and more full of things. Even a pure poet can only be enriched by whatever knowledge he makes wholly his own. And a poet who wishes to be once more as of old a prophet and a truth-speaker, will *have* to make some genuine and verified, and as we say "systematic," knowledge his own. He will have to read some science deeply and become at home in the temple of science. There is no way to overcome a division of labor without retrogression, but for one person to perform the whole of both kinds of labor. And there is no way to re-assemble the divided product, but to understand where the division lies and what are the functions and particular virtues of each part. It cannot be a mere wilful act of mixture now, a piece of intellectual mud-pie-making like D. H. Lawrence's *Fantasia of the Unconscious,* or Yeats's *Vision*—a return by sentimental fiat to the handicraft stage in the mind's history. It cannot be universal or undiscriminating. It cannot be accomplished by those blind to the difference between blowing grotesque bubble-castles of iridescent ideas and lending the warm weight of poetry to the expression of a general truth. There is no denying a stern limitation of the possibilities that lie before the literary mind in an age of science, an age which is perhaps the future history of man. I should express those limitations, however, not by saying that there will be no more great truth-speaking poets, but by saying that in the future such poets will have to be very great.

It is needless to say that if poetry and truth were once indiscriminately presented together by the same people and in the same books, poetry, once humbled of her independent pretension to *be* truth, can find ways to come back to truth and join with her to produce at times the old moving force. Poetry cannot be the criticism of life, but she can be the life of criticism. She is not the breath and finer spirit of knowledge, but she can breathe a fine spirit into knowledge. She has her ways—and she will find new ways—of enshrining, if not in the same word, yet in the same line, or page, or volume, the experience and the understanding of it—her ways of teaching by experience. They are not all destroyed because poetry and truth have in their natural growth divided, and can only sometimes and with deliberate art be recombined.

The thought turns back instinctively upon this theme

to Goethe, the only man since poetry and science parted company who did work and play creatively in both fields. His example proves that this division can exist consciously within one mind, if the mind is flexible and fertile enough, without implying a dry poetry or an unreliable observation and experiment. Goethe was, to be sure, rather a romantic natural philosopher than a modern scientist so far as concerns his theoretical speculations. His color theory had only a "literary validity," and was so estimated by the physicists even of his own day. His describing fertilization as a "spiritual anastomosis," and saying that the tails of mammals may be regarded as an indication of the *"unendlichkeit* of organic being," will show how much poetry was still mingled with his biological speculations. He was rather at the stage of Kepler than of Isaac Newton—from whose "detested theories" he was indeed hailed by Schelling as a deliverer. Nevertheless he had the faculty for matter-of-fact observation and verification by experiment, and he made genuine contributions to the most exact knowledge—none more genuine, I should say, than his remark about the nature of poetry: "What need of much definition? Lively feeling of situations and power to express them make the poet."

That a man fruitfully active in several branches of science, and with this quite matter-of-fact conception of what poetry is, should have produced perhaps the richest and most varied poems of all our modern era except those of Shakespeare, seems a sufficient proof that this division of the minds of men and of their books and language which is causing such a desolation in contemporary letters, can be in instances surmounted. We must in honesty remember, however, that besides this matter-of-fact vein in which Goethe knew so well what poetry is—in which he knew how to contrast *Dichtung* with *Wahrheit*—there was another vein, a vein of gilding and of glorification, in which he talked of poetry like Wordsworth and Shelley, and himself defined the poet as "in essence . . . universal interpreter of nature." In a modern mind endowed and occupied like Goethe's the conflict between those two views of poetry could hardly lie concealed. If the poet is distinguished by his lively feeling of situations, he cannot then in essence be distinguished by his power to interpret them. There are only these two things in question—experience and the interpretation of it—and if one is poetry, the other so far as it succeeds is science. There does remain the question then, whether a universal genius like Goethe—a thinking singer—could grow up and come to flower in a civilization which confronted him with that contradiction—a civilization which would remind him continually that the true interpretation of colors rejects the lively feeling of them, and that he must ignore the interpretation in order to express the lively feeling, and that this is true not only of rainbow colors but of all the colors of life—a civilization which would lend him no eloquent phrase out of a great tradition with which to moderate at times this sharpening conflict. I think we may wisely leave that question to the universal genius himself to answer. Of this, however, I am sure—that such a poet could live and flourish in our civilization only on one condition, that he should not attempt to blur the conflict or cling to the tradition, but should boldly face it all out to the point of understanding.

IV

THE PROBLEM OF CRITICISM

In spite of prodigious efforts that have been made to sanctify the Fathers of the New Humanism, it is plain that the profession of literary criticism is in a sad decline. There are no great critics in the world, not one even with a voice that commands attention. In previous times men of this profession were looked up to like prophets and listened to. Samuel Johnson, Lessing, Hazlitt, Sainte-Beuve, Renan, Arnold, Pater, Taine—these are among the big names in literary history. Especially in the nineteenth century this profession rose to a commanding height. "Of the intellect of Europe in general," said Matthew Arnold, "the main effort, for now many years, has been a critical effort." The century ended, however, in a debate among critics as to whether criticism has any value, whether indeed it has any existence, and since then the profession has been steadily sliding down hill. We do not even take that word "intellect" very seriously any more, but if we did it would strike us as fantastic that the main effort of the intellect of an entire continent should for many years have been concentrated on the rather narrow business of criticizing a single art. It seems as though something must have flared up and flourished there for a while, like a comet, and then died down to almost nothing. And that is exactly what happened, although it was a very great and important thing that flared up.

Those years in which the intellect of Europe was concentrated on "criticism" were the years in which the scientific investigation was gradually differentiating itself from the literary discussion of human nature. The psychological and social sciences were coming to birth. And those great critics were, at first, forerunners of these sciences, and then afterwards mediators between them and the general body of intellectual literature from which they had not moved too far away. In Taine, indeed, with his essay on "Intelligence," his ardent and too straitened effort to "explain" English literature on grounds of race, milieu and moment, you see the last of that old breed of masters merging into the new. In Anatole France, too, with his quaint combination of cynicism in literature and scientific socialism in life—the latter always conveniently forgotten by those pseudo-moralists who pounce upon him—you see this birth of a new kind of leader taking place. In Brunetière, launching himself with a false imitation of science, a kind of Origin of Literary Species, and coming to port with a visit to the Vatican and a cry against science in the name of the "supremacy absolute" of art, philosophy and religion, you see the same process failing to take place. And in William James—if I may speculate a little—you see the same process completed. James had all the gifts and motives both of heart and brain that made those great humane critics of the years preceding him. Born a little earlier, it is not hard to imagine that he would have been one of them—he would have been, that is, exactly what he was, a great student of human life. But the study of human life was dividing from the art of literature in his time, was growing specialized and intensive, building laboratories, becoming a science and a profession wholly divorced from art. And James was alert and alive in his own times, and therefore instead of another great "literary critic," we had a great psychologist with poetry on his pen.

It is natural that this new division of labor, involving the decline of a liberal profession, should have filled our libraries with "theories" as to the precise function and importance of this profession. Almost anybody these days who publishes an essay or two on the poets, or writes a thesis for an M.A. degree in English, will offer you a new "theory of criticism." T. S. Eliot has adopted two opposite views of criticism at different points in his career, graciously acknowledging his earlier mistake, and continuing to write exactly the same kind of criticism after the change that he did before. The whole argument resounds like a hollow thing. It is carried on with the intense earnestness of a talk at a tea-party where everybody is indeed earnest, but only with a dread lest there be no talk at all. The business which made literary critics great and important in times gone by—the business of understanding human nature—has been taken over by experts and left them with empty minds and hands. That is why they are talking so earnestly and so little to the point.

The very phrase "theory of criticism" belongs in my opinion, along with Brunetière's theory of literary evolution, not to the scientific study of literature but to the literary imitations of science. It is one of the minor stratagems by which men of letters, while holding aloof and insisting upon their superiority to organized knowledge, try to appropriate a little of its growing authority. A theory in the usual meaning of the term is an idea advanced to explain what something is or why it occurs. The so-called theories of criticism do not pretend to explain why criticism occurs; if they did they would go to the depths of psychology at one plunge. Nor do they attempt to define what it is; if they did, they could hardly fail to remark that it is everything they are arguing about. It is historical, æsthetic, dogmatic, philosophical, impressionistic, constructive, destructive, prescriptive, plastic, subjective, objective, evolutionary, biographical, religious, moral, rational, judicial, admirative, interpretative, personal, impersonal, social, political, economic, typographical, and even—once in a while—creative. People who are interested in books talk about them in all the ways that people who are interested in things do talk about those things. They always have and they always will. That would be, I should think, the beginning of a "theory of criticism." And I do not see why a person choosing to emphasize one of these ways of talking, or expressing his preference for it, if he were not trying to magnify the reverberations of the act, should not be content to describe it as a method.

J. E. Spingarn's formula, "Creative Criticism," is the most ingenious of these inventions, and most clearly reveals the emotional anxiety underlying them. Mr. Spingarn believes it is an "age-long self-contempt" from which he wishes to set criticism free, but we may be sure that so oppressive a sense of that contempt, and so bold a liberating stroke as to lift up the critic side by side with the artist as a creator, would hardly have come to his mind, had not criticism possessed in the past some really independent function which is slipping from it. Sensitive to the decline of a great profession—and naturally so, being a member of it—Mr. Spingarn casts about for some formula with which he may restore it to the heights. And with an audacity, as well as an erudite and easy grace of style, which can hardly fail to evoke admiration, he finds it in a declaration of the "unity of genius and taste."

"When Criticism first propounded as its real concern the oft-repeated question: 'What has the poet tried to express and how has he expressed it?' Criticism prescribed for itself the only possible method. How can the critic answer this question without becoming (if only for a moment of supreme power) at one with the creator? That is to say, taste must reproduce the work of art within itself in order to understand and judge it; and at that moment æsthetic judgment becomes nothing more nor less than creative art itself. The identity of genius and taste is the final achievement of modern thought on the subject of art, and it means that fundamentally, in their most significant moments, the creative and the critical instincts are one and the same."

It is hardly necessary to prick this engaging bubble of sophistry; it is light enough, and also sufficiently disconnected with what is substantially going on, to float up of itself in time and disappear. If in finding out what the poet was trying to express and how, the critic becomes one with the poet, and his judgment identical with the creative art, then what does the critic add besides his rather cumbersome presence to an already quite adequate situation? In attempting to exalt the critic so high, Mr. Spingarn has reduced him to nothing at all—or nothing at least but a highly self-satisfied mirror. Astonishing as it may seem, he himself concludes his panegyric by describing the art of Criticism as just a superfluous thing.

"Intellectual curiosity may amuse itself," he says, "by asking its little questions of the silent sons of light, but they vouchsafe no answer to art's pale shadow, thought; the gods are kind if they give up their secret in another work of art, the art of Criticism, that serves as some sort of mirror to the art of literature, only because in their flashes of insight taste and genius are one."

I do not suppose Mr. Spingarn fully realized in the eloquence of his peroration that he was solemnly asserting that literary critics do not think. Goethe, Lessing, Joubert, Sainte-Beuve, Renan, Arnold, Pater, Gourmont, Taine, France—all those men who for Arnold represented the main effort of the intellect of Europe for many years—are to be relieved of their "self-contempt" by the comforting assurance that they were not thinking after all, but doing something else so much nobler and more important, as standing up like "some sort of mirror" in front of a work of art so that anybody who comes around can see it by looking both ways. When Mr. Spingarn is accused by Paul Elmer More of having an "impressionistic" view of criticism, he becomes very indignant and we find on our tables a "Spingarn Enchiridion" setting forth the injustice that has been done him. And he is quite right, for he has opposed impressionism—and opposed, moreover, all the implications of this particular peroration.

Nevertheless, it stands there, this declaration of the unity of genius and taste, meaning very little but that Mr. Spingarn is worried about the declining prestige of his profession.

So long as the division of labor between poetry and science in the writing of books about human nature was not clear and sharp, the man called literary critic had a twofold function. He was, like the critic of painting or music, a man who chose among experiences offered by artists in language—a man who had specialized in the reception of these experiences and was, to some extent, delegated by the less gifted or less fortunate to choose for them. But he was also a man who judged of the validity of opinions and hypotheses *about* experience; he was a critic both of high common sense and of the beginnings of several sciences. And while yet those beginnings had not diverged too far from the art of literature, and required no very technical training for their mastery, he was indeed a great figure. What Matthew Arnold said about the intellect of Europe was not a perfectly fantastic exaggeration.

Now, however, the investigation of the mind and of human behavior and of men in society has become too intense a practical enterprise, too highly special, to be criticized by a mere brilliant intelligence whose distinguishing gift and business after all is—in the excellent language of W. C. Brownell—to *signalize qualities.* As the poetic and scientific uses of language diverge, the functions of the critic diverge also, and here too a division of labor is set up. We have our critics of science—our Bertrand Russells and John Deweys and Clarence I. Lewises, called philosophers for short, but philosophers far less than Kant was who called himself a critic—and we have our critics of literary art, our Middleton Murrays and T. S. Eliots and Elmer Mores and J. E. Spingarns, very little troubled by the advance of science and very little troubling it. These latter men are not satisfied to fall to the level of the critic of pure art—and indeed they cannot quite do so, for true or false knowledge of things named is fatally involved in any use of names—but they are also not willing to study science. They cling to a position and aspire toward a prestige that no longer exists. This is what causes them to make up all sorts of fantastic "theories of criticism," and invent strange intermediary spheres of being, which are neither science nor poetry, neither knowledge nor yet ignorance, and even in their dire groping and dismay descend to the disaster of boasting that they do not think.

The true problem for those who wish to make a profession of talking about books in an age of specialization, is the problem what kind of training will enable them without becoming quite superficial dilettantes—for in such an age we are all dilettantes—to talk sensitively about the qualities, and at the same time intelligently about the knowledge, that reaches us through books. In what way, and to what extent, can these two functions of the literary critic, which are splitting so obstinately and yet inexactly apart, be recombined. And if they cannot be recombined, what shall we do about it?

The critic of literature as poetry must have a special and mature gift for receiving and entering into the experiences that are conveyed by words. This gift can be developed by a large reading of poetic literature, a reading which to be rich and sympathetic requires a certain knowledge of history, an ability at least to tell time on the clock of ages. But it can also be developed by studying and learning the manner in which words convey experiences, by studying the psychology of poetry. A good many people are scornful of the idea that you can teach the reading of poetry. You can teach the reading of poetry just as well as you can teach swimming, if besides knowing how to do it you know how it is done. The trouble is that the teachers of poetry, still feeling that technical and real knowledge is an assault upon the prerogatives of their profession, refuse to have any traffic with the science which could tell them how it is done. In a few years it will seem incredible that a man who stands up before us as our high teacher and guide in the matter of poetic literature, a Paul Elmer More, should reject with a scornful epithet the effort of a psychologist like I. A. Richards to discover in what manner poetry accomplishes its effects. In any other sphere of being or activity in the entire range of life we should dismiss such a teacher from our consideration as an obscurantist, a man without ardent aspiration, without faith in the mind. In a literary critic we tolerate it, because these critics, these pseudo-moralists defending the prestige of their profession with high talk of the inner life, have intimidated us with the word "pseudo-science," and are still making us half-heartedly believe that they occupy some celestial intermediary sphere, loftier than real knowledge and understanding, although less lofty than the creations of the poets. We must lay aside all this motivated nonsense, and recognize that the critic of the experience which comes to us from books ought to understand how it comes.

To what extent this same man can be a critic of knowledge is no small question. It is amusing that Matthew Arnold, who defined literature as all the knowledge that reaches us through books, and poetry as that speech in which man comes nearest to being able to utter truth, nevertheless gave warning of the danger to the critic that comes from having too much knowledge! "To handle these matters properly, there is needed a poise so perfect that the least overweight in any direction tends to destroy the balance . . . even erudition may destroy it. Little as I know therefore, I am always apprehensive, in dealing with poetry, lest even that little should 'prove too much for my abilities.'" Which shows that Arnold had a good deal more sagacity than is contained in the awfully homiletical language in which he felt obliged to talk about literary art. Poetry is not knowledge, and aside from the psychology of poetry itself, which if it is a valid psychology can only assist in the appreciation of it, scientific learning is not what the critic of poetry primarily wants. The division of labor here, as even Arnold saw, is inexorable.

But there is also a division of labor within the sphere occupied by the critic of knowledge. It is obvious that one critic cannot give valid judgments about all the information—even leaving highly technical matters aside—which comes up importantly in the reading of a modern intelligent public. And accordingly we find our professional critics more and more acting as mere major-generals of a whole army of critics, each ready to be called on for judgment of a certain kind of book. This increasing specialization itself shows how the grand intellectual supremacy of the critic of literature-in-general has with the advance of humane science inevitably dwindled and crumbled away. Nevertheless, there remains the function of this major-general, the task of choosing and guiding—and blue-pencilling—all those specialists. There remains also a vast realm of writing in which opinions are either expounded or else taken for granted which lie beyond the outposts of systematic knowledge. There remain speculation and conjecture and the delight of the mind in ideas for their own sake. It is only a tendency we are discussing. Ideas valuable to any science may be born anywhere, and in general anything may happen in the world of literature as in other worlds, if people will only keep alive. But this all only the more forcibly demonstrates that our critic of knowledge in general, who has now become our general manager of critics, must have a wide acquaintance with many sciences, a keen sense of the method of science and the nature of its validity—and he must have, if he is ever to rival those great men of the past, a certain standing in the scientific world. The only way he can possibly achieve these two latter things, and save the former from being pitiful in its flightiness, is to ground himself solidly in some one branch of science. He will naturally choose, I suppose, unless accidents have led him in some other direction, a branch of what I have called the humane sciences, a science treating of the nature and behavior of men. It is appropriate for a critic of knowledge in general to be an expert in some branch of psychology or sociology, for the acquisition of knowledge is a part of the behavior of men, and is immediately conditioned by social and economic movements. Here at any rate arises the sole possibility of again combining in one great intellectual leader the critic of literature as poetry and the critic of the knowledge that reaches us through books. He would have to be a great psychologist, an authority in language, a specialist in understanding the manner in which both experience and knowledge are brought to us by books.

It may be that science will outgrow the capacities of men, and that a more loose and literary guesswork will prevail widely even where true knowledge is possible, but that will not be because of the superiority of such guesswork but because of the inferiority of men. To resist the farthest possible advance of every science into the sphere of humane letters, in the name of those great men called literary critics in the nineteenth century, who were heralds and forerunners of the process, is pedantry and obscurantism of the darkest kind. Norman Foerster has a great deal to say about the "lamentable state of our critical journals" and the "caprice and aimlessness of our criticism," and he thinks it will never be cured until critics apply "learning and the passion for truth to the study of the universal and unchanging in man." But if I show him Edward Thorndyke's classical investigation into "The Original Nature of Man," he will call it "pseudo-psychology," and sniff and walk away. And if I run after him, bringing in my hand Professor Jennings's recent book on *The Biological Basis of Human Nature,* and if I insist upon reading to him Professor Jennings's assertion that, "Anyone who declines the labor of becoming familiar with the fundamental features of the genetic system and its method of operation cuts himself off from the possibility of understanding the nature of man," he will perhaps not call this "pseudo-biology," and he will perhaps not sniff either, but he will walk away. He will walk away to his own "department" and sit behind his own desk. There is no understanding the New Humanism until you realize that those elusive barriers between the different "levels of being" are identical with the walls of the department of "Literature" in our colleges and universities.

It is quite true that our critical journals are lamentable, and that they will be so until critics have applied learning and passion for truth to the study of man. Both as critics of poetry and critics of prose they should serve their apprenticeship in this study. But instead of resisting as hostile and a kind of blasphemy the penetration here of the search for verified and valid knowledge, they should welcome it as a fulfillment of the sacred promise of humane letters. They have no other choice but to do this, or to let literary criticism dwindle and die away until it is generally regarded as a harmless parlor entertainment or a rudimentary survival like alchemy and the quack forms of therapeutics. I remember once meeting on the many-colored sidewalks of Greenwich Village a hawk-faced blade in a minister's coat who seized my hand and introduced himself with the words: "You are a literary man, aren't you? I'm in that line, myself, I'm an astrologer." I felt that I was pursuing a different line, but I do not see how those critics can, who are trying in the name of a study of the "unchanging in man" to resist the investigations of science into man's fundamental nature. By opposing instead of accommodating themselves to an inevitable division of labor, they are making of their profession a damage and a drag upon our civilization. We cannot put our literary critics in jail, I suppose, for practising without a diploma in psychology or sociology. We shall have to rely upon the milder pressure of an educated opinion. But we might begin exerting that pressure by reminding them that if they have not been licensed and jailed on this basis long ago, it is only because their function is of so much less assured and clear importance than the practice of dentistry or medicine.

V

THE TEACHER OF LITERATURE

THERE is no great difference between a teacher of literature and a literary critic, except that the teacher is more important because he talks to younger people and for the same reason more likely to fall asleep. Accordingly we find the same anxious turmoil among teachers these days that we do among critics. We find the "literary scholar," in the troubled pages of Norman Foerster, seeking an "avenue of escape" from a "besetting sense of superficiality." Professor Foerster does not deceive himself, as Mr. Spingarn does in the case of the critic, that this self-depreciation is "age-old." He is too brightly confronted with the modern cause of it, the "scientific hierachy still entrenched in our colleges and universities." "We are blinded," he cries, "with excess of scientific light." And what it means to a sensitive person to be blinded by scientific light is stated by a less high-flying professor of English, Howard Mumford Jones, as follows: "The professor's colleagues in science or psychology or mathematics . . . view him indulgently as one engaged in a futile but harmless game—something like chess, and about as important." In reading these complaints from present-day teachers of literature, remember that in 1899 Thorstein Veblen was still attacking the "position of prerogative in the scheme of the Higher Learning" accorded to the humanities, and explaining why the classics are "esteemed the most honorific of all learning." It will give you some sense of the rapid growth of interest in verified knowledge, and if you are wise with any of Veblen's wisdom, some intimation of the folly of standing against it.

At any rate the professors of literature are now plainly on the defensive, and may be seen from time to time peeping under the lids of their reading desks, and poking around in all the corners of their departments and among their old papers, trying to find out if they can just what "subject" it is they are teaching. Is it history, philology, anthropology, sociology, philosophy, ethics? It cannot very well be any of those things because they are all more competently taught in other departments. And yet in a way it seems to be all of them together and a good deal more too. If we take but a hint from Matthew Arnold's definition of literature as "all the knowledge that reaches us through books"—even without adding to it, as in accurate conscience we must, "all the ignorance too"—it will be evident that, whatever indeed the professors of literature may be doing, they are not indulging in a harmless game. It behooves us, I think, for their sakes as well as our offspring's, to look into this matter very soberly and find out if possible what, if anything, the professors of literature are teaching. After that we may be able to suggest what they ought to teach.

Among these professors themselves the turmoil assumes the form of a sort of class struggle. The patricians led by Norman Foerster, with such astute aides beyond the campus as Henry Seidel Canby, maintain the old inviolable superiority to mere facts of the "higher activities of scholarship." The specific nature of these activities Professor Foerster illumines a little by describing them as "an earnest study of the unchanging." But Mr. Canby outside the walls, realizing that the unchanging, although by definition still with us, is no longer very good journalism, describes them in a more lively way as "imagination, intuition, emotion and prophecy." Facing these genteel advocates of what is "beyond proof though not beyond reason," we have the plebeian hordes led by the redoubtable Edwin Greenlaw, who insists that the study of literature is not a hot air—I am slightly paraphrasing him—but a "learning," and that the method of learning is "research, understanding by means of investigation." Professor Greenlaw does not in the least mind being told that he "apes scientific methods," nor that he buries the "higher" faculties of his soul in an accumulation of mere historical facts. He declares on the contrary that if his opponents realize their longing to "make the study of literature purely literary" they will end by putting it out of business altogether. "No mere pedagogical debate is involved in this matter . . ." he cries. "Nothing less than the position of the humanistic studies, their right to survive, is at stake." And Professor Greenlaw has an invaluable aide in Howard Mumford Jones, who distinguishes himself among all teachers by discussing, when he writes, the actual problems of teaching—the amount of time the student of average brain and income can afford to spend on "imagination, intuition, emotion and prophecy," if he is to learn in the graduate school what he was supposed to learn as an undergraduate, and then also acquire "a sense of chronology, the historicity of events," a mere acquaintance with the methods of research, and "a knowledge of the development of the mother tongue and of the changing meaning of words." "I cannot admit," says Professor Jones, "that any portion of what I have outlined may be omitted from the training and discipline of the graduate student without damage so serious to the end and purpose of graduate training as to negate its value—that end and purpose being, as I understand it, the discovery and statement of essential truths regarding literature as it has been written by men."

I think we might summarize the conflict between these two war-camps of professors by saying that the "Left" wants literature to be made an object of investigation somewhat in the manner of ultra-violet rays or fossils or fish or chromosomes or dementia præcox or anything else. If they really cast loose and achieved all that they sometimes seem to be talking for, they would no longer be professors of literature,—not any more than an ichthyologist is a professor of fish. They would be professors of literaturology—a word so hybrid and horrendous that perhaps they would consent to call it literology for short. The members of the "Right," on the other hand, rigidly insist upon being professors of literature, and they decline to have literature placed in the same category with fish, flesh, fowl, minerals, manias, mother-complexes or anything else whatever that is a mere *object* of study. They want literature to continue a subject.

Now in order to make literature a subject, or keep it so in the face of those increasingly sceptical glances from across the campus, you have to find for it an object. And you have to find one a little more plausible in this age of specialization than that suggested in the phrase "all the knowledge that reaches us through books." You might of course frankly announce yourself Professor of a Smattering of All Knowledge, and that would certainly give you a plenty to do, but it would take all the fine edge from your title of "scholar," and moreover it would get you into undignified trouble with the philosophy department where they have an old and divine sanction for smattering. There is nothing for you to do really, as a gentleman and a scholar of literature, but to declare most emphatically that literature is not all the knowledge that reaches us through books, but is a special kind of knowledge of a special kind of thing, and then go out and make up some fairy-story which will enable you to identify that kind of knowledge or that kind of thing. It is this fairy-story that Professor Foerster and Mr. Canby, and all the host of the Patricians whom I have somewhat arbitrarily selected them to represent, are so fervently and ingeniously trying to make up.

They do not of course all make up the same story, and in fact every one of them has made up two or three conflicting stories, but that only goes to show how resolute they are and how desperate the situation with which they are confronted. I have made a little collection of forty-three different ways in which these teachers of literature as a subject describe what its object is, or how it differs from anything that can possibly become an object of scientific knowledge. Of course the simplest way to do this is to define scientific knowledge in some antique or fantastic manner which quite obviously leaves the whole study of everything bright and interesting to humane letters. Professor Foerster begins by asserting that "in its true function science is merely descriptive," which of course is neither true nor adequate to his purpose, and so he adds immediately that it "interests itself properly in the mechanical aspects of reality." But that too is hardly enough, and he soon adds that science is purely quantitative, that "as soon as one passes beyond this quantitative universe . . . one ceases to be a scientist." That Professor Foerster does not seriously mean anything by these old-fashioned remarks about science, becomes evident a few pages later when he tells us that philology as "a genuine science" has enabled us to interpret the subtle nuances of Greek words in Aristotle's *Poetics*. It becomes still more evident when he describes as "scientific" that kind of literary history which explains the relations in which a work arose—not purely quantitative relations, one would suppose, nor "properly mechanical," the history that explains them certainly not "merely descriptive" but the opposite. A little farther on this criterion too is forgotten, and we learn that "externality" is what distinguishes science. Everything is explained and taken care of by the "externality of science" and the "inwardness of art." Still a few pages and we find ourselves in a world where "scientific method" is distinguished from the method of literary wisdom by the absence in science of a certain faculty, not identifiable to logic or psychology, but known to polite letters as "natural sense." Lastly—or one would hope lastly, for there are only sixty-seven pages in this little book—we are told that "literature is more than science, since, unlike science, it is itself selective, critical." And then just at the very tip end we are reminded that what distinguishes the scientific historian from the literary scholar is that the scientist studies only change, whereas the business of the scholar is with "an earnest study of the unchanging."

These gems from *The American Scholar* do not by any means exhaust Professor Foerster's fertility in devising ways for keeping science out of the sacred precincts of literature. Science, he tells us in another book, is interested only in "things done, phenomenal happenings viewed in retrospect." Science also gives us a "motion picture of reality" in which "there are no values." Science moreover believes in "the final validity of reason," whereas literature has a similar confidence in "intellect"—at least I infer this from the statement that "the value of supernatural intuition must be tested by the intellect."

I must refrain, of course, from trotting out all the curios in my collection. Here is one which I culled from an essay by Professor L. T. More: "The false pretenses of science must be wholly abandoned, and the problems of our destiny be examined by a wise judgment drawn from human experience." As though science had not been fighting three hundred years to get experience recognized as the source of all wise judgment! And here is another from the same essay: "The fundamental definition of science excludes the processes of consciousness from its field, for it assumes that objective phenomena are to be interpreted by the mind. If we attempt to study the mind objectively, then we come face to face with the absurd paradox of a thing investigating itself by means of itself." The curious thing about this argument when examined closely is that it locates the superiority of literature to science not in that literature studies things *subjectively,* but that it studies them *with something else besides the mind.* Just what that something else is, I cannot imagine, unless it is the pen. *The pen is mightier than the mind,* would be a good motto for all these highly literary professors.

But let us turn now to Mr. Canby, and examine the six or seven ways in which he would distinguish science from literature. The function of science, he tells us, is to "measure fact," to "uncover the nature of *things,*" to "provide a technique for the control of nature itself." The function of literature, as we have seen, is "imagination, intuition, emotion and prophecy." But if intuition does not uncover the nature of things or enable us to control nature, what does it do that is worth doing? And how without imagination and prophecy can nature be controlled? Mr. Canby seems to have sensed some loose-jointedness in his own classifications here, for he places a semicolon after the word prophecy, and then cries out in what seems to me a kind of desperation that literature "is instinct with beauty, and the power of ideas." But if science provides "control," and literature the "power of ideas," what again has become of our distinction? It seems indeed to have doubled back on itself and mixed things up most astonishingly in Mr. Canby's eloquent conclusion, where he actually attributes to literature the rôle of "explanation." If we do not abandon the mere recording of literary history, he predicts, and take up the study of literature itself, "our masters, the scientists," will "return from beyond the atom to seek in the only perfect expression of mind, which is literature, some explanation of phenomena irreducible by law and experiment."

Is it not obvious in all this jumble of devout nonsense that the professors are not trying to think out a distinction, but trying by not thinking to convince themselves that a distinction exists? They are trying to convince themselves that literature is not and cannot become an object of investigation by science, but must remain a subject on a par with science having its own object. In my opinion they have but one argument in all their collection that would stand up under a ray of clear daylight, and that is the statement that scientific knowledge has to do with fact and literature with value. If I were Professor Foerster and felt called to marshal the right wing of the professors of literature in a last stand against science, I would summon them all together at an international conference in Geneva, and I would say: "My most learned friends and colleagues, we have already supplied the public with forty-three definitions of the difference between science and literature, and the public instead of waking up to the difference is going fast asleep in our faces, suspecting I fear that forty-three definitions of one and the same thing are as good as none at all. I urge you therefore in the name of mere political expediency and at whatever sacrifice to literary truth, that you appoint a committee to go over the whole stock of definitions we have so far produced and see if they cannot find one upon which we can each collect himself and then all unite together. And as a candidate for this distinguished position I respectfully urge upon your attention that one of mine where I say that literature is interested in values and science is not, for I believe that that is the most intricate and the most abstruse of all, and the one upon which we are most likely to get help from the philosophy department. I cordially invite you all therefore to rally round this definition, and I propose three cheers for the Judgment of Value." In this way, it seems to me, the right wing could keep up for a time a certain interest in confused thinking, not only in the English department, but in the world outside as well.

In the long run, however, even here they would have to yield. For there is no such thing as a judgment of value in the sense that they need it. There are judgments that things are valuable, but those are judgments of fact. And there is the judgment as to what value is, but that also is a judgment of fact. Aside from this what we call a judgment of value is nothing in the last analysis, and when all factual judgments have been eliminated from it, but an act of choice. This is not difficult to see if you stay out of those exalted regions called ethical or æsthetic, where emotions not having to do with the essence of the problem come in and confuse us with their clouds of glory. If you and I were a couple of brakemen walking the top of a freight train, and I shouted to you "Low bridge, you better duck your head!" the problem of fact and value would be involved in its whole scope and complexity. I state a fact—the bridge is low; and I imply a value —*better* duck your head. But suppose you disagree with me and show a disposition to argue the question. Your argument may take two forms. You may deny that the bridge is low enough or you high enough to require ducking, in which case only science can settle the matter—science in its most despised form of "measuring facts." If I happen to be informed that all the bridges on this section of the road have a five-foot clearance, that is scientific knowledge, and will probably convince you that you would "better" duck your head. The betterness, however, derives not only from my knowledge but from your wish, from what is assumed by us both, that you do not *choose*—as Coolidge would profoundly say—to bump your head against a bridge. Suppose, however, that you do choose to do this. Suppose that you have been reading Pascal who "plumbed the depths of man's moral nature," and, all filled up to the brim with literary truth, you have decided as he did that you would be better for a few bumps. "All right, I see," you shout back, "but I want to bump my head." Here surely is a situation which calls for judgments of value from me, if I have any, and calls swiftly. But I have none. All I can possibly do in this case as in the other is to urge you to *measure the facts*. When you did not choose to bump your head, it was the bridge we were to measure, and I had not your will to improve but only your mind. But when you do choose to bump your head it is the bump we must measure, and we must measure it from all possible points of view, and find out in what relation it stands to your past and your future and to your friends and to the world and to everything in the world in which you are interested. But that too, in so far as it is valid and systematic, is science. It is judgments of fact. Nor is this anywise altered by talking about "Standards of Value," for standards are a mere shorthand by which this long process of argumentation may be handily reduced and not every time wholly gone through with—most especially handy in this case because all I had time to say was "Don't be a damned fool!"

This simple and straight way of thinking about values, so natural to the Greeks, will be one of the last things we come back to, I suppose, as we emerge from the reign of otherworldliness. But we shall come back to it. The Patrician professors will find it impossible to give ultimate battle even upon Standards and the Judgment of Value. They will find no choice in the long run but to declare themselves either professors of a smattering of all knowledge, or professors of the knowledge that is not yet known.

Edwin Greenlaw is accurately right when he declares that "nothing less than the position of the humanistic studies, their right to survive, is at stake." And he is right in connecting the desperate position of these studies with their smug superiority to mere fact and their intolerance of scientific method. But if we turn to him and his cohorts of the "Left" for some clear championship of the advance of scientific method into the sphere occupied by these studies, we shall be sadly disappointed. All that Professor Greenlaw's argument does is to flirt with the terminology of science, and take a sufficiently bold tone against the Patricians to catch our confidence, and then turn us over bound hand and foot to the enemy. I have likened this professorial duel to a conflict of classes—a comparison which is not purely pictorial, for an association between scientific progress and the revolt of the masses against privilege is indubitable. And I cannot better define Professor Greenlaw's "historic mission," as they say in Russia, than to liken it to that of the leaders of the so-called "revolutionary democracy" in the revolutions of 1917. Abstractly they adopted the slogans of the revolting masses—expropriation and the conquest of power by the proletariat—but in every concrete issue of importance they clung to the essentials of the old property rights and the rule of their declared enemy, the bourgeoisie. They thus only prolonged the life of the old system, confusing millions of people, risking a military dictatorship, and making more difficult the triumph of the proletarian party. In a similar way Professor Greenlaw has adopted the slogans of science but clings loyally to every position that will safeguard the separate dominion of "literary truth." His book on *The Province of Literary History,* instead of overthrowing his avowed enemies, the New Humanists, will only cloud the issue and prolong their sway.

"Research," "mastery of fact," "understanding by investigation"—these words take a bold sound in his opening pages, and we think we are about to see advocated at last a department of science which will have literature as its object of study. But instead of thus facing the contemporary situation, Professor Greenlaw, as though frightened by his own voice dropping such words in the hallowed chambers of the Humanities, flies back into the past for another word which will deny their meaning, and quiet their echoes, and patch up any injury they may have done. He flies back to Francis Bacon—great man who stood just on the brink of the division between science and literature—and from him borrows that magic word "Learning," the one word in the world which will enable him to ignore the division, re-fog the issue, and turn over the sovereignty in a confusion of mind that is still essentially mediæval to the defenders of humane letters. "The investigation of literature may be permitted to talk like science," he says in effect, "but that does not mean that it is a science. Oh no, do not misunderstand me! It is a learning. The sciences are also learnings. But *so is poetry!* And thus everything remains as before."

Or to put it more respectfully, and more in his own words: We must not be awed by the "pretence of understanding without investigation" put up by those professors of the purely literary school; their scorn for our hard-headed investigation into the facts of literary history is like that of superstitious people in the Middle Ages to whom "scientific investigation . . . seemed . . . to be traffic with Satan." Scorning them in return, we must devote ourselves to the "disinterested pursuit of truth in the effort of man to understand his environment." But *on the other hand,* we must not fall into the error of Taine with his "false conception of history as a science, a view formerly held by many historians but now thoroughly discredited." We must remember—and here is the forty-fourth jewel in my collection—that "scientific research . . . penetrates the mysteries of the physical universe. The humanities, dealing with the phenomena of personality, pursue analogous researches, and, like the sciences, constitute a learning." I glance up from this pronunciamento to the shelves of my library and without a motion of my head I read the titles of three books of science devoted to research into the phenomena of personality. They happen to be *The Psychology of Character,* by Doctor A. A. Roback, National Research Council Fellow in the Biological Sciences, Instructor in Psychology at Harvard University, *The Neurotic Personality,* by R. G. Gordon, M.D., D. Sc., F.R.C.P., and *Problems of Personality,* by Doctor C. G. Jung of the University of Zurich; but they might be any one of a thousand books which could not by the wildest stretch of imagination be described, in contradistinction to science, as literature. It is the existence of these books that forces Professor Greenlaw and the professors of the Left to demand that the department of literature go in for the investigation of facts. But instead of taking his stand side by side with these books, and voicing the demand in its full scope and meaning, he borrows their gesture and intonation only, or certain phrases that they speak, and by bringing these out resoundingly, manœuvres himself into a middle position between the two actual forces in conflict. In this position, whatever his intention, he will function only as a buffer, delaying a settlement of the real issue.

It is not necessary to decide whether history is a science—although the answer to that question depends, I suspect, upon whether you read history with a view to doing something about it or not. A mere preliminary glimpse of the fringes of science in their approach to history would be enough to convince you that in writing the history of a particular thing, it would be well to determine in a precise way and with words that have meaning, what thing it is whose history you are writing. Professor Greenlaw defines literature as the "*spiritual* reaction of man to his environment," thus with one word which has no factual reference withdrawing the whole topic from the possibility of a genuine "understanding by investigation." He endorses Wordsworth's definition of poetry as "the breath and finer spirit of all knowledge," not seeing that this phrase was but a stage in the slow dying out of the view prevalent from Spenser to Milton that poetry is knowledge itself. And then after so defining poetry he raises a little fog-screen of eloquence, and when the fog lifts we find before us the same definition, or what he evidently expects us to take for the same definition, with the word *experience* slipped into the place of the word knowledge. "Poetry is the breath and finer spirit of . . . experience." This prestidigitatory or sliding-panel definition is the very last word, in this year of our Lord 1931, on the ancient question: What is poetry? And it is but one more step forward in that same dying out of the confusion of poetic literature with the literature of knowledge. As though in fear lest someone should see this, Professor Greenlaw recoils from his own too clear statement, and leaves us with the remembrance that poetry is "distilled and concentrated experience transformed into spiritual reality." And with this safely meaningless definition of what he is going to investigate and write the history of, he invites us to study literary history in a spirit of "understanding by investigation."

Is it so tragic in view of all this, if what Stuart Sherman said of our graduate schools in English is true?

"The very best men do not enter upon graduate study at all; the next best drop out after a year's experiment; the mediocre men at the end of two years; the most unfit survive and become doctors of philosophy, who go forth and reproduce their kind." It shows merely that the passion for knowledge is genuine in those who elect to pursue it.

If these professors of the Left would but take their own slogans seriously and believe in them, this pitiable and unseemly situation in the schools of literature would be healed naturally and in the way in which it must be healed. "Research," "mastery of fact," "understanding by investigation"—those words are the definition of science. If they were adopted in their full meaning and applied throughout the whole department, beginning at the word "literature" printed on the door, we should not have a department of humane letters any longer, but a branch of the department of humane sciences. It would be most directly a branch of psychology, for psychology is the science which can alone define literature and explain its forms and mechanisms in the more immediate relations in which they arise. But it would entail, more than most branches of psychology, an acquaintance with all that comes under the head of social science. For the movements of social forces that condition a work of literature are often more important than the motives of the individual which cause it.

It is for this very reason, of course, that Professor Foerster and all his colleagues of the Right Wing—differ as they may about such trivial things as God and the policies of the state—are solidary in the opinion that sociology and psychology are "pseudo-sciences," mere bastards and pretenders to any place whatever in the hierarchy of true knowledge. And it is for this same reason that the professors of the Left, while so boldly eloquent about research and investigation, and while even defending the importance of biography among the facts investigated by the literary historian, are studious to ignore the very existence of a science of the mind and motives of men. "Neither philology nor philosophy nor humanism nor social history nor textual criticism," says Howard Mumford Jones, "can utter the final word as to what literature in its essence truly is . . . and . . . by no formula however lofty or scientific or philosophical, will any of us determine why men write books or want to read them." Perhaps it is true that we shall never exactly determine that, but a more peculiar thing is that none of the sciences mentioned in this catalogue will ever even approach the question or attempt to determine it, whereas it belongs most obviously to the psychologists to make that attempt and they are making it. Professor Jones stands, I suspect, considerably to the left of Professor Greenlaw, and he has been riotous enough to tear some very sad-looking holes in the reputation of Irving Babbitt for accurate scholarship, but even he, although describing the purpose of graduate study in English as "the discovery . . . of essential truths regarding literature as it has been written by men," ignores utterly in outlining the program for such study the existence of a science of human behavior.

Nobody will pretend that psychology is more than an infant science, or that anything called sociology is altogether mature. Neither of these disciplines will have an overwhelming array of square-cornered ultimatums to deliver if admitted into the literary sanctum. But does not that make it all the easier to welcome them in? Is it not a little mysterious that scholars should recoil and cry out against the inquiring spirit of a developing science in the name of intellect and knowledge and the higher interests of the mind? There are two principal things which explain the mystery. One is that these scholars are of a certain profession, the experts in science are of another profession, and that makes it seem as though in welcoming a more integrated kind of inquiry into their field they would be welcoming themselves out of a job. They would at least be losing an extraordinary prestige that has attached to their jobs in the past. The other is that, being primarily interested in literature as an art, they dwell far more than those do whose primary interest is knowledge, in the past. And since in the past the distinction between science and literature really did not exist—the best truth available *was* largely thought out or guessed at by poets—they simply do not know how to accommodate themselves to the modern scene. They cling, with a loyal motive and a genuine concern for what is beautiful and good, to the opinion that literature is truth in a sense that science cannot be. They will continue to do so until they become conscious of the history of literature as that of a change in this very particular, a gradual splitting apart of the art which they love from the knowledge which they love as a part of it. Once they adopt into their minds enough science to see this process of change in the past, a main source of their resistance against science in the present will disappear.

The fact is that if the professors of humane letters, both Left and Right, should some fine morning draw a great breath of courage and take a plunge down the one "avenue of escape" from their "besetting sense of superficiality" which in a clear view of things can be said to exist—if they should take up, namely, the study of the humane sciences, beginning with psychology—they would find that not only this problem of adjusting the present to the past, but also the professional problem, and even to some extent the problem of superior prestige, would quite magically solve themselves. For psychology itself is sufficiently specialized and divided up in its labors so that a whole branch of it is, or may well be, devoted to the understanding of the uses of language in literature. If the professors would, at whatever cost to their knowledge of the birth-dates of the poets, humbly learn and appropriate all that psychology has to say about this general subject, they would find themselves in possession of a systematic and developing science, merging with others, and not in the least to be looked down on by them as "a futile and harmless game." As professors of this science they might in fact hand down some very important information to their colleagues in mathematical physics, for it is indubitable that a certain part of the problem with which this science is now wrestling is a problem of expression. They could moreover still insist, and with plausibility, that besides being professors of a science that stands up on a par with all others, they are something more than professors and have, if they choose to say so, a "higher activity" to perform. The activity would not be higher in the sense of being more aristocratic, or more elegant, or more scholarly, or more closely associated with the Most High God and with the relics of a priestly morality, but higher in the sense of being a more direct contribution to the values of life. They would be guides in the art of receiving experiences through words, the art of enjoying literature. It is a high art to enjoy anything to the full, and to enjoy literature, which is not a thing but a mere suggestion of things, requires an agile and expert technique. The story is told of Professor George Woodberry that once in a course of lectures on English poetry he paused in the midst of a reading from Keats. "Of course if young Keats were sitting among you," he said, "he would probably be ranked lowest in the class, but assuredly he would have the best time. You see, he was a poet. If I were running a college I would work out an experiment whereby the boys and girls who had the best time would get the highest marks. But then, I suspect I am not a real professor."

If the teachers of literature, after restoring their self-esteem by mastering everything that the appropriate sciences have to say about the nature and growth and operation of literature itself, could but realize that beyond and above that they are not real professors at all, but guides to experience, they would find their hearts happy and their hands full.

It is impossible not to pay some tribute here to I. A. Richards, who has been a pioneer in abandoning the caste prejudices of the humanities, and approaching literature with a clear motive of understanding. He has brought with him, it seems to me, and built into his psychology of poetry, a relic of the literary man's reluctance to face the stark character of the division of labor between poetry and knowledge. Although acknowledging that poetry is not knowledge, he wants still to hold for it the high rôle of guiding our acts and adjustments. He thus becomes, by inadvertence, the advocate of a sentimentalism in poetry and a deprecation of intelligence in morals and politics, which I believe are foreign to his real nature. He has still to relinquish this last thread that binds poetry to knowledge. But nevertheless he has shown in his *Practical Criticism* how fruitful a few psychological principles and modes of procedure can be in rejuvenating the outdated and pale business of "teaching literature"—how much more rich becomes the understanding as well as the enjoyment of poetry to a mind modernly alive when it is approached not as a "subject" but as a substantial object of study.

It may be that we shall never get rid of the solemn pretensions of caste complacency dressed up in the garments of "higher" truth, until we have got rid of the system of economic privilege which sanctions and backs them up with power. It may also be that until life is no longer mainly filled up with worrying about position upon one side and destitution upon the other, it will not become openly clear that joy is a noble thing, and indicates in the absence of strong signs to the contrary that all is well. Teachers of the science of literature *and its enjoyment* may have to wait a long time—they may have to wait for that far day when justice joins hands with prosperity—before their superiority to those who teach a science only, and no joy, is acknowledged. Meanwhile, however, they can stand equal to them in the public esteem, and cherish in their own hearts, if they have the audacity, a conviction that in a sanely revolutionary view of things they are the more weighty. That is the true ideal for the literary teacher, and the only way out of the humiliating position into which he is driven by the steady mounting up of scientific knowledge.

A NOTE ON I. A. RICHARDS' PSYCHOLOGY OF POETRY

I. A. RICHARDS' PSYCHOLOGY OF POETRY

I

An eminent place among books on literary criticism of recent years is occupied by those of I. A. Richards of Cambridge University. His books are distinguished by their complete abandonment of the point-of-view of literary truth, their attempt to bring a psychological science to bear upon the problems of the teacher and the critic. He offers, as I do, a definition of poetry, and his statement that "critical remarks are merely a branch of psychological remarks" is obviously akin to the thesis I am advancing. And yet I think his psychology is wrongly based, and that this is greatly retarding the conquest under his leadership of the field he has entered.

Professor Richards' first considerable work, written in collaboration with C. K. Ogden, was an attempt to simplify the logic of science and clarify its language by eliminating all the elements that go to make up what we call the meaning of a word, besides the mere "reference" to a "thing." The book was valuable in showing how many different functions besides that of referring to things are commonly fulfilled by speech—the communication of an attitude toward the thing referred to, toward the person spoken to, the fulfillment of ulterior intentions, etc. What Ogden and Richards attempted was to write a logic for scientists which would enable them to eliminate all attitudes from their use of words except that of simple reference or denotation. But in order to do this they had to ignore the great part played by attitudes in the very constitution of "things." They had to imagine a distinction between the intellectual and the active phases of man's nature far sharper than does, or can possibly, exist. The world is not composed of "things," nor our thoughts of merely "pointing to or reflecting things." It would be as true to say that the world is organized into "things" by our thoughts. And this organization is carried out in the main, especially in its earlier phases, primarily with a view to establishing attitudes and patterns of behavior. It is rather more a classification of responses to what the world presents than of the material presented.

Take even a word like Canada, for example, which has only one single "reference." When I said the other day, on crossing the border, "This is Canada," it was clear to all that I was not so much pointing to a thing as indicating a mode of behavior. Upon reflection it will become clear that that is always true of a word like Canada. The earth presents no such "thing" as Canada. The word would mean nothing at all, and would not exist, if it did not indicate modes of behavior. And this is so in varying degrees with all words. Nature does not make the distinction between a hand and an arm—and neither, by the way, does the Russian language—but we make it. And we distinguish the hand from the fingers, drawing an arbitrary line at the first joints. But we do not distinguish what comes after the second joints. That, although clearly marked off by nature and able—as well at least as Canada—to act independently, has not become a "thing." I am going over old ground, of course, and I offer these casual examples instead of citing authorities because I do not want to identify my criticism of Richards with any particular *kind* of psychology or *system* of logic. It is simply not true, as Richards asserts, that "pointing to or reflecting things is all that thoughts do." And his definition of science as "simply our most elaborate way of *pointing* to things . . . simply the organization of references with a view to the convenience and facilitation of reference," is superficial and misleading. It ignores facts which all psychologists and all logicians, no matter how they may settle with them, are compelled to take into account.

It is significant that while Ogden and Richards were arguing that scientific meaning is a pure pointing to things without attitude or indication of behavior, and saying

"Modern physics is becoming something in connection with which attitudes seem rather *de trop,*" an eminent physicist was arguing that attitudes and modes of behavior are the *only and whole* meaning of scientific concepts. "In general," wrote Professor Bridgman of Harvard, "we mean by any concept nothing more than a set of operations; the concept is synonymous with the corresponding set of operations." Professor Bridgman arrived at this operational logic, he tells us, by studying the thought-processes of Einstein. And he asserts that, although Einstein is probably unconscious of it, this "improved understanding of our mental relations to nature" is the "permanent contribution of relativity." Of course this understanding had been arrived at, starting from a basis in biology and genetic psychology, a good while before Einstein arrived on the scene. John Dewey has pointed that out, and has, in my opinion, far too modestly offered to abandon his more universal word "instrumental" for this higher-scientific term "operational." At any rate according to Professor Bridgman, Einstein's unconscious contribution only confirms that of the higher apes. And with these two strong evidences against him—whatever may lie at the end of the long and arduous dispute entailed—I do not see a ghost of a show for this too easy idea of I. A. Richards that science has nothing to do with attitude and is "simply our most elaborate way of pointing to things."

Having been thus summarily omitted from science, we need not of course be greatly surprised to see attitude and the reference to action reappear in poetry. Indeed, once they had isolated science as a pure pointing to things without attitude and without reference to behavior, it was quite inevitable, I suppose, that Ogden and Richards should turn round and define poetry as a pure evoking of attitudes and organization of behavior *without* pointing to things, and *without* reference to reality.

"A poem . . .," they say, "has no concern with limited and directed reference. It tells us, or should tell us, nothing. It has a different, though an equally important and a far more vital function. . . . What it does, or should do, is to induce a fitting attitude to experience." It is "the supreme form of emotive language. . . . As science frees itself from the emotional outlook, and modern physics is becoming something in connection with which attitudes seem rather *de trop,* so poetry seems about to return to the conditions of its greatness by abandoning the obsession of knowledge. . . . It is not necessary to know what things are in order to take up fitting attitudes towards them. . . ."

This view of poetry, wholly worked out with Mr. Ogden in *The Meaning of Meaning,* is what Mr. Richards has continued to develop, and apply to criticism and teaching, in his three other books. In his *Principles of Literary Criticism* he repeats the theme as follows:

"We may either use words for the sake of the references they promote, or we may use them for the sake of the attitudes and emotions which ensue. . . . Poetry affords the clearest example of this subordination of reference to attitude."

In *Science and Poetry* he divides both the poet and the reader of poetry into two separate streams or branches—the intellectual and the active, the thought and the emotion, the pointing to things and the getting ready to do something about them. Both streams are of course to some extent always present, but in poetry the intellectual stream "is the less important of the two." It "matters only *as a means;* it directs and excites the active stream. It is made up of thoughts . . . which reflect or point to the things the thoughts are 'of.' " But these things pointed to do not have any reality, and the statements made are not true. They are not indeed statements, but "pseudo-statements" and to believe them is "illicit" and a "profanation" of poetry. "A pseudo-statement is a form of words which is justified entirely by its effect in releasing or organizing our impulses and attitudes . . .; a statement, on the other hand, is justified by its truth, *i.e.*, its correspondence, in a highly technical sense, with the fact to which it points." With these pseudo-statements, cut off completely from the function of interpretation and of understanding, the poet regulates the active stream. He uses them "as a means of ordering, controlling and consolidating the whole experience." His "business . . . is to give order and coherence, and so freedom, to a body of experience."

In *Practical Criticism* the same theme is repeated and applied: "The poet makes a statement about something, not in order that the statement may be examined and reflected on, but in order to evoke certain feelings, and when these are evoked the use of the statement is exhausted." But since feelings are the accompaniment of attitudes, and attitudes are "preparations for action," these statements find their real value only when we learn how to use them "as a means of ordering our minds."

Such is, in brief, the device by which I. A. Richards, while accepting the inevitable division of labor between poetry and science, nevertheless proposes to restore poetry to her position of sovereignty. You remember how William Drummond in the days long past described poetry as "the mistress of human life" and the "quintessence of knowledge," and how with the separate development of science she has intermittently but steadily descended from that high place? The *coup d'état* of Ogden and Richards consists of cutting off knowledge from life, and then declaring poetry once more the mistress of life.

II

The problem so valiantly assailed by Ogden and Richards—problem of the relation between the logic of science and the psychology of the thought process—will doubtless be a long time in getting solved. To refute their psychology of poetry, however, it is not necessary to wait until that problem is solved. A psychology of poetry should rest on the psychology, not the logic, of the thought process—the psychology and biology and history of it. Everybody will concede that historically at least "the ruling interest of knowledge," as Clarence I. Lewis says, "is the practical interest of action." Science is an outgrowth of practical effort, and its connection with and dependence upon activity has always been, and is, direct and continual. Poetry was begotten upon magic ritual by day-dreams and play. To identify poetry with the use of words to convey attitudes and prepare for action, and leave to science the rôle of merely pointing to things, is to turn the most obvious history of the matter exactly upside down.

And to pretend, as Richards has to, that the interpretation of experience, the deciding what things are in terms of their relations, is—even in its highest development as pure science—incompatible with the having of emotions about things, is equally false to the most elementary psychology of the matter. The enemy of science is not emotion as such, but premature or inappropriate emotion. And this is not because science is avoiding attitudes, but because it is seeking only those which can on all occasions of a given type be successfully carried forth into complete action. Imagine that you, a poet, are walking in the woods with a zoologist. You are frightened by a rattling in the leaves, and assume an attitude of caution. That is to say, you land approximately ten feet away in the bushes. The scientist laughs at you.

"It's nothing but a garter snake," he says.

"How do you know it isn't a rattler?" you ask.

"Well, for one thing, this isn't their habitat," he replies calmly. And that word *habitat,* which is a large part of what makes his knowledge scientific and not merely practical, relaxes your attitude of caution. So much so that you soon become curiously absorbed in another "Gordian shape" that you find coiled by the pathway. But now your attitude of "disinterested curiosity" is interrupted by a hiss, or shriek from the zoologist: "Look out, that's a copperhead!" And this time it is pure science which is ten feet away in the bushes.

Science involves a severe discipline of unenlightened

impulses, and begets a habit of calmness, because it requires a calm procedure, but there is no truth in the notion that the scientific interpretation of a thing fails to evoke the appropriate emotion. It evokes it with a surer force.

III

I believe it can be shown that all Mr. Richards' troubles, all the weaknesses of his books, derive from this fundamental error of trying to cut off the organization and control of practical activity from science and bring it over into poetry. And first among these troubles I should mention the heavy labor it turns out to be, even for those vividly interested in the subject, to read his "Principles of Literary Criticism." Rarely has a man rich in new and important thoughts produced a book so tiring to the mind. We emerge on the last page with a feeling that we have been wading and plunging through a vastly important jungle of ideas, every one so overlaid and entangled with exceptions, interpolations, affiliations, methodological asides, *obiter dictums* and addendums, that no clear impression remains even of those ideas which were—we vaguely remember—brilliantly well stated and defined. We emerge—only to learn in the conclusion, that Mr. Richards spent half of his own labor on the book "in simplifying its structure, in taking out reservations and qualifications"! Well, is not that what always happens when you try to insert a body of facts into a theory which does not fit them—or any other body into any other mismade receptacle? You jam it in on one side and it springs out on the other, and you jump over there and fix it, and then you jump back here and try to get it in again before it gets out again. At last you do get it in, usually, but so much to the detriment of your receptacle that there is no great difference left between in and out.

Not only does Mr. Richards have to tend and tinker his explanation of poetry, plugging and caulking it continually with reservations and qualifications, but he has to admit that, when all's plugged that can be plugged, the thing will not work anyway. It leaves out the main thing that was to be explained. The poet uses certain words, he tells us, "as a means of ordering, controlling and consolidating" an experience. And "to a suitable reader . . . the words will reproduce in his mind a similar play of interests putting him for a while into a similar situation and leading to the same response." But "why this should happen is still somewhat of a mystery. . . ."

Is not this as much as to say, "After all, I have no explanation of poetry"? It is easy enough to see how scientific words order, control and consolidate experience. They do it by pointing to the practically important details of the experience and reminding us that in those details it is the same as certain other experiences, toward which we already know how to behave. X, the unknown quantity, or quality, is another case of the familiar A or B. That is what scientific words tell us. In the last analysis that is all they tell us, but the resulting order, consolidation and control are obvious.

Poetic words also point to details in the given experience, and also remind us that in those details it is the same as some other experience. But the details pointed to are not necessarily of any practical importance, and our mode of behavior toward that other experience would be in the highest degree inept and unsuccessful here. How can such words help us to order, consolidate and control our experience? It remains indeed a mystery. It would be truer to say that their very essence is disorder, disconsolidation and complete loss or abandonment of control.

"Tiger, tiger, burning bright. . . ."

Can anybody control a tiger by confusing him with a camp-fire? Can anybody consolidate the animal kingdom and reduce it to order by designating and classifying its members in this anarchistical fashion? Obviously not. A tiger, if you want order, consolidation and control, is not a small fire but a large cat.

IV

Another of Mr. Richards' serious troubles is that he cannot explain metaphor, and his failure to do so grows more and more distressing with each new book that he writes. In *The Meaning of Meaning,* he and Mr. Ogden merely offered a brief sweeping of the chaff to be found in the old-time grammars and books of rhetoric on this subject. The function of metaphor, they said, is to provide "new, sudden and striking collocations of references for the sake of the compound effects of contrast, conflict, harmony, inter-animation and equilibrium which may be so attained."

In the *Principles of Literary Criticism* these stock remarks of the scholiasts are happily forgotten, but metaphor appears still less to appertain to the essence of the poetic experience. "Metaphor," we read, "is a semi-surreptitious method by which a greater variety of elements can be wrought into the fabric of the experience. Not that there is any virtue in variety by itself, though the list of critics who seem to have thought so would be lengthy; a page of the dictionary can show more variety than any page of poetry. But what is needed for the wholeness of an experience is not always naturally present, and metaphor supplies an excuse by which what is needed can be smuggled in."

It is amusing to compare this with the statement of Helen Parkhurst:

"Certainly the quintessence of poetry—the pure grain of it that is left when all chaff has been winnowed away, the unalloyed gold that constitutes its substance—is little else than metaphor."

The anti-scientists will find it amusing that one psychologist describes as a surreptitious instrument for smuggling things into poetry, what another takes for little but the defining essence. However, all of Mr. Richards' books may be described as a brilliant effort to smuggle back into poetry its own essence which he has excluded by an initial error.

In his latest book, *Practical Criticism,* he has become aware of some inadequacy in this part of his theory, for he tells us that "A better understanding of metaphor is one of the aims which an imposed curriculum of literary studies might well set before itself." But he does not himself take any steps toward that better understanding. On the contrary he quite relaxes and sinks out of sight in the existing confusion. He now defines metaphor as "a shift, a carrying over of a word from its normal use to a new use"—a definition which has about as much relevance to the general substance of his book as would the leaping of a fish out of its pages. The essential theme and reason-for-being of the book was to distinguish four *different* ways in which words are *normally* used. They are used to make "sense" (the scientific way), to evoke attitude and emotion toward an object (poetry), to express emotion toward the hearer, and to carry out some ulterior intention. What can it mean when an author professing to offer us an exhaustive analysis in four categories of the ways in which words are used, suddenly forgets all about it, drops back to the crude idea of a "normal" use of words, and defines metaphor as a departure from the "normal"? It means that he has abandoned all hope of ever explaining metaphor in terms of his own categories.

In a weak effort to pull things together, Mr. Richards distinguishes two kinds of departure from what he calls the "normal" use of words—the "sense metaphor" (prosaic or scientific) and the "emotive metaphor" (poetic). "In a sense metaphor," he tells us, "the shift of the word is occasioned and justified by a similarity *between the object* it is usually applied to and the new object. In an emotive metaphor the shift occurs through some similarity *between the feelings* the new situation and the normal situation arouse." And he illustrates this by imagining two situations in which one might call a man a *swine.* "It may be because his features resemble those of a pig, but it may be because you have towards him something of the feeling you conventionally have towards pigs, or because you propose, if possible, to excite those feelings." In the first case, the metaphor belongs to science, according to his scheme, in the second to poetry. Indeed "the poet's task is constantly . . . that of finding ways and means of controlling feeling through metaphor."

See what a complicated tangle Mr. Richards has got himself wound up in, and you will understand why he cries for help from "an imposed curriculum of literary studies." There is first the *normal-scientific* way of naming things, which consists of merely referring to them as they "are." Second there is a *departure from the normal* in science, called metaphor, which consists in not naming things what they *are* but what they *resemble*. Third there is a *normal-poetic* way of naming things, which consists of disregarding what they "are," but giving them a name that will evoke emotions toward them. And fourth there is a *departure* in poetry, which can only consist of not giving them their *normal* emotive name but some other *abnormal* name which evokes the same emotion! All these four situations to be explained, and no explanation whatever is forthcoming. There is not even the hint of a reason why science departs from the "normal" in this childish fashion. And there is no explanation of the poetic departure either —except to say that metaphor is a "ways and means of controlling feeling," and this cannot explain the departure, since it is already the sole explanation of the "normal" poetic use of words.

This inextricable tangle unravels instantly when you recognize that science, or prose, or the practical use of words, does not merely point to things but organizes experience. It does so by showing that one thing *resembles* some other thing or class of things. But the resemblances in which science is interested are those which prove constant, relevant to action and reliable on a large scale. Poetry is not interested in organizing experience, but in having it, and therefore poetry transfers the names of things according to resemblances which not only cannot be relied upon in action, but can be relied upon to make action impossible. These poetic transfers of names are all called metaphor, whether they are based on sensation or emotion, and if they appear in practical or scientific talk—except as they may be introduced for mere purposes of expository illustration—then poetry is intermingling in this talk.

Science does not call an object *swine* because it resembles a pig to mere ocular perception, any more than because it resembles a pig in the emotions which its presence evokes. Science has already had its say, when we are informed that the object "is" a man. After that anybody who calls it "swine," *whether because of sensuous or because of emotional resemblance,* is a poet. He may perhaps not be one who will shake the world with his originality, but he is occupied, as poets are, with the immediate qualities of the experience.

V

Not only does Mr. Richards' psychology fail to explain the predominance of metaphor in poetry, but it fails to explain the immemorial association of poetry with metrical or monotonous rhythm. Richards is illuminating in his discussion of the effects which may be created out of the "texture of expectations, satisfactions, disappointments, surprisals, which the sequence of syllables brings about," and the combination of these with similar effects involved in the meanings of the words. He talks more wisely about the musical than the imaginative values in poetry. But the thing to be explained here is not these high and fine values created by the subtle interplay of disappointment and satisfaction, for they belong to free verse and to prose rhythm as well as to poetry. The thing to be explained by a theory of poetry is its original and eternally persisting disposition to imitate the mere sing-song beating of a tom tom. Is there any reason for this persistent effort to be monotonous? That is what we want to know. And according to Richards' theory that poetry is essentially concerned with arousing attitudes and preparations for action, I do not see that there is.

Richards himself reminds us in several places that the fundamental effect of a monotonous metre is to put us into a hypnotic sleep. "We need not boggle," he says, "at the word 'hypnosis.'" Indeed "too simple rhythms, those which are too easily 'seen through,' grow cloying or insipid unless hypnoidal states intervene." Nobody will deny, I think, that in the vast aggregate of human poetry, those simple rhythms which are easily seen through prevail to an overwhelming degree. And if the defining purpose of poetry is to evoke emotional attitudes which are "preparations for action," how shall we explain this almost universal enthusiasm among poets for putting us to sleep? Mr. Richards has made an effort to explain it, and here too the effort goes back to the days of his collaboration with Mr. Ogden:

"Emotionality, exaggeration of belief-feelings, the occulting of the critical faculties . . . all these are characteristics of metrical experiences and fit in well with a hypnosis assumption." So these young authors assured us, and Mr. Richards repeats the theme in his *Principles of Literary Criticism:*

"That certain metres, or rather that a certain handling of metre should produce in a slight degree a hypnoidal state is not surprising. But it does so . . . through the lulling effects more than the awakening. Many of the most characteristic symptoms of incipient hypnosis are present in a slight degree. Among these susceptibility and vivacity of emotion, suggestibility, limitations of the field of attention . . . some degree of hyperæsthesia," etc.

It is noticeable that the emotions—and still more "emotionality"—appear in these quotations in their antique form as a kind of interior liquid, not in their modern form as "signs of attitudes" which are "preparations for action." It would hardly be possible for a logical mind to say—much less an experienced mind to believe—that "more through the lulling than the awakening effects" a metre makes us susceptible to vivacious "attitudes which are preparations for action." Richards is compelled to let his modern view of emotion slip out of his mind here—although his whole doctrine of poetry and criticism rests upon it—because while holding to it he cannot explain why the poets should want to put us to sleep.

I think anybody who has ever been to sleep can testify to the variety of preposterous and outrageous things he has seen happen in that country, and earnestly believed to be happening, without a glimmer of the appropriate emotion or the ghost of an impulse to do anything about it. Anybody who has experimented with hypnosis will as particularly testify that the state of suggestibility, "occulting of the critical faculties," "limitation of the field of attention," "hyperæsthesia"—the openness, in short, to complete and vivid hallucination—is accompanied by the same genius for not getting unnecessarily excited.[1] You can tell a hypnotic subject that there is a lion in the room in such a way as not to produce a flicker of emotion, but if you tell him that he is afraid of the lion you will find him under the bed. It is this disposition to believe and realize to the full any experience which is suggested by the hypnotist, whether it be emotional or not, which distinguishes the hypnotic state. It is this which distinguishes the "hypnoidal" states. And it is in order to produce these states that the poets, even though they wander away at times, under pressure from their sophisticated friends in a prosaic world, perpetually recur to a metre that does not conceal or disguise its monotony. They are not interested in evoking attitudes but in conveying experience.

[1]It is hardly necessary to cite authorities in disproof of the assertion that a condition called "emotionality" is increased under hypnosis. It is simpler to ask our brilliant authors to acknowledge that they were yielding to pressure from the hypothesis rather than the facts, when they slipped this abstraction in here. There is a precocious quality in that book, *The Meaning of Meaning,* a slightly too perfect command of thousands of big words and ideas, which makes it possible to say this without denying the value of the book.

VI

Another of Mr. Richards' troubles which his initial misconception of the mind explains, is his trouble with the lovers of art. Soon after he published his *Principles of Literary Criticism,* he was assailed by the English critic of painting Roger Fry for saying that "When we look at a picture, or read a poem, or listen to music, we are not doing something quite unlike what we are doing on our way to the Gallery. . . . Our activity is not of a fundamentally different kind."

Of course it is of a fundamentally different kind, and the more so, the more in haste we are to get there. In that case, every item of our experience is interpreted either as aid or hindrance to that purposive action. When we do get there, the difference is that we are there. The tension towards a specific goal relaxes. We become generically receptive. We are, to recall Professor Herrick, not only reaching out actively "to meet the exciting agent," but "seeking new contacts." It is idle to say that this difference is not fundamental. Everybody knows, because everybody feels, that it is fundamental. Even when we insist upon *interpreting* all the pictures in the gallery, as so many of us pathetically practical mortals have to do in order to convince ourselves that we are there at all, we try to make of the interpretation itself an objective thing, an experience to dwell upon. We enjoy it; we do not merely perform it, as we did the interpretation of the sign on the bus which brought us to the gallery.

The distinction is "fundamental," but it is not absolute, or mysterious or queer. It does not in the least commit us to the rather "arty" position of Mr. Fry, who shows an inclination to put a gold frame round our mood when we are at last solemnly arrived in the gallery, and call it an "æsthetic state" unrelated to all the other states in which we have leisure consciously to enjoy an experience. There is no fundamental difference between our activity in the gallery and on the way there, provided we pause on the way there, seized as it were by the brown twang of a hurdy-gurdy, or the bright orange hues of some display of tropical fruits and vegetables—provided we pause, and pour our energy into the act of perception for its own sake.

All poets and artists know that a child's exuberant excitement about life's experience—either that or a madman's excitement about some particular experience—is what distinguishes them from prosy people. They babble about things more than is prudent or necessary because they are in love with them. When they do not know this, it is merely because they are *too* childlike, or *too* mad, to know anything about themselves. Therefore when Mr. Richards comes along with his solemn attribution to them of a deep zeal for "organizing" their experience, for "ordering, controlling and consolidating" it, working up "preparations for action" upon it—when he accuses poets, in short, of being essentially practical people—they naturally rebel and denounce him for confusing poetry with efficiency, for confusing it with "a perfectly working mental Roneo Steel Cabinet System," to quote T. S. Eliot, or Herbert Read—I have forgotten which. They have both assailed Mr. Richards upon this point, and so I suppose has every reader of his books who has ever known or been a poet. And Mr. Richards has replied with some dudgeon that he does not mean by organization "deliberate planning," and he does not mean by order "tidiness." But that does not make the slightest difference. He is too deeply wrong for any specifications or shifts of emphasis to cure him. He is wrong in his conception of science as merely referring to things and *not interpreting them with a view to action.* And so he is wrong in his conception of poetry as essentially *not* referring to things but *merely interpreting them with a view to action.* He has got the whole thing exactly upside down, and nothing but a revolution can mend him.

VII

Another trouble Mr. Richards gets into by making attitude and preparation for action a part of the definition of poetry. He becomes a painfully austere and moralistic critic. Naturally if the poet is, and the prose thinker is not, concerned with preparations for action, the burden of regulating human conduct, or trying to regulate a little of it, rests entirely upon the poet. And that is no small burden for a sensitive and childlike person to carry. It makes Richards feel compelled to preach to the poets almost as solemnly as a Sunday-school superintendent or Matthew Arnold. In fact he becomes even more melodramatically moral than Arnold in assuring us that with creeds, dogmas, and traditions tumbling and crumbling about us, and the whole human race, so to speak, on the chaos-toboggan, poetry is our only stay.

"It is capable of saving us," he cries. "It is a perfectly possible means of overcoming chaos."

I do not know anything better calculated to strike dumb the singing lips of poets than to have a learned professor step out with this anguished expression on his face, and tell them that science has given up the sponge and the whole world is turning to them in a wild last agony of not very confident hope for salvation. People like to be praised, of course, for whatever virtues they haven't got, but they don't like to be told that everything depends upon their continuing to manifest these virtues.

The poet, Mr. Richards tells us, is "the master of speech because he is the master of experience. . . . That amazing capacity of his for ordering speech is only a part of a more amazing capacity for ordering his experience."

"The poets are failing us," he cries, "or we them, if after reading them we do not find ourselves changed; not with a temporary change such as luncheon or slumber will produce . . . but with a permanent alteration of our possibilities as responsive individuals in good or bad adjustment to an all but overwhelming concourse of stimulations. . . ."

Imagine talking that way to Sappho—or Catullus, or François Villon, or Bobbie Burns! I do not mean that poets are bad. They are just as good as anybody else. But it is assuredly a little unfortunate to come along in the name of psychological understanding and talk to them in this preachy-preachy tone. It reminds me of St. Francis urging the birds to be good.

Matthew Arnold had this to justify him in his rather heavy hopes of poetry—that he believed true judgment was an intrinsic part of it. He defined poetry not as an arbitrary evocation of emotional attitudes to life,—a preparation for action divorced from any determination of the facts to be acted upon,—but as a "criticism of life." He believed that in poetry "Our race, as time goes on, will find an ever surer and surer stay," because in poetry our race will find true ideas—because "for poetry the idea is everything." This is exactly the opposite of Mr. Richards' opinion, although quoted by him in the title-head of his *Science and Poetry*. For him the idea—or the "intellectual stream," as he calls it—is a "minor branch" of the poetic experience. "It matters only *as a means;* it directs and excites the active stream." And to believe that it gives this direction and excitation by stating any truth or offering any valid criticism of anything, is "illicit" and a "profanation."

Thus his dreadfully moralistic preachment to poets, and his solemn transfer of the whole burden of human salvation to the backs of these rather bewildered minstrels, lacks altogether the plausibility in good sense that Arnold's saintly view of poetry had. The poet is to save us, according to Richards, not by telling us what things are, and so how to take up fitting attitudes towards them. "It is not necessary to know what things are in order to take up fitting attitudes towards them." All that is necessary is to listen to a *line of talk*—for that is the good American equivalent of pseudo-statement—which will leave us in "a strong emotional attitude which feels like belief," although we know quite well that no facts and no true ideas have been adduced or alluded to.

In one place Mr. Richards describes this emotional attitude as one of genuine although "objectless" belief, but his usual position is that "the most important among our attitudes can be aroused and maintained without any belief entering in at all." And to this arousal he looks for salvation against the break-down of belief itself, and the moral and political chaos which he sees ensuing.

"Countless pseudo-statements," he cries in warning, —"about God, about the universe, about human nature, . . . about the soul, its rank and destiny,—pseudo-statements which are pivotal points in the organization of the mind, vital to its well-being, have suddenly become for sincere, honest and informal minds, impossible to believe. . . . This is the contemporary situation. The remedy . . . is to cut our pseudo-statements free from belief, and yet retain them, in this released state, as the main instruments by which we order our attitudes to one another and to the world."

Mr. Richards' nightmare apprehension of an impending chaos seems to me a malady very similar to Joseph Wood Krutch's literary despair. Richards describes the transition from the "Magical View" of the world to the "scientific," not as a discovery that nature is neutral—a rather belated discovery, one would think, since it happens to have been true all along—but as an increasingly "dangerous" process called "Neutralization of Nature." Man "has to face the fact," he cries, "that the edifices of supposed knowledge, with which he has for so long buttressed and supported his attitudes, will no longer stand up, and, at the same time, he has to recognize that pure knowledge is irrelevant to his aims. . . ."

A glance into Russia at the robust composure and good health with which the bulk of the people there have effected the transition from a belief in magic and superstitious religion in its most archaic forms, to modern machine agriculture, atheism and a materialistic philosophy, should be sufficient to explode this hot-house idea of the manner in which man's attitudes are buttressed—and also enough to put to shame the assertion that knowledge is irrelevant to a man's aims. How can knowledge be irrelevant to a man's aims if he has any serious intention of achieving them? It is not the neutralization of nature that is troubling Mr. Richards, but the neutralization of the language in which practical and scientific people talk about nature. It is not the irrelevance of pure knowledge to man's aims, but the inappropriateness of the language of pure science to the *expression* of his aims, which causes this professor to see advancing a "chaos such as man has never before experienced."

And since this is a purely literary chaos, Mr. Richards is naturally satisfied with a purely literary salvation from it. Nobody who seriously foresaw such a disaster descending upon the human race as he delineates could possibly look to poets for deliverance—much less to the universal enthronement of sentimentalism in the form of a definition of poetry. In his *Practical Criticism*—his most empirical and wisest book—Mr. Richards tells us that "A response is sentimental if it is too great for the occasion." And as though this succinct remark were not enough to condemn and wipe out utterly his own doctrine of poetry, he adds: "We cannot, obviously, judge that any response is sentimental in this sense unless we *take careful account of the situation.*" The idea that the race is going to be saved from chaos by the universal propagation of sentimental responses in the form of poetry, is so fantastic that it seems a mere act of courtesy to insist that Mr. Richards is not talking about the problem of life in a world of science at all, but about the problem of poetry in a world of scientific terminology.

For Richards is not a sentimentalist, and not a man naturally disposed to delude himself with hollow and fantastic ideas like this. His own ardent labors toward a science of poetry and a scientific attitude in criticism stand there to demonstrate that. He has been led into this untenable position by a deep and admirable love of poetry, and by following out doggedly and with a fertile brain the implications of an error in psychology.

When poetic diction is defined as suggesting the qualities of experience more than practical interpretation demands, we are quite prepared to find the poets in their extreme moments ignoring the practical interpretation altogether, and regaling us with a mere line of talk. We find them more occupied with "what it feels like" to believe something than with whether it is true. In this they are irresponsible rather than sentimental, and we accord them a "poetic license" here as elsewhere, knowing it is not their specialty to conceive things truly but to live them vividly. We slake our own thirst for experience in their poems, and we should be rash to allow a little thing like truth or the meanings of words to stand between us and the fountain of life. Nevertheless we also know, and they know too, that vivid experience must not be confused with good judgment, nor good judgment long ignored or forgotten. Something greater and not less than mere poetry is in progress, when a poet enriches with the living colors of experience an interpretation of it that is true.

NOTES AND REFERENCES

NOTES AND REFERENCES

Page 4

Professor Eddington: *The Nature of the Physical World*, p. [illegible]. Eddington's device for introducing mysticism is to assume that the qualities of things which poetry dwells on are unreal, and then because that makes poetry, and indeed the very significance of life, seem false or bad, to assert that these qualities must be signs of facts, therefore be "significant" of something, must indicate some "true relation of the world to ourselves." If he would see in the first place that the qualities are just as real as the relations between them discovered by science, he would not have to resort to a remedy to them by pretending that they have some significance beside those which science discovers: that in some mysterious way they [illegible] their [illegible] of indicating relations and give some more "intimate" knowledge—[illegible] a knowledge which nobody knows. [illegible] not merely matter-of-fact realities he need not gratuitously endow them with mystic meaning. Frederick Harrison, in his [illegible], does a similar thing. See note [illegible].

Page 6

Professor Watson: In his *Behaviorism*, chapter I, he relates how behaviorism began as a scientific method, and only gradually grew into a tendency to declare itself a philosophy of being—a process of development which is not often so frankly acknowledged.

Page 7

Francis Bacon: "And as the vision of light itself is something more excellent and beautiful than its manifold use, so assuredly the contemplation of things as they are, without superstition or imposture, without error or confusion, is in itself a nobler thing than a whole harvest of inventions." From *The Advancement of Learning*.

Clarence I. Lewis: *Mind and the World Order*, p. [illegible].

Page 9

Herbert Spencer: Quoted by John Langdon Davies in his *New Age of Faith*.

"False Messiah": The reference is to *Science the False Messiah*, a book by C. E. Ayres.

Page 11

Professor Huxley: *Science and Culture*.

Eckermann: *Conversations with Goethe*, p. [illegible].

NOTES AND REFERENCES

Page 5

Professor Eddington: *The Nature of the Physical World.* Professor Eddington's device for introducing mysticism is to declare that the qualities of things which poetry dwells on are unreal, and then because that makes poetry, and indeed the very enjoyment of life, seem false or bad, to assert that these qualities must in spite of their unreality be "significant" of something, must indicate some "true relation of the world to ourselves." If he would see in the first place that the qualities are just as real as the relations between them discovered by science, he would not have to justify a return to them by pretending that they have some significance besides those which science discovers, that in some mysterious way they reduplicate their labor of indicating relations, and convey some more "intimate" knowledge—albeit a knowledge which nobody knows. In short, if he would not unjustly deprive them of matter-of-fact reality, he need not gratuitously endow them with mystic meaning. Frederick Barry, in his *Scientific Habit of Thought* does a similar thing. See note to p. 221.

Page 6

Professor Watson: In his *Behaviorism,* chapter I, he relates how this *ism* began as a scientific method, and only gradually got up the nerve to declare itself a philosophy of being—a process of degeneration which is not often so frankly acknowledged.

Page 7

Francis Bacon: "Just as the vision of light itself is something more excellent and beautiful than its manifold use, so, without doubt, the contemplation of things as they are, without superstition or imposture, without error or confusion, is in itself a nobler thing than a whole harvest of inventions." From *The Advancement of Learning.*

Clarence I. Lewis: *Mind and the World Order,* p. 128.

Page 9

Herbert Spencer: Quoted by John Langdon Davies in his *New Age of Faith.*

"False Messiah": The reference is to *Science: the False Messiah,* a book by C. E. Ayres.

Page 11

Professor Huxley: *Science and Culture.*

Hilaire Belloc: *Conversation with an Angel,* p. 211.

Page 15

The Bookman: January, 1930.

Page 20

Laura Riding: The quotations are from pp. 85, 57, and 19 of *Contemporaries and Snobs.*

Page 21

T. S. Eliot: The quotations are from *The Sacred Wood,* p. 68, and *The New Criterion,* January, 1926. The quotations about emotion I have culled from *The Sacred Wood, Homage to John Dryden,* in the *Hogarth Essays,* first American edition, and *Religion Without Humanism* in the collection, *Humanism and America.*

Page 23

Gorham B. Munson: *Destinations,* p. 124.

Page 25

Professor Babbitt: The quotations are from *Humanism: An Essay at Definition,* p. 43 of *Humanism and America;* from *Masters of Modern French Criticism,* pp. 112 and 52; and again from *Humanism and America,* p. 32. The assertion that Professor Babbitt is a "psychologist" will be found in an article on *The Individualism of Irving Babbitt,* by Bernard Bandler II, in *The Hound and Horn,* Autumn, 1929.

Page 26

Professor L. T. More: *The Pretensions of Science,* in *Humanism and America,* p. 6.

Page 27

Humanism, An Essay at Definition: Humanism and America, p. 25.

Page 31

Ivor Winters: *Poetry, Morality and Criticism,* p. 310 of the collection called *The Critique of Humanism.*

Allen Tate: The quoted phrases are from an essay called *The Fallacy of Humanism,* pp. 160 and 163 of *The Critique of Humanism.*

T. S. Eliot: *For Lancelot Andrewes,* Preface.

Page 32

Irving Babbitt: *Humanism and America,* p. 39.

Paul Elmer More: *The Bookman,* vol. LXXI, no. I, pp. 7 and 9.

Page 33

"A strong book": *Democracy and Leadership,* pp. 246, 212, 203, 273, 209, 200, 196.

Page 35

"At the opposite extreme": *Rousseau and Romanticism,* pp. 104 ff.

Pages 36–7

Thorstein Veblen: *The Theory of the Leisure Class,* chapter XIV.

Professor Babbitt: *Humanism and America,* pp. 36, 37, 38, 51, and *Democracy and Leadership,* p. 202.

Page 40

Professor Babbitt: *The Forum,* February, 1930.

Paul Elmer More: *Criticism,* in *The Shelbourne Essays,* Seventh Series.

"Limit their desires": *Humanism and America,* p. 48.

Page 42

Malcolm Cowley: *Humanizing Society,* in *The Critique of Humanism,* p. 75.

Professor Babbitt: *Democracy and Leadership,* p. 210.

Page 43

"Immediate data of consciousness": *Democracy and Leadership,* pp. 293 and 323.

"Corruption of ethics": *Democracy and Leadership,* p. 230.

"Deny this ethical will . . .": *Democracy and Leadership,* p. 225.

Page 46

"Subordinate the intellect": *Democracy and Leadership,* p. 195.

T. S. Eliot: *The Sacred Wood,* p. 68, and *The New Criterion,* January, 1926.

Pages 48–9

T. S. Eliot: *The Sacred Wood,* p. 131; *Homage to John Dryden,* The Hogarth Essays, first American edition, 1928, p. 205.

Dryden: *On Translating the Poets.*

Page 51

"Predilections of the leisure class": The quotations are from Thorstein Veblen's *Theory of the Leisure Class.*

Page 52

Professor Babbitt: *Democracy and Leadership,* pp. 270 and 312.

Page 53

T. S. Eliot: *Experiment in Criticism, The Bookman,* vol. LXX, no. 3, also published in the collection *Tradition and Experiment in Present-Day Literature.*

The Sacred Wood, p. 68.

Page 57

I. A. Richards: *The Principles of Literary Criticism,* p. 25. See also *Practical Criticism,* p. 11. "That the one and only goal of all critical endeavors, of all interpretation, appreciation, exhortation, praise or abuse, is improvement in communication may seem an exaggeration. But in practice it is so."

Page 58

Most of the phrases quoted on this page are from *A Survey of Modernist Poetry,* by Robert Graves and Laura Riding. It is from this book that I have paraphrased—to put it mildly—the explanation of Cummings's poem. The poem is to be found on p. 76 of his *is 5.*

Page 62

Paul Rosenfeld: *Men Seen, Twenty-four Modern Authors.*

Page 64

Gertrude Stein: The quotation is from one of her pieces appearing in *Transition,* an English magazine published in Paris, and largely devoted to the Cult of Unintelligibility. The passage from Joyce is also taken from parts of *Work in Progress* published in *Transition.*

Page 68

Maiakovsky: *Pro Eto.*

Page 73

Aubade: The poem and its explanation appear in Miss Sitwell's *Poetry and Criticism,* the poem in her *Bucolic Comedies.*

Page 80

"La fille de Minos . . .": The line from Racine is quoted by Abbé Henri Bremond in his book *La Poésie Pure.*

T. E. Hulme: His poems were published by Ezra Pound at the end of his volume *Ripostes.*

Page 81

Robert Briffault: *The Mothers,* vol. I, pp. 17–22.

Page 84

Hart Crane: Letter in *Poetry,* October, 1926.

"Paris": The poem is from E. E. Cummings's *is 5.*

Pages 86–7

T. S. Eliot: *The New Criterion,* January, 1926.

Gorham B. Munson: *Destinations,* p. 3.

Virginia Woolf: *Mr. Bennett and Mrs. Brown,* The Hogarth Essays, first American edition, p. 14.

Page 88

Cummings: *is 5*, p. 91.

Page 89

Allen Tate: Introduction to Hart Crane's *White Buildings*.

"British Admirers": Laura Riding and Robert Graves, *A Survey of Modernist Poetry*, pp. 289–90.

Page 93

"The usual assumption": "The nature of technique need not be further elaborated; it is enough to mention once more its governing principle, which is *communication*."—Lascelles Abercrombie, *The Theory of Poetry*, p. 151.

"The poet writes in order to communicate."—John Livingston Lowes, *Convention and Revolt in Poetry*, p. 94.

"But poetry itself is a mode of communication."—I. A. Richards, *Practical Criticism*, p. 11.

Stevenson: Quoted by MacCracken and Sandison in their *Manual of Good English*, chapter I.

John Stuart Mill: *Poetry and Its Varieties*, in *Dissertations and Discussions*, vol. I.

Page 94

"Far from being one": F. Cudworth Flint in *The Symposium*, vol. I, no. 3.

Page 95

"Letter to Harriet Monroe": *Poetry*, October, 1926.

Page 105

Robert Graves and Laura Riding: *A Survey of Modernist Poetry*, p. 151. "The purpose of printing in book-form poetry construed in this private sense is not to convert it into a selling product but merely to give it an identity separate from the author's. . . ."

Page 106

Jean Piaget: My quotations are from *The Language and Thought of the Child* and *The Child's Conception of the World*.

Page 111

Eda Lou Walton: *The Nation* for August 6 and July 2, 1930.

Edmund Wilson: *The New Republic*, November 13, 1929.

Page 113

Mark Van Doren: *The Poetry of Hart Crane*, in *The Theatre Guild Magazine* for June, 1930.

Allen Tate: The quotation is from a book review.

Page 114

T. S. Eliot: Preface to his translation of *Anabasis.*

Ivor Winters: *Poetry, Morality and Criticism,* in *The Critique of Humanism,* p. 320, footnote.

Page 117

Marcel Brion: This quotation and that from Robert Macalmon are to be found in *Our Exagmination Round His Factification For Incamination of Work in Progress,* a book of eulogies of James Joyce published by Shakespeare & Co., 12 rue de l'Odéon, Paris.

Edmund Wilson: *Axel's Castle,* p. 207.

Page 121

John Dos Passos: From a letter to the press in praise of E. E. Cummings's play *him,* produced at the Provincetown Playhouse.

Page 125

Sainte-Beuve: *What is a Classic?* in his *Essays,* translated by Elizabeth Lee.

"Society as a whole": I quote the phrase from Edmund Wilson's *Axel's Castle,* p. 2. "Romanticism, as every one has heard, was a revolt of the individual. The 'Classicism' against which it was a reaction meant, in the domain of politics and morals, a preoccupation with society as a whole; and, in art, an ideal of objectivity."

Page 126

Robert Graves: *The Future of the Art of Poetry, Hogarth Essays,* first American edition, p. 172.

Page 127

Rebecca West: *A Last London Letter, The Bookman,* October, 1930.

Havelock Ellis: *The Dance of Life,* p. 141.

Page 128

Karl Marx: *Capital,* p. 384 of the English translation by Eden and Cedar Paul—the only good English translation.

Drummond of Hawthornden: Quoted by W. P. Ker in *The Art of Poetry,* p. 10.

Page 129

Kepler: Quoted by E. A. Burtt in *The Metaphysical Foundations of Modern Physical Science,* p. 48.

Sir William Osler: *The Old Humanities and the New Science,* pp. 5 and 34.

Page 131

"In 1645": J. Wallis, quoted by Preserved Smith in his *History of Modern Culture,* vol. I, p. 166. I owe much to this excellent book.

Hobbes: *Leviathan,* part I, chapter 5.

Page 132

Erasmus Darwin: His poem *The Temple of Nature* opens in this way:

> "Say, Muse! how rose from elemental strife
> Organic forms, and kindled into life. . . ."

A somewhat different mode of approach from the voyage of the *Beagle.*

H. G. Wells: *The Science of Life,* written in collaboration with Julian S. Huxley and G. P. Wells, Introduction, p. 3.

Page 134

Professor Whitehead: *Science and the Modern World,* chapter V, p. 107.

Page 135

E. E. Kellett: *The Whirligig of Taste* is the title of his book.

Milton: *Reason of Church Government.*

Page 136

John Dryden: *A Defense of an Essay of Dramatic Poesy,* and *Dramatic Poesy, Epistle Dedicatory to the Right Honorable Charles, Lord Buckhurst.* Dryden was delightfully frank in lowering the standards of literature and elevating its social status. "I confess my chief endeavors are to delight the age in which I live," he says in the same essay, and writing on *The Dramatic Poetry of the Last Age,* he says that the "greatest advantage of our writing" proceeds from conversation, for "in the age wherein those poets lived, there was less of gallantry than in ours; neither did they keep the best company in theirs." In his essay on *The Proper Wit of Poetry,* he said that he had found two military men, a Prince and a General, "incomparably the best subject I ever had, excepting only the Royal Family."

Page 137

Thomas Hobbes: The Preface, *To the Reader, concerning the Vertues of an Heroique Poem.* I quote from J. E. Spingarn's excellent collection, *Critical Essays of the Seventeenth Century,* vol. II, p. 67.

Page 138

Sidney: *Defense of Poesie.*

Spenser: Quoted by Edward Dowden in *Spenser, the Poet and Teacher.*

Page 140

Joseph Glanville: Quoted by Preserved Smith, *History of Modern Culture,* I, p. 168.

Page 141

Zola: *Le Roman Experimental.*

Footnote: By "prophets of confusion" I mean to suggest such books as Scott Buchanan's *Poetry and Mathematics.*

Page 142

Blake: The quotation is from S. Foster Damon's *William Blake, His Philosophy and Symbols,* chapter XIV, p. 89.

Wordsworth: Introduction to the *Lyrical Ballads, Prose Works,* vol. II, p. 79.

Page 143

Shelley: *Defense of Poetry.*

Page 145

Keats: The phrase quoted is from a letter reproduced by Clarence D. Thorpe in *The Mind of John Keats,* an interesting book which presents the opposite view from mine.

Page 146

Matthew Arnold: In *Literature and Science,* for instance, he describes poetry and eloquence as "The criticism of life by gifted men, alive and active with extraordinary power at an unusual number of points."

Hardy: Introduction to *The Dynasts.* In an article in *The English Review* (vol. 38, p. 666) Agnes Stewart ingeniously opposes those who say that Hardy, "having no message, had no will to creation." She says that the message was there, but he didn't know it. It "came from his unconscious which was in advance of his conscious mind." She thus links him up underground with Freud and Einstein, with the advance of knowledge.

Stephen Benét: *John Brown's Body.*

Page 147

Robert Bridges: As an example we may take these lines about sex, which no one will denounce at least as an erotic poem:

> "First among the lowest types of life we think to find
> no separation of sex: plants in the next degree
> show differentiation at puberty with some signs

of mutual approachment: next in higher animals
an early differentiation, and at puberty
periodic appetite with mutual attraction
sometimes engaging Beauty. . . ."

—*The Testament of Beauty,* p. 90.

Alfred Noyes: *The Torch-Bearers* is the title of a dramatic trilogy devoted to the lives of great scientists.

John Stuart Mill: *Poetry and Its Varieties, in Dissertations and Discussions,* vol. I. "Poetry is feeling confessing itself to itself in moments of solitude, and embodying itself in symbols which are the nearest possible representation of the feeling in the exact shape in which it exists in the poet's mind."

Page 148

Robert Frost: *Education by Poetry, in The Amherst Graduates' Quarterly,* February, 1931.

Page 149

Archibald MacLeish: *Einstein* and *Ars Poetica,* in *Streets of the Moon.*

Page 150

Poe: *The Poetic Principle.*

Page 153

Gautier: Quoted by George Brandes in vol. V of his *Main Currents in Nineteenth Century Literature,* p. 299.

Page 154

Axel's Castle: The definition is on pp. 21–22.

Page 155

Walter Pater: From the *Conclusion* of *The Renaissance.* This conclusion was omitted from the second edition lest "it might possibly mislead some of those young men into whose hands it might fall," but reprinted in subsequent editions, the young men having presumably all been misled.

Here is the essential passage:

"Not the fruit of experience, but experience itself, is the end. A counted number of pulses only is given to us of a variegated, dramatic life. How may we see in them all that is to be seen in them by the finest senses? How shall we pass most swiftly from point to point, and be present always at the focus where the greatest number of vital forces unite in their purest energy?

"To burn always with this hard, gem-like flame, to maintain this ecstasy, is to succeed in life."

Page 157

Zola: *Le Roman Experimental.*

"To know the best": The quotation is from Matthew Arnold, *Literature and Science,* in *Discourses in America.*

Page 162

Herbert Read: *The Form of Modern Poetry,* an essay in *The Symposium,* vol. I, no. 3.

T. S. Eliot: *Homage to John Dryden, Hogarth Essays,* first American edition, p. 210.

Edwin Arlington Robinson: "It seems to me that poetry has two outstanding characteristics. One is that it is indefinable. The other is that it is eventually unmistakable." Quoted by Louis Untermeyer in *The Forms of Poetry.*

Page 164

"Poetic subject": In one of his prefaces, speaking of the "subordinate character of expression," Arnold says literally that "all depends on the subject." In another he says: "The same tragic stories were handled by all the tragic poets." All the tragic poets were, then, in the essence of the matter identical.

Page 165

George Santayana: *Poetry and Religion,* p. 251.

Miss Edith Sitwell: The metaphor is from her poem *Aubade,* quoted on p. 73.

Miss Helen Parkhurst: *Beauty, An Interpretation of Art and the Imaginative Life,* p. 208.

Page 167

John Stuart Mill: *Poetry and Its Varieties,* in *Dissertations and Discussions,* vol. I.

Page 168

E. E. Cummings: *is 5,* p. 82.

Page 170

Miss Edith Sitwell: *Poetry and Criticism.*

Page 171

Robert Graves: *The Future of the Art of Poetry, Hogarth Essays,* first American edition, p. 185.

Hart Crane: *Letter to Harriet Monroe, Poetry,* October, 1926.

Page 172

Professor Whitehead: *Science and the Modern World,* p. 125.

Coleridge: *Biographia Literaria,* chapter XIV.

Page 174

Clarence I. Lewis: *Mind and the World Order,* p. 6.

Page 176

Professors Greenough and Kittredge: *Words and Their Ways in English Speech.*

Hopkins: *Poems of Gerard Manley Hopkins,* p. 89.

Page 177

Andrew Lang: *History of English Literature.*

Page 178

Edward Sapir: *The Musical Foundations of Verse,* in *The Journal of English and Germanic Philology,* vol. XX, no. 2.

Professor Snyder: *Hypnotic Poetry,* p. 20.

Page 181

Professor MacDougall: I think this statement occurs in his *Outline of Abnormal Psychology.*

Page 183

"Thrilling point": I borrow this phrase from Edmund Spenser, in whose time the word *thrill,* which is related to *drill,* meant little more than to pierce. It is one of those phrases which have acquired more poetic quality through changes in the language than they originally had.

Page 186

"Her paps are like fair apples in the prime": The two lines are juxtaposed in a quotation from Greene's *Eclogues* by Taine in his *History of English Literature,* Book II, chapter I, sec. 2, subsec. v.

Page 189

Hugo Münsterberg: *Grundzüge der Psychologie,* I (1900).

Professor Montague: *Consciousness a Form of Energy,* in *Essays Philosophical and Psychological in Honor of William James* (1908).

Page 190

Professor Margaret Floy Washburn: *Movement and Mental Imagery* (1916).

Page 193

John Dewey: *The Reflex Arc Concept in Psychology, Psychological Review,* July, 1896.

Page 194

Jennings: *The Behavior of Lower Organisms,* p. 116.

Page 195

The Will to Live: Journal of Philosophy, Psychology and Scientific Methods, vol. XIV, no. 4.

Neurological Foundations of Animal Behavior: Pp. 17 and 18.

Page 197

William James: *Principles of Psychology.*

Page 198

Margaret Floy Washburn: *The Animal Mind,* pp. 42–43.

Page 201

Conrad Aiken: *A Basis for Criticism, The New Republic,* April 11, 1923.

Floyd Henry Allport: *Social Psychology,* chapter IV.

Page 203

Professor Herrick: *Introduction to Neurology,* chapter XVIII, pp. 297–98.

Page 205

John Dewey: *Experience and Nature,* vol. I, p. 388. On the same page he says: "The present confusion, deemed chaos by some, in the fine arts and æsthetic criticism seems to be an inevitable consequence of the underlying, even if unavowed, separation of the instrumental and the consummatory."

Page 209

H. L. Mencken: *A Footnote to Criticism,* an essay in the collection, *Criticism in America.*

Edmund Wilson: *Axel's Castle,* pp. 39, 120, 221.

Joseph Wood Krutch: *The Modern Temper,* p. 142. "The death of tragedy is, like the death of love, one of those emotional fatalities as the result of which the human as distinguished from the natural world grows more and more a desert."

Houston Peterson: *The Melody of Chaos,* p. 5.

Anatole France: Preface to vol. IV of *La Vie Litteraire.*

Jules Lemaître: *Chateaubriand,* p. 223.

Page 210

Professor B. H. Bode: *Concerning the Teaching of English,* in *The English Journal,* May, 1929.

Page 211

Matthew Arnold: *Literature and Science,* in *Discourses in America.*

Page 214

Joseph Wood Krutch: *The Modern Temper,* chapter I.

Page 215

Edna Millay: The sonnets alluded to are all in her recent volume, *Fatal Interview.*

Page 219

H. L. Mencken: *The Poet and His Art,* in *Prejudices, Third Series.*

Page 220

Henri Poincaré: *The Foundations of Science,* Introduction and pp. 93 and 325.

Page 221

Francis Bacon: The quotations are from *The Advancement of Learning.*

Frederick Barry: *The Scientific Habit of Thought,* pp. 33–34. Although Professor Barry goes to this extreme in recognizing the element of "convenient fiction" in science, he nevertheless clings to the Baconian view that to be fictitious is the essence of poetry, identifying "poetical" with "imaginative" (p. 234), and telling us how the Newtonian astronomy destroyed "the poetic dreams of ages" (p. 249). I think this error is the principal reason—unless it be a mere loss of nerve—why his admirable book collapses like a tired balloon in the concluding paragraph. Having attributed a character of "unreality" to both science and poetry, he begins to realize on page 274—perhaps because just then somebody invited him to go swimming—that there *is* such a thing as reality and that people are at times interested in it. He therefore forgets his brilliant argument, just completed, that there is no essential difference between facts, theories, laws and hypotheses—that all are in essence pragmatic interpretations of experience—and as though he had been telling us that science is in a peculiar sense "theoretical," suddenly announces that "Beyond theory . . . there is room for a science of immediate experience, richly complete." Just what this "science" of immediate experience might be, and how related to the real science which he has been telling us includes everything from "fact" to "rational conjecture," would seem a question of some importance. Professor Barry dismisses it in two sentences: "This science knows the world not abstractly, but in its wholeness as æsthetics knows it, or religion, which supplement and give new value to knowledge. But it is the business of the scientist to provide knowledge itself. . . ." We have, then, a *science* which *knows* the world, but whose function is not to *know* but to give new value to *knowledge,* and set off against this *science* and this *knowing* which gives value to *knowledge,* we have again the *scientist* whose business is to provide *knowledge itself.* In this unseemly puddle Professor Barry's ardently reasoned discourse suddenly comes to an end.

It seems to me that such puddles are inevitable if we abandon the idea that science tells us what things "are," and yet cling to the idea that the essence of poetry is to tell us what they are not. Reality thus gets no place in the language of man, and the door stands open to every quack doctrine of mystery.

The *Æsthetics* of Benedetto Croce is a puddle very similar to this, he having inherited from Vico the idea that the experience of things is a kind of knowledge—which he calls intuition and identifies with artistic expression—and that this knowledge can be abruptly distinguished from logical or conceptual knowledge. There is no reason for making these abrupt distinctions except the desire to find support for some belief or attitude that cannot be supported by real knowledge. The passage from knowledge *about* to experience *of*, like that from prose to poetry, is not broken by any sharp divisions. The sole sharp division here—for those who have courage—is that between pure experience which is *not* knowledge at one extreme, and pure knowledge which contains no hint of possible experience at the other. (Compare the note to p. 8 on Professor Eddington's mystery. And for my use of the word *experience*, see John Dewey's introduction to his *Essays in Experimental Logic*. Those who do not like it will find support in Morris R. Cohen's *Reason and Nature*, pp. 35 ff. and 452–4.)

Page 222

Professor Lowes: *Convention and Revolt in Poetry*, pp. 18–19. Professor Lowes's book provides a lively introduction to many exquisitely chosen verses of poetry, but it is fundamentally unsound because of his want of attention to psychology and the logic of science. His identification of "illusion," in the sense in which the sea's touching the rim of the sun is an illusion, with the unreality of invented characters like Hamlet—or even Hamlet's father's ghost—puts him so far off the scent of the true essence of poetry that much of what follows becomes a mere effort to beat his way back by any means he can.

He says that "the very essence of poetic truth is accepted illusion," and again "the supreme truth of poetry . . . is inviolate consistency with itself." But then, quoting Blake's "Tiger, tiger burning bright," he cries: "There is not a shred of fact about that. Yet it is truth at white heat." Does he mean "accepted illusion at white heat," "consistency with itself at white heat"? Obviously not. Both these things liquefy before they reach white heat. He means truth to the immediacy of a real experience.

A. C. Bradley, in his *Oxford Lectures on Poetry*, improves a trifle upon Professor Lowes's position when he says that poetry and life's experience "may be called two different forms of the same thing." They are "analogues." There is a connection between them, but it is a "connection underground." He does not explain what that connection is, except to say that the one has reality but does not satisfy the imagination, while the other satisfies the imagination but has not full reality. The phrase "satisfy the imagination" must be put down, I am afraid, as a very imperfect effort to say any clear thing. In general I can see no identifiable fact underlying Mr. Bradley's mysterious talk about an underground connection between poetry and reality, except the quite obvious one that words can suggest the qualities of things in their absence, and even in their non-existence. It can do this in their real presence also, however, and the question whether the things are present or absent, real or unreal, is thus irrelevant to the definition of poetic speech. Mr. Bradley, of course, is not mainly talking about poetic speech, but about "poems" as objects of art—trying valiantly to defend these objects from being judged essentially from the standpoint of ulterior ends—and that permits him to be impressive and valuable and yet noncommittal as to the essential problem of the material out of which they are composed.

Lascelles Abercrombie in his *Theory of Poetry* states the thing in its true terms when he says: "The value of things in poetry is the value of experience simply as such." But because of a frankly, and rather fliply, expressed ignorance of psychology, and an equally frank dread of the problems of logic—ignorance and dread of efforts more strenuous than his to find valid conceptions in the sphere he has entered—he fails to stand firm upon this excellent formulation. He thinks it is necessary to add that experiences in order to enter into poetry must not only be enjoyed for themselves, but must be "significant." With that word *significant* he of course plunges us back into the very confusion from which his definition, if he had stuck to it, would have delivered us. "I do not propose to meddle," he remarks, "with that vexatious problem, the *meaning of meaning*." Which is to say: I do not propose to face the problems which I have raised with my word *significant;* I have brought the word in for the purposes of literary truth only.

The fact is that Mr. Abercrombie brings in his word *significant,* because he does not know how in terms of his original statement to explain the presence of metaphor in poetry. He does not see how the "primitive relish for experience," the "virtue of delightedly conscious activity," which "bears its value on the face of it," can be enhanced in one situation by comparing that situation with another. (He will never find out, you may be sure, so long as he persists in keeping his skirts clear of the "watery soil" of psychology.) And so he tells us that "we must try to form some tolerably precise notion of poetic significance," and that it "must be the notion of a significance that does not require to be argued in order to be effective," etc., etc., destroying effectively the clear distinction he had drawn between poetry in its essence and the practical or scientific way of talking.

Page 226

Coleridge: *Biographia Literaria,* chap. xiv.

Page 228

Grant Overton: *The Philosophy of Fiction.* "The history of fiction is simply the history of the decay of plot."

Sherlock Bronson Gass: *Modernism and the Novel,* in *The Forum* for May, 1928.

Grant C. Knight: *The Novel in English,* pp. 369–370.

Virginia Woolf: *Mr. Bennett and Mrs. Brown,* in *The Hogarth Essays,* first American edition.

Page 229

Storm Jameson: *The Georgian Novel and Mr. Robinson.*

Charlotte Brontë: The dedication of *Jane Eyre.*

Page 231

Dostoyevsky: From a private letter published in *The New Criterion,* June, 1926.

The Bookman: September and October, 1928.

Page 236

Panferov: From an interview in a Moscow paper translated in *Les Nouvelles Littéraires,* Paris, June 20, 1931.

Page 238

Aldous Huxley: *Subject-Matter of Poetry,* in *On the Margin.*

Page 239

Edna Millay: *Euclid alone has looked on Beauty bare,* a sonnet in *The Harp-Weaver.*

Archibald MacLeish: *Einstein,* in *Streets of the Moon.*

Shelley: From *Prometheus Unbound.*

Page 240

Matthew Arnold: *The Study of Poetry,* in *Essays in Criticism.*

Sacheverell Sitwell: Preface to *The Gothic North.*

Julien Benda: *Belphégor.*

Page 243

Emerson: A contrasting of "intellect" against "science" will be found in the Essay on Experience.

Page 246

Morris Cohen: *Reason and Nature,* p. 367.

Page 248

Goethe: I quote from *Goethe's Literary Essays,* selected by J. E. Spingarn, pp. 178 and 133.

Page 249

Keats: From a letter.

Page 251

Conrad Aiken: The quotations are from *A Basis for Criticism, The New Republic,* April 11, 1923; *The Blue Voyage,* quoted by Houston Peterson in *The Melody of Chaos,* p. 21, as representing Aiken's own views; *The Future of Poetry,* in *The New Freeman,* vol. III, no. 7; and from a personal letter quoted by Peterson, p. 205.

Page 252

The Bookman: The quotation is from T. S. Eliot in the issue of November, 1929.

H. G. Wells: The quotation is from his reply to a request from Harrods, Ltd., to write advertising for them.

Page 256

Goethe: The quotations will be found in a discussion of Goethe's contributions to science by Eric Nordenskiöld in his *History of Biology,* in *Conversations with Eckermann,* Saturday, June 11, 1825, and in *Shakespeare as Playwright,* in *Goethe's Literary Essays,* p. 186. My idea of a matter-of-fact vein and a vein of glorification in Goethe I derive from George Brandes's *Wolfgang Goethe.*

Page 258

Matthew Arnold: *The Function of Criticism at the Present Time,* in *Essays in Criticism.*

Page 260

T. S. Eliot: *The Perfect Critic,* in *The Sacred Wood.*

Page 261

Creative Criticism: This little book is to be republished with additions this fall by Harcourt, Brace & Co.

Page 264

W. C. Brownell: *Criticism,* p. 16.

Page 265

J. E. Spingarn: In his *Creative Criticism,* p. 9, Mr. Spingarn expressly dismisses "evolutionary science" as "a useless weapon in the field of æsthetic thought."

Page 266

Paul Elmer More: *A Revival of Humanism,* in *The Bookman,* March, 1930—"The pseudo-scientific treatises of Mr. I. A. Richards . . ."

Page 267

Matthew Arnold: Quoted by W. C. Brownell in *Criticism,* p. 11.

Page 269

Norman Foerster: *The American Scholar,* pp. 42, 40, and 51. The quotation from Professor Jennings's book is on p. 3.

Page 272

Norman Foerster: *The American Scholar,* pp. 27, 52, and 42.

Howard Mumford Jones: *Graduate English Study, Its Rationale,* in *The Sewanee Review,* 1930–31.

Thorstein Veblen: *The Theory of the Leisure Class,* chapter XIV.

Page 274

Mr. Canby: *Scholarship,* in his volume called *American Estimates.*

Edwin Greenlaw: *The Province of Literary History* (1931).

Page 276

"Forty-three different ways": The commonest of all these ways of keeping science out of the temple of literature is to identify science with a philosophy of absolute determinism, which leaves to literature every kind of discussion which implies the reality of choice. However, since Einstein apologized in the public press for being such an old fogy as to go back to the *abandoned doctrine* of determinism, this device has rather lost its force. "I know very well," Einstein was reported as saying (New York *Times,* March 17, 1931), "that my conception of causality as a part of the nature of things will be interpreted as a sign of senility. I am convinced, however, that the concept of causality is inherent in matters relating to natural science."

Another style in the literary man's attack on science is to declare that scientific opinion itself shows no fixed points, nor even a line of progress, but merely a succession of fashionable dogmas. To this an enduring answer has been made by Henri Poincaré in his chapter on *Science and Reality*:

"At the first blush it seems to us that the theories last only a day and that ruins upon ruins accumulate. To-day the theories are born, to-morrow they are the fashion, the day after to-morrow they are classic, the fourth day they are superannuated, and the fifth they are forgotten. But if we look more closely, we see that what thus succumb are the theories properly so called, *those which pretend to teach us what things are.* But there is in them something which usually survives. If one of them has taught us *a true relation,* this relation is definitely acquired, and it will be found again under a new disguise in the other theories which will successively come to reign in place of the old." (*The Foundations of Science,* p. 351. The italics are mine.)

Page 277

"Purely quantitative": A. E. Heath in his article on *Science and Education,* in F. S. Marvin's collection *Science and Civilization,* has an able refutation of the idea that quantitative statement is the criterion of science. See also *Qualitative Thought,* by John Dewey, in *The Symposium,* vol. I, no. 1.

Page 278

"Another book": *American Criticism.*

L. T. More: From the essay in *Humanism and America* entitled *The Pretensions of Science.*

Page 281

"There is no such thing as a judgment of value": If my treatment of this all-important question seems brief, the reader will find a long enough one, and to much the same effect, in Ralph Barton Perry's *General Theory of Value.*

Page 287

Stuart Sherman: *Graduate Schools and Literature,* to be found in the volume *Shaping Men and Women.*

Page 292

George Woodberry: The incident was recalled by Harold Kellock in an article, *Woodberry—A Great Teacher,* in *The Nation,* vol. 130, no. 3369.

Page 298

"Pointing to or reflecting": *Science and Poetry,* pp. 14 and 52, and *Principles of Literary Criticism,* p. 265.

Page 299

"Modern physics is becoming": *The Meaning of Meaning,* p. 159.

Professor Bridgman: *The Logic of Modern Physics,* pp, 2, 5, 7.

John Dewey: *The Quest for Certainty,* footnote to p. 111.

"Too easy idea": In justice to Ogden and Richards it must be said that they have a sufficiently complicated way of establishing this over-simplification of science. They begin with a quite obvious remark, and one from which a valid psychology of poetry might have flowed almost automatically:

"All experience, using the word in the widest possible sense, is either enjoyed or interpreted (*i.e.*, treated as a sign) or both, and very little of it escapes some degree of interpretation." It was perhaps by accident that the word "enjoyed" dropped in here, as though experiences could not be painful without interpretation. But it puts the authors in the more complete accord with my own thesis, and makes it seem most natural to continue: *Words are used to communicate the enjoyment as well as the interpretation of experience—in poetry the first element predominates, in practical and scientific language the second.* Instead of continuing that way, Ogden and Richards permitted the enjoyment of experience to drop out of sight forever—only to reappear, at least in the austere remark of Richards that "it is not the intensity of the conscious experience, its thrill, its pleasure or its poignancy which gives it value, but the organization of its impulses. . . . There are plenty of ecstatic instants which are valueless." They let all this "valueless" matter drop out of sight, and proceeded to divide the interpretation of experience, or what we call the interpretation of it, into two nearly water-tight compartments: (1) pointing to it, which is real interpretation, or science; and (2) evoking attitudes toward it, which is not interpretation at all, but poetry.

The manner in which Ogden and Richards eliminate from interpretation, and so from science, the element of attitude—or response, or adaptation, or reaction, or anything of that active and profitable kind—is the central mystery of their book on *The Meaning of Meaning.* And although it is wrapped up in an almost impenetrable darkness of language, I believe that if the reader will be patient I can show him at least a fumbling glimpse of what it is. On page 53 the authors are still talking a simple language, the language of biology and psychology. They are explaining the "peculiarity of interpretation" as consisting of the fact that "when a context has affected us in the past the recurrence of merely a part of the context will cause us to *react in the same way* in which we reacted before." The italics are mine, but they are hardly necessary, because the authors are here making no secret of the fact that "reaction" and "adaptation" and "attitude," and indeed action itself, are the essence of the process of interpretation. They illustrate it with the famous dog who came running to the table when he heard the dinner bell, and the famous chicken who did not eat a yellow-and-black caterpillar because having pecked him once before she found him bitter. Interpretation in these cases consisted of *reacting* to a *part* of an experience, the sound of the bell and the colors of the caterpillar, as though the whole experience were there—a meat-bone dropping benignly from the table, a bad caterpillar-taste in the mouth. To the dog, you see, the bell "means" a meat-bone; to the chicken the yellow-and-black "means" a bitter taste. But how can a yellow-and-black color *mean* a bitter taste? We say that it is "directed towards" or "refers to" a bitter taste. But what is this state of being directed towards or referring to a bitter taste? What *is* meaning? This can only be answered by asking how it arose. What caused the sensation of yellow-and-black to mean, or refer to, a bitter taste? Was the cause anything else but a bitter taste? Then why not end all arguments and resolve all mysteries—and most particularly the mystery of how to reconcile psychology with logic—by defining "meaning" as "being caused by"?

Let us go over it once more: A sensation of yellow-and-black which *means* bitter taste is one which has been experienced in the same context with bitter taste in the past. That is the only thing which distinguishes it from sensations of yellow-and-black which mean nothing. A bitter taste is the *cause* of its meaning, and a bitter taste is also *what* it means. Then *meaning* something and *being caused by* something are the same.

If this sounds to you a little topsy-turvy and upside-down, and almost like a kind of ingenious joke, I think you are perfectly right. The bitter taste that a black-and-yellow caterpillar means is not the same bitter taste as the one which caused him to mean it. There are two different experiences involved and the relating them together is an act of the mind. In my opinion, it is only in a world already organized into "things," and classes of things, by the interpretative action of the mind that the act of interpretation could be so inactively conceived.

However, it is not my task to criticize this theory of meaning in detail. I merely wanted to play fair with Ogden and Richards by showing that they have at least a sufficiently arduous, erudite and abstruse manner of effecting the separation of reaction from interpretation, and so negotiating the leap from the psychology of interpretation to a purely denotative logic. The chicken sees a yellow-and-black object and recoils from it in a way that may be described psychologically as the automatic result of a former coincidence of yellow-and-black object with bitter taste. And if the chicken happens to be conscious and to be saying that the black-and-yellow caterpillar *means* bitter taste, that is merely another way of saying that the process is taking place in this way *because of* a bitter taste. The black-and-yellow sensation does not *perform the act of* meaning bitter taste, but the meaning bitter taste is merely the *being a part of* such a process. Thus, although conceding to begin with that the essential thing in interpretation is "reaction," the authors wind up by asserting that "To be an act of interpretation is merely to be a particular member of a psychological context of a certain kind." And they add, "We shall, in what follows, speak of . . . interpretations . . . as references." In this way—or in some such way, for I cannot pretend to have penetrated the darkness completely—reaction is dropped out of interpretation, and attitude or reference to action out of science.

"A poem, they say . . .": *Meaning of Meaning,* pp. 158–9.

Page 300

Principles of Literary Criticism: pp. 267, 273.
Science and Poetry: pp. 13, 59, 61, 26, 55.

Page 301

Practical Criticism: pp. 354 and 349.

Page 302

Clarence I. Lewis: *Mind and the World Order,* p. 85.

Page 304

"The poet uses certain words": *Science and Poetry,* pp. 26–7.

Page 305

The Meaning of Meaning: p. 240.
Principles of Literary Criticism: p. 240.
Helen Parkhurst: *Beauty,* p. 208.

Page 306

Practical Criticism: pp. 221–223.

Page 308

"Texture of expectations": *Principles of Literary Criticism,* p. 137.

Page 309

Hypnotism: *Principles of Literary Criticism,* pp. 138, 144.
"Emotionality": *Meaning of Meaning.* p. 240.
Principles of Literary Criticism: p. 143.

Page 311

Roger Fry: *Transformations,* p. 2, quoting *Principles of Literary Criticism,* p. 16.

Page 313

"It is capable of saving us": *Science and Poetry,* p. 82. The quotations immediately following are from pp. 41, 39 and 43.

Page 314

"It is not necessary to know": *Meaning of Meaning*, p. 159. The quotations immediately following are from *Principles of Literary Criticism*, pp. 279 and 280, and from *Science and Poetry*, pp. 61 and 60.

Page 315

"Magical View": *Science and Poetry*, pp. 47, 52.

Page 316

"A response is sentimental": *Practical Criticism*, p. 258.

DATE DUE

44098	5Feb'65		
46065	7Sep'6		
39474	10 Feb'66		
54826	13Mar'67		
54826	24Mar'67		
52847	26Oct'67		
39593	1Jun'68		
MAY 17			
DEC 05 '81			
AUG 11 '82			

GAYLORD PRINTED IN U.S.A.